The Politics of Violence

The Politics of Violence
The New Urban Blacks and the Watts Riot

David O. Sears
University of California, Los Angeles

John B. McConahay
Yale University

Houghton Mifflin Company / Boston
Atlanta / Dallas / Geneva, Illinois / Hopewell, New Jersey / Palo Alto / London

The publishers below have granted permission to reprint or adapt the following material for this book:

One figure from "Black Invisibility, the Press, and the Los Angeles Riot," *The American Journal of Sociology,* Vol. 76, No. 4, January 1971 by Paula B. Johnson, David O. Sears, and John B. McConahay by permission of the University of Chicago Press. © 1971 by The University of Chicago. All rights reserved.

One table from "Racial Socialization, Comparison Levels and the Watts Riot," *The Journal of Social Issues,* Vol. 26, 1970 by David O. Sears and John B. McConahay by permission of *The Journal of Social Issues* and the Society for the Psychological Study of Social Issues.

Five tables reprinted from "Black Attitudes Toward the Political System in the Aftermath of the Watts Insurrection," *The Midwest Journal of Political Science,* Vol. XIII, No. 4, Nov., 1969 by David O. Sears by permission of the Wayne State University Press. Copyright, 1969 by Wayne State University Press.

Five tables from "The Politics of Discontent" by David O. Sears and John B. McConahay in N. E. Cohen (ed.), *The Los Angeles Riots: A Socio-Psychological Study* (New York: Praeger, 1970) by permission of Praeger Publishers.

Two tables from "Participation in the Los Angeles Riot," *Social Problems,* Vol. 17, No. 1, 1969 by David O. Sears and John B. McConahay by permission of *Social Problems* and The Society for the Study of Social Problems.

Five tables from "Riot Ideology in Los Angeles: A Study of Negro Attitudes," *The Social Science Quarterly,* Vol. 49, 1968 by David O. Sears and T. M. Tomlinson by permission of *The Social Science Quarterly,* The Southwestern Social Association, and The University of Texas at Austin.

Printed in the U.S.A.
Library of Congress Catalog Card Number: 73-5247
ISBN: 0-395-11927-8

974.49405
S439p

Contents

Introduction

This is a book about the political and social psychology of the Los Angeles Watts Riot of August 1965, an event that changed the course of American race relations. We shall attempt here to formulate, and to subject to rigorous empirical test, a comprehensive social psychological theory of urban mass violence. Two basic questions will be addressed: (1) Can riot participation rightfully be interpreted as a political act? (2) What were the major political effects of the riot? We shall also develop an alternative theory of riot participation, constructed from the observations and generalizations made by other observers, and then subject it as well to rigorous empirical test. In most instances, our focus is upon the psychology of the individual citizen, whether black rioter or white voter, rather than upon the political system, government policies, or the views of articulate leaders.

The primary data base for this book is a survey with two samples of black respondents: (1) the "Curfew Zone" sample, consisting of 586 residents, aged 15 and above, representative of the large area of Los Angeles cordoned off for curfew purposes during the riot. The Curfew Zone contained most of the blacks in Los Angeles, so this sample is approximately representative of blacks living in Los Angeles; and (2) the "arrestee" sample, consisting of 124 residents of the Curfew Zone who had been arrested during the rioting. This sample was obtained in a variety of rather informal ways. It cannot be regarded as representative of the nearly 4,000 blacks who were arrested during the rioting, but it is useful for purposes of comparison.

Both samples were interviewed with the same interview schedule, during late 1965 and early 1966, by black interviewers living in the Curfew Zone. The cooperation received from the respondents was unusually gracious, especially considering the circumstances, and the completion rate was quite good, despite the lengthy interview schedule. To a lesser extent we have also referred to data collected simultaneously from a large sample of whites living throughout Los Angeles County, from Mexican Americans living in the Curfew Zone, from a survey of white voters in the suburban San Fernando Valley in 1969, and from a content analysis of racial references in Los Angeles newspapers from 1892 through 1968.[1]

While our primary goal has been to formulate and validate a theory about participation in and endorsement of mass violence, we also have attempted to address the larger questions that have puzzled so many concerned citizens, and which have important social implications. Principal among them are four: (1) Why did the riot happen in 1965, of all times, in the midst of what was apparently an unprecedented national civil rights effort, with the most sympathetic white public, President, Congress, and judiciary in history, and in the midst of great prosperity? (2) Why did it happen in Los Angeles, of all places, generally thought to be among the most pleasant, open, and egalitarian of American cities? (3) Was the riot politically meaningful in origin; that is, did it grow out of no longer tolerable social conditions that had to be reformed if further riots and miseries were to be avoided? Or was it a politically meaningless explosion, generated mainly by criminals, malcontents, or a few agitators, who managed to dupe hapless innocents? (4) What were the political consequences of the rioting? Did it lead whites to further sympathy for black people, and at long last spur them out of lethargy into remedial social action, or did it create a massive backlash that abruptly terminated the sympathetic consensus and thrust for civil rights progress? Did it horrify and terrify decent black citizens into a renunciation of all forms of confrontation, or provide for a general uplift in black pride and black solidarity, or fuel the advocacy of militant action and racial violence? Did race relations move into a more mature and realistic era, or regress into greater suspiciousness, hostility, and distance?

These are questions that are fundamental both for an understanding of "Watts" as an historical event and for the farreaching decisions on social policy that must be made in its wake. While others have addressed these same questions at other levels of analysis, we feel we have some unique insights to contribute to them, as will be seen. Thus we hope this book will both serve the need for rigorous theory-testing and lend greater insight into the larger political, social, and historical implications of the Watts Riot.

Before presenting our theory and data, however, there are some other, more philosophical issues that we must comment upon. To start with, there is a very natural suspicion of white social scientists writing about blacks. Indeed, we ourselves have a healthy respect for our own limitations

---

[1]The methods utilized in drawing each of the samples used in this volume are summarized in Appendix A. They are also given in greater detail in Tomlinson and TenHouten (1970). For the two surveys of whites' attitudes, see Morris and Jeffries (1970) and Sears and Kinder (1971). The content analysis is described in Johnson, Sears, and McConahay (1971).

as students of blacks' lives, society, and minds. Nevertheless, we do not subscribe to the view that only blacks should write about blacks, any more than we believe that only whites should write about white racism or that de Tocqueville had no business writing about Americans. And we have chosen a level of analysis in this book that we think is appropriate to our own level of understanding; we have not attempted to portray life in the ghetto, or to analyze clinically the thoughts and feelings of any particular person. Rather, the book rests on some rather straightforward and general social science theory, which we hope will prove relevant to ethnic groups of all kinds in many nations.

Perhaps a few words about our political biases would be appropriate as well. We both probably could be located somewhere between the new radicals and the older academic liberals. The theories we develop in this book have grown out of our thinking about society more generally. However, the biggest mistake a social scientist can make is to imagine that society, or individuals, simply work the way he would like them to— whether that makes them into angels or devils. Most of what has been written about the riots has been written in that vein. It is political propaganda thinly disguised as scholarship, with little effort to test it against systematic empirical data.

We too have strong moral convictions about race relations. We have tried to protect ourselves against wishful thinking in three ways: we have tried to test our theories as rigorously as we could with the best empirical data we could gather; we have tried to formulate alternative theories that were as plausible as possible, and to give them as fair a test as we could; and we have tried to be honest about the discrepancies between our theories and the data. We regard ourselves as scholars rather than as pamphleteers or activists. There is no way that we can completely screen out the influence of our biases on our work. Hopefully, we have presented enough of the data so that others can judge our work fairly.

Finally, we wish to avoid any misunderstanding about our use of the term "riot." We offered our respondents their choice of terms for their discussions of the events of August 1965, and the term chosen most commonly by blacks and whites alike was "riot" (see Chapter 10). Many blacks did use such terms as "insurrection" and "rebellion," and we are sensitive to the symbolic importance various terms have (for example, one would not refer to the events of 1789 as "the Paris riot"). For simplicity's sake, though, we have decided to use the term "riot" because it was used overwhelmingly in the media and by most of our respondents. Our data indicate, as will be seen, that it was more of a "rebellion" than a "riot," but we will let our data speak for themselves and not try to prejudge the case by selecting a less commonly used word.

An event such as the Watts Riot cannot be separated from its broader social and historical context. It cannot be understood as an isolated incident precipitated by some chance events and fueled by greedy impulse. The racial and political conflicts in our society that triggered the rioting in August 1965 are as old as America itself, and, indeed, they are fundamental to our society and to our way of life. They were there in August 1965; they are with us still, if anything more strongly and tragically than ever, as we put this book into print; and they will be with us for decades to come. As we will attempt to show, they have been undergoing great changes for a considerable time, changes even the most sophisticated of observers have not been sufficiently aware of. Our primary argument is that "Watts" was a profoundly important historical watershed, both because it grew so directly out of these historical changes and because it represented a rallying cry and a sign for the future. In the long run, the importance of "Watts" is not the temporary crisis it created, but what it tells us about the underlying state of the body politic. The story it tells, as will be seen, leaves us much to be concerned about, yet, in a longer-range sense, much to be hopeful about.

Acknowledgments

A project of this magnitude requires the inspiration and effort of many persons. Therefore, we must express our deepest gratitude to the many others who participated in the Los Angeles Riot Study (LARS). Our early work in LARS was done with Tommy Tomlinson, Diana TenHouten, Raymond Murphy, James Watson, and Nathan E. Cohen. The final shape of the project and many of our ideas stem from this fruitful interaction and collaboration.

Our other colleagues in the early years of the LARS project also facilitated our work in many ways: J. Cohen, Vincent Jeffries, Selma Lesser, Richard Morris, Stanley Plog, Walter Raine, and Harry Scoble. Many interviewers, coders, and respondents gave freely of their time and energy. To each of them, we owe a special debt of gratitude.

We also want to thank those who have worked with us in the years since "Watts" and LARS, during the period when the data were analyzed and re-analyzed and the manuscript was written and rewritten. Richard P. Longaker spent countless hours with us poring over many drafts of the manuscript. Paula B. Johnson, Richard E. Whitney, Donald R. Kinder, Fred Hornbeck, and Daniel L. Rourke provided intellectual stimulation and worked tirelessly with the computers at three different universities as well. Ronald P. Abeles, Lois Crawford, Karen Stanley Ebeling, Thomas Pettigrew, Harvey Reed, Robert T. Riley, and Esther Spachner also made important contributions to our perspective and analysis. The editors at Houghton Mifflin constantly provided us with vigorous and informed criticism of our efforts. We must give special thanks and recognition to Sura Boxerman, who typed more drafts of this manuscript than anyone could contemplate. Finally, we must thank Diane Straus who compiled and re-compiled the references for various drafts and who proved invaluable in her help with the last-minute details of getting the book into its final form.

We are also grateful to the publishers and authors who have permitted us to reprint material from some of our previously published writings.

The original data collection was supported by a grant from the Office of Economic Opportunity to the UCLA Institute of Government and Public Affairs, Nathan E. Cohen, Principal Investigator. Our own subsequent work on this monograph was supported by grants to David Sears from the National Science Foundation and the National Institute of Mental Health and by a predoctoral Research Fellowship from the USPHS to John McConahay. John McConahay also received support from the Center for the Study of the City of the Institution for Social and Policy Studies of Yale University. Computation support and assistance were supplied by the UCLA Health Science Computing Facility, the Central Computing Network at UCLA, the Claremont College Computing Center, and the Yale University Computing Center.

Finally, we owe the most special debt to Shirley McConahay who made her own important contribution to this book and who put up with a lot on the way, and to Juliet and Olivia Sears and John, Susan, and Mary K. McConahay, to whom, ultimately, this book is addressed.

David O. Sears
John B. McConahay

The Politics of Violence

Los Angeles Times photo

Arrest Causes Near Riot In Negro Area of Coast

LOS ANGELES, Aug. 11 (UPI) — A near riot was touched off here tonight by the arrest of a drunken driving suspect. Hundreds of persons, many of them throwing rocks, were involved and all available police units were summoned.

A police car was surrounded by part of the crowd in a predominantly Negro neighborhood. At least one woman was hospitalized.

The trouble started when California highway patrolmen arrested the drunken driving suspect. As the crowd gathered, the suspect turned on patrolmen, and officers made three arrests, two for resisting arrest.

The driving suspect was identified as a Negro. The arresting patrolmen were white.

1　The Fires of August

America was born in violent revolution and reared in violent conquest of her frontier. Her domestic tranquility has been shattered repeatedly by racial, ethnic, and labor riots. Since 1860, one out of every five of her presidents has been assassinated. Since 1776, she has fought nine major wars. In addition, she has intruded forcefully, if not violently, into the affairs of numerous sovereign countries, ranging from Haiti and Panama to the USSR. And she has experienced a major civil war. Yet, the burning, looting, and small arms fire that blitzed her cities in the mid-1960s reached levels of domestic violence which were virtually unprecedented.

In the preceding 50 years, race riots marred the American dream of racial harmony at a rate of slightly more than one a year, but most of them were small in scope and concentrated during the two world wars (Lieberson and Silverman, 1965). Suddenly, in the "long hot summers" from 1964 to 1968, violence became commonplace. During these five years there were 239 riots serious enough for the local enforcement agencies to require outside assistance (Downes, 1968). Furthermore, the nature of racial violence changed radically during the mid-1960s. In previous years, it had consisted mainly of lynchings and other attacks in which blacks were the sole victims. In the 1960s, angry blacks were attacking white authorities and destroying white property in the ghettoes.

Americans were surprised by both the outbreak and the intensity of these events. Today, white and black Americans stand polarized and fearful, dreading a future of small racial wars and crime in the streets. This book is an attempt at understanding the violence that swept through our urban scene. By examining the Watts Riot in considerable depth, we hope to illuminate not only what happened in Los Angeles but also what occurred in Newark, Detroit, Cleveland, Chicago, New York, and elsewhere. We hope to illuminate as well the violence that persists today in many other forms and that shows so little sign of relenting.

A Routine Arrest

The rioting in Los Angeles followed from a routine arrest, one of many made every day in every part of the city. At 7 p.m., Wednesday, August 11, 1965, Marquette Frye, age 21, born in Wyoming and reared in Los Angeles, drove north on Avalon Boulevard. His brother Ronald was with him in the car. The two had been celebrating Ronald's return to Los Angeles from the service and had consumed several "screwdrivers." In a hurry to get home for dinner, Marquette exceeded the speed limit and weaved his car in and out of traffic in a manner which attracted the attention of another motorist, a black, who notified the first police officer he encountered. The officer, Lee Minikus of the California Highway Patrol, gave chase and caught up with Frye at 116th Street and Avalon, an area in the South Central part of Los Angeles known as Watts.[1]

At the outset, there was nothing unusual about the incident. All participants played their expected roles. As he climbed from his motorcycle, the arresting officer, in his black leather outfit and white crash helmet, resembled a cross between a Prussian cavalry officer and an astronaut. Marquette Frye, the man to be arrested, was neatly attired in tapered, cuffless trousers and a tailored sport shirt. He stepped out of the auto to meet the advancing officer and began to act happy, friendly, and humorous in an attempt to "shuck the cop." Minikus put Frye through a series of sobriety tests and decided to make an arrest for speeding and drunken driving. Frye entered into the tests wholeheartedly and even offered to walk the line backwards.

Minikus asked all of the questions necessary, according to the standard procedure, to fill in the arrest citation, including the color of Frye's hair. Frye answered all the questions, noting that he had black hair and that he was black all over. To emphasize this last point, Frye danced up and down in place, showing his ankles and arms.

Marquette Frye's antics during this routine arrest attracted people from the area who lingered in the streets to escape the stifling early evening heat in their apartments and houses. This crowd behaved in the usual way, joking with Frye and at the same time wondering why black people were always being arrested by white police.

Following the routine for cases of drunken driving, Officer Minikus radioed for his partner, Bob Lewis, asking him to help with the arrest and to call a tow truck and a car to transport Frye to jail. Bob Lewis reached

---

[1]In the brief narrative that follows, we have relied upon the carefully documented chronicle by the journalist Robert Conot (1967) and the report of the official commission appointed by Governor Brown, usually called the "McCone Commission" (Governor's Commission on the Los Angeles Riots, 1965), for most of the "facts" concerning the course and direction of the riot. Since it is not our primary purpose to write a chronicle of the events, generally we have accepted the "facts" agreed upon by these two sources.

the scene quickly, as did a tow truck and the arrested man's mother, Mrs. Rena Frye, who had been summoned by a friend. At this point Frye became belligerent and began to argue with the arresting officers. The officers were prepared for this contingency and responded with the usual procedures for dealing with a recalcitrant arrestee.

Officer Minikus went after Frye with a riot baton, Officer Lewis sent out a code 1199—"Officer Needs Help"—over the radio, and Officer Bennett, who had just arrived with the car to take Frye to jail, attempted to disperse the crowd by pushing them back with his shotgun. The crowd moved back, Minikus and Frye struggled for control of the riot baton, and Ronald Frye argued with Lewis. At this point, Officer Wayne Wilson arrived in response to the 1199. He went into action immediately, dispatching Ronald Frye with baton blows in the stomach and ribs. Then he belted the struggling Marquette Frye on the forehead. A jab to the stomach finally subdued him, and Minikus and Lewis led him to the car, his head locked in the arms of Minikus. Mrs. Frye and Ronald Frye attempted to help their kinsman and they, too, were arrested.

The crowd, seething with anger, swelled to over 100 persons. Nevertheless, the officers who poured into the area with sirens screaming knew the procedures for dealing with such situations. They moved the crowds away from the scene and attempted to disperse them with businesslike shoves and advice to go home. As the Fryes were led off to jail, the crowd began to disperse and so did the police. However, Officer Vaughn felt someone spit upon him and he and other officers rushed into the crowd to bring the culprit to justice. They dragged a young woman in a barber's smock, which resembled a maternity dress, from the crowd and threw her into a police car. Upon seeing this, the crowd became an outraged mob. Someone threw a bottle at the departing police vehicles and then a stream of rocks, bottles, bricks, and other missiles burst from the mob. The Watts Riot had begun.

The Violence Spreads.   For the sake of simplicity, we shall speak of the riot in later chapters as if it had been a single event. It was, however, a very complex series of many events during the hours that followed the Frye arrest. For the first two days of the upheaval, the police department stuck by its usual procedures, as the level of riot activity escalated from a few hundred people limited to the vicinity of 116th Street and Avalon Boulevard to several thousand people in many mobs scattered throughout a 46-square-mile section of the city. The book of police contingency plans recommended withdrawing so as not to create undue agitation and provocation in the area. Thus, on the first evening, August 11th, the police withdrew from 116th and Avalon, leaving it in the hands of a very angry mob. The mob threw rocks, bottles, and debris at the police and motorists who ventured or stumbled into the area but there was no looting, no burning, and no shooting.

During the afternoon of August 12th at a meeting in Athens Park, John

Buggs, the Los Angeles County Human Relations Commissioner, enlisted youth gang leaders and others to spread a rumor that the riot was off and that the word was to "cool it." In return Buggs promised that white police would be removed from the ghetto that night. When Buggs approached Deputy Police Chief Roger Murdock with word of the agreement, Murdock berated him for dealing with criminals, telling him that the police knew how to put down a riot and that the police department would demonstrate who ran the town.[2] The contingency plan for civil disturbances of this sort called for the police to display their superior strength by returning in force. So, following this standard procedure, they returned in force. Around 5 p.m. the first looting occurred. The first burning followed shortly afterwards. Quickly, a large portion of Los Angeles was in flames and thousands of people were in open revolt against the agents of law and order.

The police set up a war room, designated the Emergency Control Center or ECC, in a downtown skyscraper. As is the custom in military head-quarters, in the ECC the police expected to receive reports and issue orders which others would promptly carry out. Having issued the orders, the ECC sent word to Lt. Governor Glenn Anderson (the Governor, Edmund G. ("Pat") Brown, was vacationing in Greece), at 1:45 a.m., Friday, August 13th, that they were nearing control of the riot.

The riot was not under control, however. Things were not going according to the scenario written by the police officials in their planning sessions. The law enforcement personnel were following the usual procedures but the blacks were not playing their designated parts. The unflappable Police Chief William Parker was "perplexed." He had never seen anything like it before.

Business as Usual.   Others did not have to face the rebellion as directly and they went on with their customary business. In Sacramento, Lt. Governor Anderson left at 7 a.m. for Berkeley to attend a meeting of the Board of Regents of the University of California. At 9 a.m., in Los Angeles, Mayor Sam Yorty hopped a plane for San Francisco in order to address the prestigious Commonwealth Club, to further his bid for the governorship in the next election.

Shortly after Yorty left, Chief Parker decided that the National Guard would be needed to restore order. At 11 a.m. when the formal request for the National Guard finally had passed through official channels to Lt. Governor Anderson, he was at the regents' meeting (which, ironically, was concerned with raising out-of-state tuition in retaliation against the "outside agitators" responsible for the Berkeley student rebellions of 1964). Anderson hesitated to take such a drastic step. He wanted more information. Thus, he decided to fly to Los Angeles and have a meeting with the black

[2]Gary Marx (1970, p. 19) recounts a somewhat different version of Murdock's reply to Buggs' offer: "I don't want to hear anything you have got to say; you're part of the problem. I know how to run a riot and we are going to handle it our way."

leadership and the directors of the law enforcement agencies most involved: Chief Parker, Sheriff Peter Pitchess, and Highway Patrol Commissioner Bradford Crittenden. All three, however, were too preoccupied with other business to attend. Pitchess was vacationing in Canada, Crittenden was on business in Oregon, and Chief Parker was, in accordance with the emergency plan, directing the ECC operations atop the downtown skyscraper.

Though there was a commercial flight every half hour from nearby San Francisco to Los Angeles, which took about 50 minutes, Anderson decided to drive the longer distance from Berkeley to Sacramento in order to fly in the governor's official plane. Unfortunately, that plane was being used, far to the North, on other business, for the State Department of Parks and Recreation. Had he taken a commercial flight, Anderson would have arrived in Los Angeles at 1 p.m. Following the appropriate procedure, however, he took the governor's official plane and did not arrive in Los Angeles until 3:45 p.m.

In Los Angeles, meanwhile, the burning had resumed at 1:20 p.m.

Riot Control.   After deliberations with the Commander of the California National Guard and Police Chief Parker, the Lt. Governor decided to impose a curfew upon the areas of Los Angeles he thought affected by the rioting. This included the area mainly delimited by Alameda Street on the east, Crenshaw Avenue on the west, Adams Boulevard on the north, and Rosecrans Avenue on the south. This was then called the "Curfew Zone." Inside the zone, a dusk to dawn curfew was imposed, and people were not allowed to go in or out of its exits. The Curfew Zone included most of the blacks in Los Angeles, and it thus created a genuine ghetto.

As the military and civil authorities began to cordon off the Curfew Zone, the violence continued to escalate. Around 6 p.m., Friday the 13th, a stray policeman's bullet ricocheted from a building and killed 20-year-old Leon Posey, Jr. His was the first death. By 5:15 a.m., Saturday, when the National Guard was fully deployed, 16 people were dead, including one fireman and one policeman. Friday night and Saturday morning marked the high tide of violence. Eighteen more people would die in the next four days but the size and intensity of the Friday night conflict would not be equalled. By Monday night there were only sporadic incidents; the stringent curfew established by the police, sheriffs, and National Guard was for the most part effective. On Tuesday, August 17th, the curfew was lifted. The Watts Riot was over. But it had left a bitter legacy and many questions to be answered.

Size and Scope of the Riot

The central and foremost fact about the riot is that it was massive—in terms of the size of the affected area, the amount of damage done, and the forces necessary to suppress it.

Curfew Zone during Los Angeles Riot, and Surrounding Area

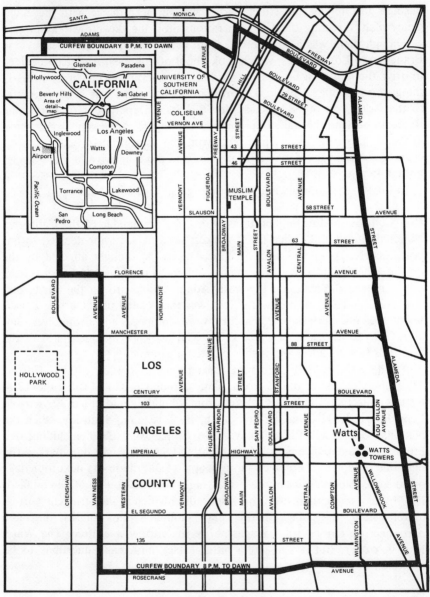

Adapted from © The New York Times, August 16, 1965.

The rioting lasted six days. For the first three days, the legally constituted authority of the City of Los Angeles and the State of California was overthrown in major parts of the Curfew Zone. For the last three days, the most stringent military rule applied to a domestic crisis in almost half a century prevailed in that zone. At the time, this response to a domestic problem was extraordinary, although in time it was to become more commonplace.

The extent of personal tragedy cannot be accurately calculated but it is reflected in part by the number killed and injured and the amount of property damaged. Thirty-four persons were killed and at least 1,032 were injured seriously enough to require treatment. Virtually all were black. In addition 3,952 were arrested, of whom 60 per cent later were convicted. Almost 1,000 buildings were damaged, burned, looted, or destroyed; total property damage was estimated at around $40,000,000 (Governor's Commission, 1965).

The amount of territory subjected to this holocaust was equally impressive. The Curfew Zone that was completely sealed off by the National Guard and police covered 46.5 square miles—an area one and one half times as large as Manhattan and larger than the City of San Francisco. It also contained a population that could have placed it among the 25 largest U. S. cities, ahead of Fort Worth and Louisville. And it was more than 80 per cent black.

In order to restore order in this area and stop the destruction, 13,900 National Guard troops, 934 police, and 719 sheriff's deputies were required.

Number of Participants.   The number of blacks involved in the rioting was staggering. Much of the violence took place at the hands of small groups as well as large mobs. Furthermore, it was widely scattered, with attacks at odd times and at a variety of places. Thus, the riot resembled a series of small and scattered brushfire wars more than a single holocaust. Since the participants were spread over such a large area, frequently they had to travel some distance to reach the action. It was not always a matter of stepping from one's home into the mob. Hence, to estimate the number of participants means not to gauge the size of a definite crowd or mob at its peak but to estimate the number of people involved at one time or another in a widely varying series of events occurring over a six-day period.

The most direct estimate of participation rates is based upon the following question, asked of black respondents in the survey conducted by the authors: "We are not interested in the details of what you actually did, but just generally, would you say that you were: very active, somewhat active, or not at all active?" In the Curfew Zone sample, 4 per cent reported being "very active" and 18 per cent, "somewhat active," for a total of 22 per cent who claimed some form of activity.

To determine blacks' perceptions of the extent of riot participation, each respondent was asked: "What per cent of the people in the area participated?" The mean estimate of respondents was that 20 per cent of the area

Wide World Photos

Los Angeles Times photo

residents had joined in. Approximately 20 per cent participated, then, regardless of whether participation rates are assessed by determining the proportion of respondents claiming to have been active or by asking respondents to estimate how many of the area's inhabitants had been active.

A third set of estimates derives from the respondents' reports of what they saw during the riot. Each one was asked whether or not he had seen shooting, stones being thrown, stores being looted, stores being burned, and crowds of people. The distributions for these several questions are shown in Table 1.1. Perhaps most noteworthy is that the looting of stores, burning of stores, and large crowds of people—the most visible manifestations of the disturbance—were each seen by over half the sample.

TABLE 1.1

Curfew Zone and Arrestee Samples:
Indexes of Riot Participation

RIOT PARTICIPATION	CURFEW ZONE SAMPLE ($n = 586$)	ARRESTEE SAMPLE ($n = 124$)
Self-reported activity		
"Very" or "somewhat" active by self-report	22%	62%
Perceived community involvement		
Mean percentage of community perceived as participating	20	33
Percentage who perceived own neighborhoods as being "very" or "somewhat" active	52	82
Events personally witnessed		
Saw shooting	20	48
Saw stones thrown	29	67
Saw stores burning	54	81
Saw stores being looted	60	87
Saw crowds of people	60	90

Note: See p. 9 and Appendix A for survey questions and methods of drawing samples.

The label "rioters," in layman's usage, is applied usually to people who break windows, throw Molotov cocktails, and shoot or snipe at police, and also to those who take advantage of disturbance and disruption of the social order to loot stores already broken open. "Spectators," on the other hand, include those who constitute an audience for the more aggressive acts of others but who do not loot, burn, or shoot. No doubt numerous "spectators" felt they had been active in the riot, and indeed were quite close to the criminal activity, but they must be distinguished from the "rioters."

In analyzing our data, this distinction can be made by combining the measure of self-reported activity with that of events witnessed. The precise classifications are given in Table 1.2. We classified as "rioters" respondents who saw looting, burning, large crowds of people, *and* said they took part in the riot. These constituted 15 per cent of the Curfew Zone sample and represented our best estimate of the proportion in the area (among those 15 years of age and over) who actually participated in the rioting (for the technical details of how these levels of participation were computed, see Sears and McConahay, 1969, 1970a). The exact content of their participation remains somewhat ambiguous, of course, but clearly they were close to the major criminal activities and said they were personally involved.

Another 31 per cent were classified as "close spectators." These were respondents who saw looting, burning, and large crowds of people, but who said they were "not active." They too were close enough to view the most common criminal acts but said they themselves had not been involved in them. Presumably they made up the vociferous crowds of people on the streets but their role was mainly a supportive one.

TABLE 1.2
Percentage at Each Level of Riot Participation

RIOT PARTICIPATION LEVEL	CURFEW ZONE SAMPLE	ARRESTEE SAMPLE
Rioters: "Active" by self-report. And saw looting and burning and crowds.	15	52
Close spectators: "Not active" by self-report. But saw looting and burning and crowds	31	26
Distant spectators: Saw some looting, burning, or crowds of people, but not all three.	27	18
Saw some criminal activity (saw only looting; saw looting and crowds; saw looting and burning).	10	12
Saw no criminal activity (saw only burning; saw only crowds; saw only burning and crowds).	17	6
Stay-at-homes: Did not see looting, burning, or crowds of people.	27	4
	100	100

Note: The number of cases here is 523 and 116, respectively. The remainder of each sample is not considered because data are missing on at least one of the four measures (self-reported activity, having seen crowds of people, and having seen stores looted and burned).

"Distant spectators" constituted those who saw little of the riot's criminal activity but who did see some of its more visible manifestations. Twenty-seven per cent of the sample fell into this category. Presumably these respondents ventured from their homes during the disturbance in order to obtain food, go to work, or for other reasons, but they were not active in the riot and they were not in the crowds consistently enough to see all of the major kinds of events.

The "stay-at-homes" were those who said they had not seen crowds of people, or the burning of stores, or the looting of stores. Apparently, they had been too far from the riot to see any of its most common manifestations. A sense of how absorbing these events were to the population of the Curfew Zone may be gained by noting how few people claimed to be in this least involved category—only 27 per cent.

Thus far, we have been speaking in terms of percentages but, if we are to gain a clear, concrete impression of the magnitude of the disturbance, we must deal with numbers of people. We can do this by multiplying these percentages by the number of black people (15 years of age and over) living in the Curfew Zone. Since there is some ambiguity about this population base, we can only estimate the number of participants within a reasonable range (for a detailed summary of our computations, see Sears and McConahay, 1970a). Our best estimate is that between 31,000 and 35,000 adults in the Curfew Zone were active as rioters at some time during the week-long upheaval. About double this number, between 64,000 and 72,000 persons, were involved as close spectators.

To help Americans gain a sense of the scope and magnitude of "Watts," it is instructive to compare it with other significant events in American history. Thirty-four persons were killed in Watts while five were killed in the Boston Massacre. The 1,032 wounded in Watts are almost equal to the British losses in the Battle of Bunker Hill and two and a half times greater than the American losses in that battle. At least 31,000 black people actively participated in the rioting—the equivalent of three combat infantry divisions or one and a half times the maximum number of troops under General Washington's command in the American War of Independence. The 16,000 National Guardsmen, sheriff's deputies, and policemen necessary to control the outburst were equal to the strength of the Union forces at the start of the Civil War and almost equal to the 17,000 troops necessary to conquer Cuba in the Spanish American War. The Watts Riot was of vast and unprecedented magnitude, by any standard.

Subjective Perceptions of Riot Proximity. Subjectively, most residents of the Curfew Zone experienced the riot in a personal way. It was not merely an abstract set of far-away events seen on television or read about in the newspaper. It was close enough to have a major direct impact upon most residents of the area.

The immediacy of the riot can be illustrated in four ways. First, our respondents perceived the rioting as being spread throughout the vast area of the Curfew Zone. Each respondent was asked: "How active were the people in your neighborhood?"; 15 per cent replied "very active" and 37 per cent "somewhat active." Thus, over half of the Curfew Zone residents perceived some activity occurring in their locale and/or engaged in by their neighbors. Second, even many of those who said that they *personally* were "not active" felt close to the rioting. Forty-three per cent of those in the Curfew Zone sample who said they themselves had not been active described the people in their neighborhood as being either "very" or "somewhat" active. Furthermore, even those who said their neighborhood was *not active* also estimated that 14 per cent of the residents in an area the size of San Francisco had participated actively in a week-long insurrection that, for about half that time, had successfully overthrown constituted legal authority (Sears and McConahay, 1970a).

Finally, as we reported above, a majority of the area's residents had witnessed the main events of the riot—the crowds, the burning, and the looting (see Table 1.1). The riot, therefore, represented a subjectively large and absorbing experience for most Curfew Zone blacks, an event that touched their lives in such a way as to make even the most timid a vicarious participant.

No doubt the riot was a highly novel as well as an absorbing experience. Normally, only a small fraction of any community's residents witness violations of "law and order," whether personal assaults in the streets, police brutality, burglaries in the home, or mass demonstrations that turn into confrontations with the authorities. Usually these events are experienced only secondhand, if at all. The immediacy of any such experience is severely diluted when one's sole contact with it is through a newspaper story, a few moments coverage on television, or the belated tale of a friend of a friend.

Therefore, the attitudes of the crowds toward the rioting are of particular importance for an understanding of the later interpretations of the riot offered by black leaders and the black public (see Chapters 9 and 10). Anecdotal observations from the riot reported in the press suggested that opposition to the rioting was rather uncommon among the spectators. They were not reported to be at all hostile to what was going on, and they even entered into what was described as a holiday or carnival spirit. Indeed, in our survey, when we asked "who tried to stop it?," only a rare respondent cited the crowds in the streets (15 per cent) or blacks in general (3 per cent). Those most often cast in that role were the authorities (38 per cent), black leaders (21 per cent), or, dismally, "nobody" (16 per cent) (Sears, 1966).

Our data show that the "close spectators," who presumably composed the crowds in the streets, overwhelmingly described the riot events in negative terms, expressing their dislike of the bloodshed, burning, and destruction. However, they described the rioters in more sympathetic terms, as mistreated and suffering people, rather than in harshly negative and moralistic terms, as most whites did. And they were highly optimistic about the riot's effects, feeling that whites would be led to pay more sympathetic attention to their problems. The crowds then seem to have been quite ambivalent about the riot but they by no means repudiated it. Thus, they must have formed a rather permissive, if ambivalent, audience for the more enthusiastic rioters (see Sears and McConahay, 1969, for the complete data).

Validity of Participation Measures.   How do we know that those who said they were active "really" were active? That is, how valid are those participation measures? The validity question is always one of the most difficult problems for psychological and social science research. Since it deserves a more thorough and detailed treatment than we can give it in this chapter, we have devoted Appendix C to it and to related questions. Here we shall give a brief summary of our attempts to assess the validity of our self-report measures.

One criterion for establishing validity is reliability (that is, consistency across various measurements). We think that the reliability of our 15 per cent estimate of activity beyond watching and cheer leading is quite good. It was based upon a combination of two measures: events witnessed and self-reported activity. We feel it is the most conservative estimate that can be obtained from these measures, since other means of calculating the level of participation (using other measures) yield a figure of about 20 per cent. Hence, our estimate meets two standard criteria of reliability: it is consistent and is based upon multiple measures of the entity.

Second, our estimate of the rate of participation is not affected by time. Those interviewed in January or February were as likely to report themselves active as those sampled in October (Sears and McConahay, 1970a). If respondents were distorting to make an impression upon our interviewers or to avoid punishment, one would expect an increase of reported activity over time, since the fear of punishment would decline with the passage of time subsequent to the event.

Finally, those arrested in the riot serve as a criterion group in which most were known to have been active (though of course some surely were erroneously arrested, due to the chaos). If our measures have any validity, then the arrestees should have been more likely to report themselves active, to make higher estimates of area and neighborhood participation, and to have seen a greater number of events. As shown in Table 1.1, this was indeed the case. The arrestees were much higher in every category. They saw more, they rated their neighborhoods more active, and they were more likely to report themselves active.

These tests do not indicate that our measures have perfect validity, by any means. Obviously they may include some error. However, they are valid enough for our purposes, which for the most part call for an analysis of the antecedents of riot participation, rather than estimations of the exact rate of participation. To protect ourselves against chance findings due to errors, most of our analyses of riot participation below are repeated over three independent indexes of participation: (1) comparisons of arrestees with the Curfew Zone sample as a whole, and, within the Curfew Zone sample, those (2) "very" or "somewhat active" versus "not active," and (3) high in events witnessed (that is, having seen at least four of the five riot events listed in Table 1.1) versus low in events witnessed. Thus, we feel sufficiently confident of our participation measures to proceed on the basis of them.

Analysis

Our primary concern in this book is with the riot as a political instrument. This devolves into two basic issues: (1) can riot participation rightfully be interpreted as a political act? and (2) what were the major political effects of the riot? In both cases our focus is upon the psychology of the individual citizen, whether black rioter or white voter, rather than upon the political system or government policy.

This book, then, has two main parts. In Chapters 2 through 7, we attempt to answer our first question by posing various political and non-political theories about the origins of riot participation and presenting empirical tests of them from our survey data. In Chapters 8 through 12, we are concerned primarily with the aftermath of the riot and its psychological effects upon individuals. In Chapter 13, we present a summary and a look into the future.

"Watts" was a landmark event in American race relations. It closed one era and opened another. It may have opened a Pandora's box but it also created exciting opportunities for America to develop into a truly mature, multiracial society. An in-depth examination of this event can be, we feel, a benefit to us all.

2 Who Were the Rioters?

Whites in Los Angeles (and throughout the North) were unprepared for a ghetto uprising of the magnitude of "Watts." A nationwide opinion poll in June 1963 revealed that only 20 per cent of northern whites expected "racial trouble" in their community in the "next two or three years" (Erskine, 1967). Even as late as June 1965 the opinion polls were showing that only 20 per cent expected "many riots" that summer (Schwartz, 1967). When the rioting erupted in Watts, Los Angeles whites responded initially with bewilderment and amazement.

In the face of such novelty, political leaders, journalists, the public, and social scientists asked: Who were they? Who could possibly have been rioting in the palm-lined Eden of Southern California? Soon, there were almost as many answers to this question as there were reporters to transcribe them; everyone had a theory. Yet the riot itself, like a giant projective test, was so vast, so remote, so diffuse, and so heterogeneous, and whites were so ignorant of the black ghetto, that the theorizer had only the barest, provocative, most ambiguous clues. Ignorance, however, inhibited virtually no one from speaking out and offering a theory, but usually the theory told more about the theorizer (and his political biases) than about the people of South Central Los Angeles.

Popular Theories of Rioting

Theories of crowd behavior and mass movements usually fall into one of two categories: those stressing convergence and those stressing contagion as mechanisms to account for the behavior of participants (see Milgram and Toch, 1969). *Convergence* theories emphasize the social and psychological characteristics of participants that predispose them to converge upon a place where the action is likely to occur. For example, peace demonstrations have been largely a convergence of those predisposed against the Vietnam war; pep rallies are largely a convergence of sports fans rooting for a particular team. *Contagion* theories emphasize the immediate environmental forces acting upon an individual who by chance happens to be near the action and is caught up in the spirit of the moment as the excitement spreads contagiously through the crowd. Parades, for example, tend to attract bystanders almost indiscriminately.

Contagion theories were especially popular with both white leaders and the white general public as explanations of who rioted, for by their very nature such theories derogate the rioters and rob the event of any political significance. They imply that only the most conventional changes are in order, usually emphasizing the need for more and better trained police to put out the dangerous spark or to contain the violence before it spreads. Convergence theories also can be used to derogate the rioters and rob the event of political significance but their effectiveness in this depends upon the predisposing motives and characteristics imputed to the rioters, as will be indicated later in this chapter.

The most popular contagion theories stated that the rioters were the unwitting dupes of communist or Black Muslim conspirators or other outside agitators; that they were simply caught up in the action because of proximity; and/or that they saw the beginnings of the riot on television and, like lemmings, rushed out to their own (and society's) doom. We will take up each of these in more detail in Chapter 7, as part of our attempt to construct a single, coherent, and comprehensive contagion theory, the "random outburst theory." The remainder of this chapter, and the succeeding four chapters, are devoted to various convergence theories.

White observers ascribed a wide variety of characteristics to the rioters, and political bias seemingly had much to do with these ascriptions. Political conservatives tended to view the rioters as deviant and disreputable, as hardened criminals, as ungodly drifters, as lazy and chronic troublemakers, as rebellious youths working off their "animal spirits," and so on. Clearly, they were people to be repudiated and the primary response to them should be harsh social control.

The other popular version of a convergence explanation, to which liberals were more drawn, saw the rioters (and the riot more generally) as a product of social ills. Sometimes this version emphasized the rioters' own social and personal handicaps, produced by poverty, unemployment, lack of education, broken homes, and, for newcomers from the South, cultural shock. At other times it blamed the conditions in which blacks lived, amid widespread police brutality, southern (or northern) racism, underfinanced schools, delapidated housing, and poor public transportation.

All of these convergence explanations, whether favored by liberals or conservatives, shared certain comforting characteristics. First, the prime causes selected by whites generally cast the blame for the riot outside their own sphere of responsibility. Communists, southern whites, the heat, the excitement, the liberals, civil rights agitators, the police, the conservatives, or the blacks themselves were responsible for the violence. The whites proposing the theories were not to blame. Second, since the theorists were not responsible, others would have to make the sacrifices necessary to bring about change. Blacks would have to resist their criminal impulses or invite control by the police forces. Southern whites would have to change their ways so that southern blacks would not want to migrate to Los Angeles. Civil rights leaders would have to tone down their rhetoric. A minimum of inconvenience for the theorist was involved.

These theories differed most dramatically, perhaps, in their estimates of the political implications of the riot. Conservatives generally favored theories that would deny it any political meaning. If the individual rioters were deviant and pathological, the trouble lay in these individuals, and the main solution lay in controlling their behavior better through coercion, or in inducing conformity to what was assumed to be a relatively satisfactory status quo.

The tenacity with which the white community, especially its Establishment, espoused the nonpolitical view of the riot is revealed in the theories of participation suggested by the McCone Commission, the group of business and civic leaders appointed by Governor Brown to investigate the rioting. After (1) labeling the riot an "insensate rage of destruction," the commission proposed that (2) participants were a small fraction of the ghetto (2 per cent or 10,000 persons) who were marginally related to the ghetto community, as drifters (principally criminals), unemployed, and dropouts from the educational system, and that (3) participants were newcomers to Los Angeles from the South who had been attracted by California's liberal welfare policies and who turned to violence when the expectations they brought with them were not fulfilled. These three views of the participants—a senseless mob, riffraff, or southern newcomers—all robbed the violence of any political significance and relegated it to the realm of the irrational and pathological (Governor's Commission on the Los Angeles Riots, 1965, pp. 1, 4–6, 24, and 71). The problems were not the collective problems of a large black community living in a predominantly white society riddled with racism; they were merely the individual peculiarities of a few deviant and uncivilized troublemakers.

This basic issue—whether the rioters were socially pathological or whether the riot revealed something amiss with society and the political system—was the central battleground of the various theories of participation or interpretations of the riot, and consequently of all of the systematically and unsystematically gathered data on it. The political implications of each view differed enormously. If the rioters were socially pathological, they would have to be ostracized or "corrected." No major changes in society, or in the distribution of power, would be necessary. If social ills were at fault, as many liberals contended, then the solutions lay in social changes that would remedy these ills. New social programs, reduced discrimination, and police retraining would be necessary. Note, however, that the liberals' views did not imply any very fundamental changes in power, either. There would be no need to disrupt "business as usual," no need to change "standard procedures." Mostly the reforms they advocated were to be generated and administered by those already in positions of some power. In this sense warmed-over New Deal programs did not differ very much from new armament for the police department. But liberal theories did open the door for a critique of social institutions, and thus ultimately for a general critique of the political status quo.

If the riot really did have a political meaning, if it was an expression of something really wrong with society, the ensuing social conflicts and sacrifices were bound to be more serious and to affect more of those in power. Our data must be viewed, then, as addressing this basic question about political power in America, as well as testing our more academic theories.

Theories of the Convergence of Pathological Rioters

As we have noted, then, most of the convergence theories of participation proposed by whites tended to derogate the rioters as criminals, riffraff, ne'er-do-wells, school dropouts, or products of unhappy childhoods. Since the motives and characteristics that predisposed the rioters to converge upon the action were seen as pathological, the riot to a large extent was deprived of political meaning. In this section, we shall test empirically the most popular of these lay theories.

The Rioters as Riffraff.   Perhaps the most common theory (and certainly the most attractive to many white authorities) held that the rioters were the dregs of society, the riffraff. This theory of riot participation had three major themes: (1) the rioters were a small, almost infinitesimal fraction of the ghetto population (the McCone Commission estimate); (2) they were principally criminals, thugs, drifters, and the ungodly who did not represent the typical ghetto resident and who had few, if any, ties to the ghetto community; (3) they were overwhelmingly rejected and repudiated by the decent folk of the community.

This sort of theory has a long (if not honorable) history. For example, it was King George's explanation for the various events preceding the American War of Independence. Louis XVI and his cabinet ministers proposed the riffraff theory to account for the disorders of the French Revolution (Rudé, 1967). Recently, it was invoked by every mayor of every city hit by a disturbance in the mid-1960s (Fogelson, 1967; and Fogelson and Hill, 1968). Los Angeles too had its riffraff theory exponents. Mayor Yorty and Chief of Police Parker vied with one another to see who could heap the most scorn upon the hoodlums and thugs who supposedly had carried out the bidding of the communists.

The riffraff theory has many current supporters. Is it true? Or, more properly, is it supported by our data? Clearly and emphatically, no. We have indicated already that well over the McCone Commission's estimate of 2 per cent of ghetto residents (or 10,000) were involved at a level beyond being passive spectators. In Chapter 1, we estimated conservatively that at least 31,000 were active participants, and that another 60,000 were close spectators of the action.

Not all of these people could be criminals. Data published by the Los Angeles Probation Department indicate that 56 per cent of the juveniles (aged 10–18) actually arrested and referred to them during the riot had had only one or no previous contact with the police, that 57 per cent never had been on probation before. In addition, 48 per cent attended church frequently or weekly and 53 per cent were doing average or better in school (Los Angeles County Probation Department, 1965, pp. 5–7 and 24–25). A great many of these young people, then, could not legitimately be called criminals or thugs.

Our data, too, indicate that the rioters were not unusually ungodly. Riot participation was significantly related to church attendance ($X^2 = 10.04$, 5 *df, p* < .05) but in a curvilinear fashion: those who attended religious services more than once a week were the *most* likely to report themselves active in the riot (35 per cent), while those who attended once a month were least active (13 per cent active). The non-attenders were in between (25 per cent). This failure to find a simple negative relationship is an important refutation of the riffraff theory because it shows that those who were most involved with perhaps the most important social institution in black society—the church (Dollard, 1937; Frazier, 1966; Drake and Cayton, 1962)—were not the least involved in the rioting. On the contrary, those who attended church most often were most likely to have participated in the upheaval.[1] The rioters then were not principally the drifters and the ungodly.

Finally, the rioters were not condemned or repudiated by their community. While blacks expressed much distaste for the death and destruction of the rioting itself, the most respectable and eminent figures in the black community (see Chapter 9) and the black public in general (see Chapter 10) expressed sympathy for the rioters. Most blacks, elite and mass alike, felt the rioters were embodying, in a mass protest, the just complaints of black Americans in general. They did not simply repudiate them as common criminals.

The Underclass Hypothesis: The Riffraff Theory Reformulated.   Another version of the riffraff theory, more popular among academics, saw the rioters as victims of social ills rather than as disreputable criminals and

---

[1]The curvilinear relationship was most persistent. It remained essentially undiminished with age, sex, social class, urban and rural socialization, political efficacy, cynicism, or other political attitudes controled. For more detailed analyses of the role of religion in this event, see McConahay, 1970a and b.

thugs. In this version they were identified as coming from some "under-class" of ghetto society—from the unemployed, the uneducated, the welfare recipients, or the lower classes. The McCone Commission, as already noted, gave a prominent place to the underclass theory, both in its analysis and in its recommendations for more education, better transportation, and job retraining. A variant of this theory was implied in the Kerner Commission's (1968) recommendations regarding employment, education, the welfare system, and housing. Anthony Oberschall, a sociologist, wrote one of the earliest attacks upon the riffraff theory in its crude form. Nevertheless, he proposed that the riot was "a massive, violent, *lower-class,* Negro outburst which stopped short of being an insurrection" (1968, p. 340, emphasis added). He suggested that the gains of the civil rights movement benefited the southern and middle-class blacks but did not do much for the lower-class, urban ghetto dwellers. Thus, the lower classes turned to burning and looting in response to grievances against the police and white society.

The most entertaining statement of the underclass hypothesis is found in Edward C. Banfield's book of speculations on urban problems (1970). In a chapter entitled "Rioting Mainly for Fun and Profit," Banfield declares that the rioters were lower-class, young Negro males who worked off their "animal spirits" and looted a few stores along the way. In his opinion, the grievances expressed by blacks and their leaders were entirely rationalizations for what in the main was merely meant as harmless fun.

These theories which recast the riffraff hypothesis in sociological under-class terms are appealing to academicians and liberals who are mostly sympathetic toward blacks. First, it is easy to document the great differences in employment, income, and quality of education between whites and blacks: since whites did not riot, these class differences appear to correlate with riot participation at this aggregate level. Second, by formulating the theories in sociological terms, one can avoid the stigma of being a "law-and-order person." Since the rioters are not criminals but simply people with nothing to lose, the problem is not one of law enforcement. Third, it is possible to infer that it was not the failure of liberal social policies that contributed to the rioting but rather that we need a more vigorous application of liberal social policies in order to elevate the underclass and give each person a "piece of the action." Fourth, since such theories are social and not racial, they are not subject to a charge of racism. Finally, and perhaps most important, formulating the theories in social and economic terms implies that the conditions that precipitated the riots can be altered by means which would not seriously inconvenience most whites—or at least most liberal academicians, politicians, and others of the professional class. Instead, they would seriously inconvenience working-class whites, who would face tougher competition for jobs and for places in the educational structure.

The underclass theories are quite appealing, but were they supported by the data? Unfortunately, they were not.

One characteristic of the underclass is its lack of formal education. Americans of every political persuasion are fond of proposing education as a solution to violent racial conflict. Implicit in this proposal is the theory that those with less education are more likely to turn to violence than those

TABLE 2.1

Riot Participation as a Function of Education and Subjective Social Class (Curfew Zone Sample)

SOCIAL CLASS INDEX	RIOT PARTICIPATION INDEX	
	Self-report (percentage active)	Events witnessed (percentage high)
Own education	$(n^* = 554)$	$(n = 472)$
Not high school graduate	20	32
High school graduate	26	33
Some college	24	31
	$X^2 = 0.7$, 2 df, n.s.†	$X^2 = 0.1$, 2 df, n.s.
Father's education	$(n = 513)$	$(n = 434)$
Grade school	25	23
Junior high	25	40
High school	22	33
College	21	31
Other; don't know	19	31
	$X^2 = 2.3$, 4 df, n.s.	$X^2 = 5.3$, 4 df, n.s.
Mother's education	$(n = 522)$	$(n = 440)$
Grade school	25	24
Junior high	18	36
High school	30	38
College	18	23
Other; don't know	22	22
	$X^2 = 6.5$, 4 df, n.s.	$X^2 = 10.8$, 4 df, $p < .05$
Subjective (self-reported) social class	$(n = 527)$	$(n = 450)$
Lower	29	35
Working	21	34
Middle and upper	22	24
	$X^2 = 2.2$, 2 df, n.s.	$X^2 = 5.7$, 2 df, n.s.

*n indicates "number of cases"   †n.s. denotes "statistical nonsignificance"

with more of it. However, we did not find that the educational underclass was any more likely to riot than those who had more formal education. The data summarized in Table 2.1 reveal no significant difference in participation rates among respondents with a grade school, high school, or college education. In Detroit and Newark, the rioters actually were significantly *better* educated than the non-involved (NACCD, 1968, p. 75) but age was not controlled in that study, so this result may have been an artifact of the negative correlation between age and education. In our own sample, controlling for education had no effect; at all age levels, education was unrelated to our measures of riot participation. So, in all three instances—Watts, Detroit, and Newark—the rioters were, if anything, drawn from those who had slightly more rather than less education than the nonrioters.

A variety of other methods assess social class more directly and they yield similar results. Table 2.1 also summarizes the associations between participation and objective measures of social class, such as father's and mother's education, and a more subjective measure, self-reported social class. Overall, it appears that the effects of these factors were minimal to nonexistent, since only one of these six relationships was statistically significant and it was not in the direction predicted by the underclass hypothesis. Similarly, those arrested in the rioting (our arrestee sample) did not differ on any measure of class from those in our Curfew Zone sample. Finally, as with education, controlling for age did not reveal any obscured relationships between these characteristics of the underclass and riot activity.

Unemployment was one attribute of the underclass that did relate to riot participation when controls were introduced. At the gross (uncontrolled) level, self-reported activity was not related to being employed or unemployed (Murphy and Watson, 1970, p. 224), nor were events witnessed or being arrested. However, when we controlled for age and sex of the respondent, a statistically significant relationship emerged between unemployment and our indexes of riot participation. Unemployed young (under 30) males were more likely to report themselves active (75 per cent versus 40 per cent for the employed), to have seen most of the riot events (90 per cent versus 45 per cent for the employed), and to have been among the arrestees (34 per cent unemployed in the arrestee sample versus 15 per cent unemployed in the Curfew Zone sample). All of these relationships were statistically significant, even with the reduced numbers resulting from the controls. Employment was not a factor in producing participation among women of any age or among men who were over 30 years old.

Other characteristics of the underclass—low levels of income and receipt of welfare—do not support the underclass hypothesis, however. We found no relationship between receiving or not receiving welfare and riot participation and no relationship between income level and riot participation. The Kerner Commission also reported finding no relationship between income and participation and concluded that, even though more affluent blacks were not residents of the areas from which they sampled, "the rioters are not necessarily the poorest of the poor" (p. 75). Murphy and Watson, also using data from the Curfew Zone sample (1970, p. 225), discovered that persons living in less affluent areas of the Los Angeles Curfew Zone were no more likely to report participation than those in more affluent areas.[2]

On balance, then, we found little support for the riffraff theory's more refined cousin, the underclass theory. Of all of the hundreds of relationships that could have emerged in our data, only two were significant. One, between employment and riot activity among young males, supported the underclass theory. The other, mother's education and participation, was directly contrary to it. All other relationships were nonsignificant. The picture that emerged was that the rioters were not drawn from one particular social class. Every stratum of the ghetto contributed its share of rioters.

Family Life Breakdown.   In the months preceding the Watts outburst, Daniel Patrick Moynihan authored a United States Department of Labor report entitled *The Negro Family: The Case for National Action* (1965). This paper, known as "the Moynihan Report," brought together census data and the results of several studies in history, sociology, and psychology. Moynihan called attention to what he felt was the severe disorganization and decay of the black family, particularly among lower-class urban blacks. He argued that this disorganization or destruction immersed the black American in the "tangle of pathology." Moynihan traced the roots of black family disorganization to the severity of American slavery where marriage was not recognized and father and mother and child were all apt to be sold at the whim of the slave master.

The weaknesses of the black family allegedly were heightened by urbanization and especially by the rapid urbanization resulting from the migration of blacks from the rural South to the urban North. The newcomers became enmeshed in the "tangle of pathology" whereby children from broken homes received less education, were more unemployable, had a greater tendency toward crime, married earlier or had illegitimate children, had more children, and were unable to live in stable family relationships—all of which produced another generation of children from broken homes who received less education, had a greater tendency toward crime, and so on.

In the report, Moynihan did not attempt to link broken homes and mob violence. He stated that he wanted to call the plight of the black family to the attention of the top policy makers of the Johnson Administration in

---

[2]Like the Kerner Commission's surveys, our sample area excluded the most affluent black residential areas. However, these areas represented a relatively small number of people. Murphy and Watson (1970) did find that those whose houses were neatly kept, a possible indicator of middle-class life style, were less likely to report activity than those whose housekeeping was not as meticulous. However, this measure is difficult to assess without more information about the reliability of our interviewers as judges of housekeeping.

order to mount a massive effort aimed at breaking the tangle of pathology. However, in the final days of the Watts holocaust, articles appeared in the *Los Angeles Times* (August 14th), the *Wall Street Journal* (August 16th), and the *Washington Post* (August 17th), expressing the thesis that "Family Life Breakdown in Negro Slums Sows Seeds of Race Violence" (the *Wall Street Journal,* August 16, 1965). These articles, and others that followed, credited this thesis to Moynihan and indeed Moynihan stated this view explicitly in an article appearing in the September 18th issue of *America* (Rainwater and Yancey, 1967, p. 139ff).

Moynihan's report was just the thing to produce maximum feasible misunderstanding. Conservatives did not like his suggestion that massive federal intervention was necessary, white liberals thought it was terribly impolite of him to mention flaws in the black character, and blacks were enraged by the manner in which his data could be used to blame blacks for their plight. However, many psychologists found the broken homes hypothesis appealing. Here was a truly psychological hypothesis to account for a large-scale social phenomenon. Hence, we included in our interview schedule several questions designed to assess family structure and generational relationships. These factors also failed to relate to riot participation in any way.

The participation rates differed very little between those reared by both parents and those reared in a broken home of one sort or another. For example, 22 per cent of those reared by both parents and 25 per cent of those reared only by the mother reported themselves active. Hardly a significant difference! This held true when we controlled for age and sex of the respondent and when we compared the arrestee and Curfew Zone samples. Thus, the "family life breakdown" hypothesis seems no more valid than the riffraff and underclass hypotheses.

Youthful Animal Spirits. The hypothesis that young men in particular were likely to riot, because of their "young, male animal spirits," has been stated most forthrightly by Banfield: "Young men are naturally restless, in search of excitement, thrills, 'action' " (p. 187). "Apparently, the [Frye] incident was mainly important as a pretext for a rampage by teen-age Negro boys" (p. 195).

Indeed, age was the most powerful and consistent demographic factor, other than race, in riot participation. We found a strong relationship between age and all of our measures of riot participation: 32 per cent of those under age 30, and 16 per cent over, said they were active; and 41 per cent and 25 per cent, respectively, were high in events witnessed. And indeed young men in particular were most active: 41 per cent of the men under 30 reported themselves active versus 22 per cent for the entire sample and 48 per cent versus 32 per cent were high in events witnessed. Furthermore, our arrestee sample included proportionately many more young men than either our Curfew Zone sample as a whole or census figures for blacks living in South Central Los Angeles. In our Curfew Zone sample, 15 per cent were young (aged 15–29) males; in the census, 18 per cent were young males; but in the arrestee sample, 52 per cent were males between 15 and 29 years of age (Sears and McConahay, 1969).

Clearly, then, the most outstanding characteristic of the riot participants was youth. The young were most likely to claim participation. The young were most likely to have seen a large number of riot events. The young were most likely to have been arrested. And the young males were the most active of all. Any theory that seeks to account for riot participation must be linked to the age factor.

Southern Newcomers.   Finally, the southern newcomer hypothesis successfully seduced almost every white observer of the riots. It represented the merging of two separate streams of respectable scholarship, on the South and on migrants in general. Many have commented upon the unusually violent history of southern life (Banfield, 1970; Cash, 1941). Blacks in particular have borne the brunt of this violence, from the beatings of slaves through post-Emancipation lynchings to the violence that greeted the civil rights movement in the years just before the rioting. Black people fleeing the South's oppression and brutality therefore might bring North with them a deep anger which could explode into violence. In addition, southern Negroes coming North with high hopes for a better life might become violent upon discovering the illusory nature of their hopes.

Similarly, the newcomer hypothesis has had a long history as an explanation of urban violence. Plutarch and Livy invoked it to account for the mob violence that preceded the fall of the Roman Republic (Lupsha, 1969, p. 280). Mass society theorists expect migrants to be generally rootless and violence-prone (Kornhauser, 1959). Since newcomers often come from rural areas, it is reasonable to suggest that they may suffer "culture shock" when they arrive with little preparation for the rate, stresses, and complexities of life in the urban ghetto. Thus, they may become alienated and hostile and turn to violence against the system that they perceive as the source of their woes.

But the southern newcomer hypothesis has more than just reasonableness and plausibility on its side. In the minds of northern mayors and police chiefs, this theory serves the same functions that the "outside agitator" theory has served for southern mayors and police chiefs. Both theories shift the locus of responsibility away not only from government officials but away from the community as well. Since the rioters (or protesters) are from outside the community, or at least have spent their formative years outside the local ghetto, the community and its leaders cannot be blamed for what has happened.

The policy implications of the southern newcomer hypothesis are also reassuring. Except for some patching of the local social fabric in order to restore the "harmony" that existed before the "ill prepared" or

TABLE 2.2

Riot Participation as a Function of Age and Length of Residence in Los Angeles (Curfew Zone Sample)

LENGTH OF RESIDENCE	AGE			
	15–29	30–44	45+	All ages
Percentage reporting themselves active	$(n = 212)$	$(n = 172)$	$(n = 173)$	$(n = 580)$
Born in Los Angeles or arrived before age seven	37	7	*	31
Arrived before 1946	*	20	14	16
Arrived 1946–1960	38	17	16	23
Newcomers (after 1960)	17	26	*	19
X^2	7.82	2.49	1.40	9.81
df	2	3	1	3
p	$<.025$	n.s.	n.s.	$<.025$
Age effect $(X^2 = 19.61, 2$ df, $p<.001)$	32	18	14	
Percentage high in events witnessed	$(n = 172)$	$(n = 147)$	$(n = 154)$	$(n = 492)$
Born in Los Angeles or arrived before age seven	52	38	*	49
Arrived before 1946	*	33	20	23
Arrived 1946–1960	43	30	20	33
Newcomers (after 1960)	23	20	*	22
X^2	9.52	1.56	0.33	16.70
df	2	3	1	3
p	$<.01$	n.s.	n.s.	$<.001$
Age effect $(X^2 = 15.67, 2$ df, $p<.001)$	41	30	20	

*These cells had observed frequencies of less than 10. The entry in this and most subsequent tables on riot participation is the percentage active of those characterized by both row and column. For example, 37% of all those who were both 15–29 years old at the time of the survey *and* native to Los Angeles reported themselves "very active" or "somewhat active" in the riot. The remaining 63 per cent of such respondents said they were "not active" or did not answer the question.

"hate-mongering" southerners poured into an area, the necessary changes and sacrifices are to be made in the South—far away from Los Angeles or Detroit or Newark.

The McCone Commission, in its report on the Los Angeles riot, carried the southern newcomer hypothesis one step further. It deplored the increase in welfare costs in the years preceding the violence and suggested that California's generosity in this regard had attracted large numbers of black and Spanish-speaking Americans to Los Angeles (p. 71). Attracted to Los Angeles by dreams of welfare luxury, the southern blacks were filled with a "special measure of frustration and disillusionment" (p. 4). Thus, not only were the rioters outsiders but they were ungrateful outsiders. In this form, the southern newcomer hypothesis suggested to the people of Los Angeles that the white community should avoid any feelings of guilt over its contribution to the conditions that produced the riot. Indeed, it had done too much, rather than too little, for the blacks. Hence, the appropriate response to the riots was indignation.

Our survey data from Los Angeles lend little support for either the southern or the newcomer aspect of the southern newcomer theory. First, we looked at the relationship of riot participation to length of residence in Los Angeles. The natives and long-time residents were much more active in the riot than the newcomers, as shown in Table 2.2.

Obviously, this finding might have been distorted by the relationship between age and length of residence in Los Angeles. But it proved not to be. When we corrected this by holding age constant (looked at the effects of length of residency within a given age group) we found that, among the young, the natives and long-time residents were still twice as likely to report themselves active as the recent arrivals (37 per cent and 38 per cent versus 17 per cent). A similar effect was obtained when participation was indexed with the events-witnessed scale, as shown in Table 2.2. Thus, surprisingly enough, it appears that the newcomers were by far the *least* active members of the black ghetto.

Nor were the rioters especially likely to be ex-southerners. In accordance with the theoretical analysis we will present in the next chapter, we defined a native as one who was born in Los Angeles or who arrived there before his seventeenth birthday.[3] As shown in Table 2.3, the southern migrants

---

[3]Those who arrived in Los Angeles before age 17 are included in our definition of "native" because early political socialization is central in our theorizing and the best current evidence indicates that this socialization is roughly complete only by mid-adolescence. Hence, if we had used a younger cut-off point, we would have classified falsely some Los Angeles-socialized respondents as "migrants." This evidence will be discussed in detail in the next chapter. We depart from this practice in only two places. In some of our analyses of the acquisition of racial attitudes (see Chapters 5 and 10) we used an earlier cut-off age because of the evidence that racial attitudes are generally acquired earlier in life than are most political attitudes (see Chapter 3). In Table 2.2 we used an earlier cut-off age because we wanted a rather conservative definition of native for this analysis, perhaps our most basic and certainly one of our most important findings. We have done the analyses presented in Table 2.2 with both more and less restrictive definitions of nativity but, except for changes in the cell sizes, the results are essentially unaltered for those arriving before age 17.

TABLE 2.3

**Riot Participation as a Function of Age and Place of Origin
(Curfew Zone Sample)**

PLACE OF ORIGIN	AGE			
	15–29 ($n = 212$)	30–44 ($n = 172$)	45+ ($n = 173$)	All ages ($n = 580$)
Percentage reporting themselves active				
Los Angeles natives	37	9	*	28
Northern migrants	19	17	17	19
Southern migrants	24	21	15	20
X^2	5.0	2.7	2.4	4.4
df	2	2	1	2
p	<.08	n.s.	n.s.	n.s.
Percentage high in events witnessed				
Los Angeles natives	52	43	*	48
Northern migrants	37	21	17	26
Southern migrants	20	28	21	25
X^2	14.7	3.4	1.0	23.5
df	2	2	1	2
p	<.001	n.s.	n.s.	<.001

*Cells had observed frequencies of less than 10.
Note: First entry is percentage reporting themselves somewhat or very active. Second entry is percentage reporting having seen four or five major riot events.

generally were less likely than the natives to have participated. The right-hand columns of this table indicate that the natives witnessed significantly more riot events (48 per cent high in events witnessed for natives' versus 25 per cent for southern migrants) and reported themselves more active (28 per cent versus 20 per cent for southern migrants) than others in the Curfew Zone. Furthermore, the Los Angeles natives were disproportionately represented among those arrested (48 per cent versus 31 per cent of the random sample).

Again, because of the strong relationship between age and place of origin, we repeated these analyses with age controlled, as also is shown in Table 2.3. The young natives were significantly more active than the young southern migrants in events witnessed and marginally more active according to self-reported activity.[4] Among the older age groups, the differences were inconsistent in direction and not statistically significant. For the crucial young age group, then, the natives, rather than the ex-southerners, were the most active.[5]

Caplan and Paige's survey for the Kerner Commission discovered data quite consistent with ours. They found that northern natives were significantly more active than southern migrants (NACCD, 1968, p. 332). In both Detroit and Newark, 74 per cent of those claiming participation were northern-reared. On the other hand, only 36 per cent of the nonrioters in Detroit and 52 per cent of the nonrioters in Newark were from the North. Clearly, in all three cities local northern natives were disproportionately represented among the rioters, while southern newcomers were the least active.[6]

[4]Since our sample included persons of age 15 and above, we could conceivably have classified as "natives" some 15- or 16-year-olds who had just arrived in Los Angeles. However, as it turned out, all "natives" over 15 had arrived before age 8 (not surprisingly; see our discussion of migrants' ages in the next chapter). Still, we were concerned that some young persons we called "natives" might have been in Los Angeles for a rather small portion of their entire lives. To analyze the effects of relative proportions of lifetime in Los Angeles upon riot behavior, we devised a Percentage of Lifetime in Los Angeles Index (number of years spent in Los Angeles divided by age in 1965). Among the young, 15-29 years old, 72 per cent of the natives as opposed to 0 per cent of the northern and southern migrants had spent 50 to 100 per cent of their lifetime in Los Angeles. Most importantly, among the young, percentage of lifetime in Los Angeles was not related significantly to riot participation for the natives or the northern or southern migrants. For example, for the young natives (by our definition), 50 per cent of those spending less than one third of their lives in Los Angeles versus 53 per cent of those spending 75 per cent to 100 per cent of their lives in Los Angeles, were high in events witnessed. This lack of effect of percentage of lifetime indicates that the broader categories of native versus northern migrant versus southern migrant are the crucial ones.

[5]The major inconsistency in the pattern was provided by the northern migrants. On some measures they were almost as active as the natives, while on others they were the least active group. This may result from the small number of northern migrants in our samples (making for unreliability) or from the fact that they came mainly from medium-sized cities, not large urban ghettoes, and thus differed from the natives in some important respects besides place of origin.

[6]Attempts to test the southern newcomer hypothesis at the aggregate level (across cities) have yielded mixed results. The hypothesis was partially supported in a study by Wanderer (1969). He found a strong correlation (.833) between riot severity in 1967 and mean percentage increase of nonwhites in the total population of a given city from 1950 to 1960. Similarly, a study by the Lemberg Center for the Study of Violence at Brandeis University found a higher proportion of southern blacks in three riot cities than in three "matched" nonriot cities during 1966. Contrary to these results were those of Lieberson and Silverman (1965). They compared 76 "matched" pairs of riot and nonriot cities during the years 1913-1963. Their results suggested that riot and nonriot cities did not differ with regard to black in-migration. Similarly, Williams (1964) used a random sample of cities and found that tensions were no higher in cities with rapid growth in black population than in those with stable

Who Were They?

We have presented in this chapter a series of theories commonly invoked to explain urban rioting. Although they serve to shift the blame and to rob the riot of much of its political significance, the riffraff, underclass, family life breakdown, and southern newcomer theories are all inconsistent with our data. Each proposes a single demographic factor as the key to understanding who the Watts rioters were, but each in large part fails to offer an adequate explanation. Indeed, of all the demographic variables implied by these popular theories, and normally employed in socio-psychological research, only age, place of origin, and to a lesser extent, sex, had a significant relationship with riot participation. What theoretical sense do these variables make?

One theory of why many young people participated in urban rioting, although accurate, has a somewhat tautological ring to it. This theory, popular with some laymen and historians, proposes that the young were the most active in the riots because the young historically always have been the most active in civil disorders of this sort. While this theory does point to the most readily identifiable group among the participants, it does not explain very much. Hence, social scientists usually attempt to account for the great participation rates of the young by referring to their superior physical vigor (or "animal spirits") and/or their low level of socialization and integration into the community (or the status quo).

There is no denying that young people are vigorous and active and probably physical vigor is a factor in rioting. It does not account for all participation, however, for physical vigor was not the only distinguishing characteristic of the rioters. Since rioting seems to be so counternormative, a theory utilizing the concepts of integration into the community and socialization to its norms and values appears to be a potentially fruitful approach to understanding the phenomenon of urban violence. However, as

---

populations. Each of these aggregate studies has a flaw that makes it impossible to test the southern newcomer hypothesis. Matching always raises methodological difficulties, since one never can be sure that matching was along the appropriate dimensions (Campbell and Stanley, 1963). Also, the proportion of blacks (usually measured by "nonwhites") in a city could increase by in-migration from North or South, by a high birth rate among blacks, by a rapid out-migration of whites, or by a combination of all three. Finally, even if these aggregate studies concurred in their support of the southern newcomer hypothesis, we still would have no assurance that the rioters actually were the new arrivals. A rapid growth of population might create conditions that make the outbreak of violence highly likely. However, local people who resent the crowding created by the influx of newcomers might go on the rampage rather than newcomers or the rioters might be both natives and migrants in common cause. Finally, some third variable might make the city highly attractive to in-migrants *and* also highly volatile. Thus aggregate analysis can tell us a little about the population makeup of cities that riot but it tells us nothing whatever about the demographic characteristics of individual rioters.

reported above, we discovered that those who should have been most socialized and integrated into the community, that is, those who were Los Angeles natives, were significantly *more* active than either group of migrants. Furthermore, with age controlled, the effects of local socialization were strongest among the young. The young natives, who should have been much more integrated and socialized to the norms and values of the community than the young migrants, rioted to a much greater extent than the migrants did. Thus, the usual form of the socialization hypothesis, that the young riot because they are least socialized to the existing system, appears untenable.

We suggest that another form of the socialization hypothesis is more plausible. What is important is not the degree of socialization and integration but rather the nature of the community norms to which a young person is socialized. Those who see rioting as reflecting a lack of integration into the community may have misunderstood the nature of the norms dominant in northern urban ghettoes, especially the norms dominant among the young. In reality, mainstream socialization may move young northern blacks part of the way toward, rather than away from, collective violence. The aim of this book is to pursue this line of reasoning; to attempt to formulate a socialization hypothesis that fits the demographic findings of this chapter into a more general theory of urban violence.

3   A Theory of Urban Rioting

The most important empirical finding to emerge from Chapter 2 is the high rate of riot participation among the young blacks reared in Los Angeles. In this chapter we wish to suggest that these young natives constitute an identifiable group, whose psychology, individual and collective, is so different from that of others in the ghetto that we have called them "the New Urban Blacks."[1]

The New Urban Blacks have four distinguishing characteristics. They generally are under 30 years of age, were born in the North (or West) or arrived there before the age of 17, were socialized in an urban setting, and have at least a high school education. In this chapter we shall show that, in the pre-riot years, after a half century of demographic changes, people with these characteristics finally achieved numerical dominance among young adults in black ghettoes. Then we shall attempt to spell out, at a theoretical level, the social and political psychology that mediates between these demographic characteristics and participation in urban violence. Most specifically, we shall attempt to answer the question: What social-psychological changes, resulting from the demographic trends, were sufficiently profound to spur a sudden surge of rioting? After formulating the hypotheses in this chapter, we shall test them with empirical data in later chapters.

Demographic Origins of the New Urban Blacks

The demographic changes affecting the Afro-American population during the twentieth century are generally well-known but the radical nature of

---

[1]Though we think we were the first (see Sears and McConahay, 1970b, a reprint of a report first published in 1967), we are not the only social scientists to have noted the emergence of a new ghetto person (see Caplan, 1970).

these changes has surprised even informed observers. Therefore, our purpose in presenting the data in this section is not to document that blacks have changed demographically; rather it is to emphasize the dramatic extent of these changes, before spelling out their implications for urban violence.

Relative Size.   The proportion of blacks in the American population has not altered appreciably in this century. It reached a zenith of 21 per cent at the peak of the slave trade in 1770, gradually declined under the onslaught of white immigrants to a low of 9.7 per cent in 1930, and stood at 10.6 per cent in 1960. The proportion of blacks is expected to increase only slightly in the next few decades (Taeuber and Taeuber, 1966, p. 102).

Northernization.   On the other hand, the geographical distribution of blacks has altered considerably since the beginning of World War I. As shown in Table 3.1, the percentage of blacks in the South declined by only three points in the fifty years from 1860 to 1910 but in the next 50 years it declined by 30 points, that is, ten times as fast as in the previous period. In 1910, at the beginning of the major Southern migration to the North,

TABLE 3.1

**Migration of the Black Population to the North:
Distribution of the Black Population by Region, 1860–1970**

Year	South	Northeast	North Central	West
1860	92.2%	3.5%	4.2%	0.1%
1870	90.6	3.7	5.6	0.1
1880	90.5	3.4	5.9	0.2
1890	90.3	3.6	5.8	0.4
1900	89.7	4.3	5.7	0.3
1910	89.0	4.9	5.6	0.5
1920	85.2	6.5	7.6	0.8
1930	78.7	9.7	10.6	1.0
1940	77.0	10.7	11.0	1.3
1950	68.0	13.4	14.8	3.8
1960	59.9	16.0	18.3	5.8
1970	53.0	19.2	20.2	7.5

Sources: Dept. of Commerce, Bureau of the Census, *Negro Population, 1790–1915*, pp. 33, 43–44; *Negroes in the U.S., 1920–1932*, p. 5; *Historical Statistics of the U.S., Colonial Times to 1957*, pp. A71, 122; *Statistical Abstract of the U.S., 1969*, p. 27; and U.S. Bureau of the Census, *Census of Population: 1970, General Population Characteristics*, Final Report PC (1)-B1, United States Summary.

only 11 per cent of the black population lived outside the South. By 1966, this was estimated to have increased to 45 per cent (Bureau of Labor Statistics, 1967).[2]

As the northern black population has increased, its northern-bred off-spring gradually have replaced the older southern migrants. During the decade of the 1950s, the balance between the southern migrant and the northern native finally tipped. In 1950, nonwhites living in the West came almost equally from the South and from the West. By 1960, western-born nonwhites outnumbered the southern-born by more than two to one. Thus, from 1910 until recently, the northern ghettoes have been populated mainly by recent migrants from the South (who, incidentally, have tended to be less literate, less skilled, and older than the natives). Today, this is no longer the case. The northern natives have become numerically dominant among young adults in the ghetto.

Urbanization.   In 1900, the black population was predominantly rural (77 per cent) but, since the turn of the century, blacks have moved from the countryside to the cities of both the North and South at a rate greater than that of whites. Consequently, the formerly predominantly rural black population has become highly urbanized, even more urbanized than the white population. In the North and West, the areas where most of the riots have occurred, the black population is almost entirely urban, as shown in Table 3.2.

Youth.   Both the white and black populations have become more youthful in the last two decades but the blacks have done so at a relatively greater rate. In 1950, the median age was 30.7 and 26.2 years for whites and blacks, respectively. By 1967, these figures were estimated at 29.0 and 21.2 years, respectively (*Statistical Abstract*, 1968, p. 26). Thus, in 17 years, the "youth gap" had increased from 4.5 to 7.8 years; and 55 per cent of the black population was under age 24.

If present trends continue, we can expect steady increases in the proportion of blacks who are in the most riot-prone age groups (adolescence and young adulthood). This is due to the higher birth rates and shorter life expectancies among blacks (Taeuber and Taeuber, 1966, pp. 153–156). This prediction is quite tentative, however, because birth rates fluctuate enormously over time and increasing levels of education among blacks will probably decrease fertility rates and increase life expectancy. Nevertheless, it is a safe bet for at least the next two decades, since the people already have been born.

[2]Throughout this section we have used population estimates as close as possible to the year of the riot (1965). However, preliminary data from the 1970 census indicate that, since 1965, all of these trends have continued and in some cases have accelerated.

TABLE 3.2

Urbanization of the Black Population:
Percentage of Blacks and Whites Living in Urban Areas, 1900–1970

	BLACKS					WHITES
	United States	Northeast	North Central	South	West	
1900	22.6	76.8	64.4	17.2	67.8	42.0
1910	27.3	81.4	72.6	21.2	78.7	48.0
1920	34.0	86.9	83.4	25.2	76.7	53.2
1930	43.7	89.0	87.8	31.7	82.6	57.6
1940	48.6	90.1	88.8	36.5	83.0	57.5
1950	62.4	94.0	93.8	47.7	90.3	64.3
1960	73.4	95.7	95.7	58.4	93.0	69.6
1970	81.3	97.0	97.3	67.3	96.9	72.4

Note: Entry is percentage of race classified as urban dwellers by the Census Bureau.
Sources: U.S. Bureau of the Census, *Population Trends in the U.S.: 1900–1960*,
Technical Paper No. 10, U.S. Government Printing Office, Washington, D.C., 1964,
p. 140; U.S. Bureau of the Census, *Census of Population: 1970, General Population
Characteristics*, United States Summary.

Education.   The deficiencies in educational opportunities for blacks are
well known. However, post-World War II increases in black educational
attainments are astounding. In 1940, black men aged 25–29 averaged 6.5
years of education. By 1962, the average was 11.0 years. The racial differential has not been eliminated but it has been reduced. In 1940, whites had,
on the average, 4.0 more years of education than blacks; by 1962, the
difference was only 1.5 years (12.5 versus 11.0) (Taeuber and Taeuber,
1966); by 1970, the median difference was less than half a year. In 1970,
the major discontinuity was at age 35: below that, the racial difference in
education was 0.5 years or less in every age group, while it was 1.2 years
for those aged 35–44, and 3 years or more for those over 45. Thus those
under 30 at the time of the rioting were quite different from their elders in
their educational background (*Current Population Reports: The Social and
Economic Status of Negroes in the United States*, 1970).

Accompanying these changes in formal educational attainment has been
an equally astounding decrease in the illiteracy rate. In 1900, 35 per cent
of blacks 20–24 years old were illiterate. Today, illiteracy virtually has been
eliminated from that age group. Approximately 0.5 per cent of all blacks
aged 14–24 are illiterate. This signals, among other things, a radically increased potential for politicization.

Residential Segregation.   Segregation has remained a central fact of life for blacks in this country. As blacks moved to the North and into the great cities, they were herded together in the most dismal and ancient surroundings urban America could offer. Consequently, there was (and is) a high degree of residential segregation in every city with any sizable black population (Taeuber and Taeuber, 1966). Moreover, blacks have been crammed increasingly into the "central cities" of the largest metropolitan areas. In 1900, only 54 per cent of blacks residing in metropolitan areas were in central cities. By 1960, the figure was 80 per cent. In contrast, the white population was withdrawing from the central cities, decreasing from 63 per cent to 48 per cent over the same period (Taeuber and Taeuber, 1966, p. 133).[3]

Thus, both the characteristics of the cities and of their dark ghettoes have changed during this century. The central cities are no longer exclusively the preserves of white immigrants, for the blacks have sufficient numbers to challenge the white ethnic dominance. And in the segregated, crowded, but expanding ghettoes, the older, less literate, and rural southern-socialized blacks are being replaced by northern, urban, better educated young people —by the New Urban Blacks.

The New Migrant.   Even the newcomers to urban life are not what they used to be. The characteristics of migrants themselves have changed in a way that simply reinforces the other population trends we have been presenting.

There is substantial evidence that prior to 1950 migrants from the South were of lower status than northern natives on several dimensions, as Taeuber and Taeuber have shown (1966). Migrants were especially low (relative to northern natives) in educational attainment. However, the low status stereotype no longer applies to the typical new arrival. Starting in the 1950s, black in-migrants to major metropolitan areas have tended to *raise,* rather than to lower, the average status level of the destination population. Today, for example, black in-migrants are more likely to have graduated from high school than are the blacks already living in major cities of the South and North alike. The same is true for occupational levels; in-migrants are more apt to be engaged in white-collar occupations than are the natives of the host population (*Mobility for Metropolitan Areas,* 1963,

[3]Census data for 1970 reveal *exactly* the same proportion of metropolitan blacks living in central cities as in 1960. See *Current Population Reports,* 1971, p. 13. Blacks who moved to the so-called suburban "ring" areas normally did not experience suburban life as it is described in the Sunday supplements. Most often, blacks migrated to "industrial suburbs," where they continued to live in segregated neighborhoods, or occasionally they moved to "Negro suburbs" (Taeuber and Taeuber, 1966, pp. 134–136). The housing in these areas was better, the schools were better, and the density of population was reduced. But normally the housing was not as new, or the schools as good, or the vistas as spacious, as in the more affluent white suburbs. In this sense residential segregation remains complete, even in suburban areas.

pp. 146–147). Thus, migration, in itself, no longer tends to disorganize the ghetto schools with poorly prepared children; to flood the job market with unskilled labor; or to fill the streets with friendless, aimless, "alienated," and homeless itinerants.

Most important for our analysis, the migrants tend to be quite young. Geographically mobile nonwhites are five years younger than the total nonwhite population and tend to be in either their twenties or the five-to-nine year age bracket (*Mobility for States,* 1963, p. 1). There are two consequences of this influx of young adults and minor children. First, migration lowers the overall age level of the destination population. Second, as the young children get older, they are socialized in the ghetto. In combination with those actually born there, such socialization swells the ranks of those who have adopted the political and social norms of the northern ghettoes.

These changes in geography, age, and education were sufficient to convert the predominantly southern, agrarian, uneducated, and residentially stable black population of Booker T. Washington's time into today's mobile, urban, young, northern, and educated black population. No longer is the Afro-American population dominated by the rural southern blacks. And increasingly today the northern natives—the New Urban Blacks—are coming to dominate the northern ghettoes. And this is especially true in Los Angeles.

The Changing Los Angeles Black Population. Blacks (like whites) began moving to Los Angeles much later than to the major industrial centers of the East. There was very little migration of blacks to Los Angeles until the 1940s. By 1960, however, the young natives had gained numerical superiority over the southern migrants in Los Angeles, just as they had elsewhere in the country. In 1950, 48 per cent of the California nonwhites between 10 and 19 years of age had been born in the South; by 1960, this had decreased to 33 per cent. Persons who were aged 10 to 19 in 1960 would be, in 1965, 15 to 24 years old, the age group most active in the rioting.

This trend is illustrated further in our sample of Los Angeles Curfew Zone residents interviewed after the riot. Table 3.3 reveals dramatically the recency of the appearance in Los Angeles of a substantial number of natives. Only among the youngest age group (15–29) do the native-born and native-bred predominate: 58 per cent were natives. In the middle and oldest age groups, the proportion of natives was quite small: only 21 per cent and 8 per cent, respectively. In the older generation, southern migrants were dominant.

In years gone by, southern origins normally also meant rural socialization, so in the past southern migrants to Los Angeles typically were *not* urban in origin in contrast to northern migrants (32 per cent versus 63 per cent, respectively). Hence, as a result of the big increase in the number of natives, and some influx of young, urban northerners into Watts, the proportion that is urban in origin is much greater among the young than among the old (62 per cent versus 39 per cent, respectively).

TABLE 3.3

Age and Place of Origin of Blacks in Los Angeles
(Curfew Zone Sample)

PLACE OF ORIGIN	AGE			
	15–29	30–44	45+	All ages
*Los Angeles natives**	58%	21%	8%	31%
Northern migrants	13	18	20	17
Southern migrants	30	61	72	53
	100%	100%	100%	100%

*"Natives" are those either born in Los Angeles or migrating to Los Angeles before age 17. See Footnote 3 in Chapter 2.

Finally, education (and status) has increased with the growing numbers of natives and northern migrants as opposed to the older generation of southern migrants in the Los Angeles ghetto. The young (under 30) in our sample were more than twice as likely to have attended college as the old (45 and over) (28 per cent versus 13 per cent). And many of the young could be expected to continue further with their education, contributing to an even greater generation gap.

In Los Angeles and across the nation, then, the demographic profile of the black population has changed radically. Blacks are increasingly northernized, urbanized, and residentially segregated. At the same time, blacks are forming a younger, more vigorous, and better educated population. As a consequence, the ghettoes are rapidly becoming dominated, numerically at least, by young, urban, educated, and northern socialized residents, by the New Urban Blacks. And the evidence indicates that this trend will accelerate, so that the emerging New Urban Blacks also represent the wave of the future.

We shall now present our hypotheses about what these changes have meant for the political and racial attitudes of blacks, their personal expectations, and thus their riot participation. In later chapters we shall examine what these trends tell us about the future.

Early Political Socialization

The first major consequence of this demographic shift is that the early political socialization of the New Urban Blacks has differed considerably from that of the older, southern blacks, with major and enduring effects upon their racial and political predispositions. Before discussing this question, we must consider first the more general one of the enduring effects of early political socialization. Here we might note in passing that our approach is formulated in terms of social learning theory, rather than in terms of cognitive development (e.g., Piaget) or psychodynamic (e.g., Freud) theory.

The Psychology of Enduring Dispositions.   If attitudes acquired during childhood political socialization are to be of any social consequence, they must leave strong and stable residues in adulthood. More formally, in adulthood they must be (1) stable over time, (2) consistent across various related contents, and (3) capable of determining opinion on newly arising attitude objects. Research conducted in the last decade on political socialization, and on adult political opinions, has pinpointed certain areas of public opinion in which American opinions consistently meet these criteria. The clearest are (1) group identity, (2) racial prejudice, (3) political party identification, (4) affection or disaffection for various symbols of the nation and the political system, and (5) political involvement. Political opinion in other areas generally tends to be neither very convincingly socialized in childhood nor very stable, consistent, or powerful in adulthood, frequently declining to the status of what Converse (1970) has called "non-attitudes" (Sears, 1969a; Sears and Whitney, 1973).

The socialization of group identity, racial prejudice, and political party identification all appear to take place in pre-adolescence, for most American children. This has been documented repeatedly in the cases of racial attitudes (Proshansky, 1966), social class (Hyman, 1959), nationality (Lambert and Klineberg, 1966), intergroup antagonisms (Proshansky, 1966; Lambert and Klineberg, 1966; Zellman and Sears, 1971), and party identification (Easton and Hess, 1962; Greenstein, 1965). None of this implies that the family's influence is overriding on these matters; indeed, the best evidence is that the child acquires such attitudes rather broadly—from the social environment around him, including the family and also peers, teachers, relatives, and to some extent the media. Finally, the best evidence is that these attitudes normally change very little in adolescence (Jennings and Niemi, 1968b).

Affection or disaffection for the nation and political system also has been shown repeatedly to be socialized in late childhood (Easton and Dennis, 1969; Greenstein, 1965; Hess and Torney, 1967). How specific this socialization is to particular symbols of the system, such as the flag, the President, and the police, is still mostly a matter of speculation, as are the family's and the school's relative contributions to such socialization (Jennings and Niemi, 1968a; Sears, 1968a). And while it seems clear that children develop such attitudes relatively early in life, there is evidence that their attitudes continually evolve through adolescence. Increasingly cynical attitudes toward the political system and the police seem to be characteristic of adolescence (Easton and Dennis, 1969; Jennings and Niemi, 1968b).

Significant variations in subjective political involvement (and in its overt manifestations, such as amount of political information, extent of media exposure, and political participation) also can be detected in pre-adolescent children (Hess and Torney, 1967). Normally we would expect that political sophistication, too, would depend upon the degree of subjective political involvement acquired by the individual in late childhood and early adolescence. Here too there is evidence of continual evolution through adolescence, with, however, substantial increases in political involvement and sophistication taking place (Jennings and Niemi, 1968b).

Hence it is appropriate to regard pre-adolescent socialization as critical to group identity, racial prejudice, and party identification, but political socialization appears to continue well into adolescence in the case of affection and disaffection toward the political system and various dimensions of political involvement.

Attitudes in these several domains also appear to be more stable over both the long and the short term than are most other social and political attitudes and dispositions. Panel studies have demonstrated short-term stability most convincingly. For example, Converse (1964) has shown that racial attitudes and party identification are more stable over two- or four-year periods than are any of a variety of other political attitudes tested. Long-term stability is more of an unknown, since longitudinal studies of attitudes have been conducted on only a few, rather specialized, and usually highly politicized samples (Bloom, 1964; Newcomb *et al.*, 1967). Nevertheless, these retrospective reports indicate that relatively few people change their basic attitudes to any extent and very few change political parties (Campbell *et al.*, 1960, p. 147). Finally, even aging, or social or geographic mobility, may not influence party or racial attitudes as much as is generally believed (Barber, 1965; Campbell *et al.*, 1960; Sears, 1969a). Thus, the weight of the data supports the hypothesis that those basic racial and political attitudes acquired in early socialization are quite stable and long-lasting.

Systematic tests of the internal consistency of these dispositions have been uncommon. Any available indications suggest that at least racial attitudes, party identification, and political involvement show great consistency across a variety of different indexes of disposition. For example, attitudes toward a variety of different racial policies tend to be rather consistent (Converse, 1964), party identification tends to be highly consistent with stands on partisan issues and with partisan candidate choice (Sears, 1969a), and there is much consistency among various dimensions of political involvement, such as voting rates, information, party campaign work, and campaign donations (Milbrath, 1965).

The last of these three criteria, power of controlling opinion or behavior with respect to newly arising attitude objects, is perhaps the most difficult to test. Nevertheless, this has been documented repeatedly for racial attitudes (Becker and Heaton, 1967; Sears and Kinder, 1971), party identification

(Sears, 1969a), and political involvement (Milbrath, 1965). And the influence of intergroup antagonisms upon attitudes toward various freedom of speech issues has been demonstrated (Zellman and Sears, 1971).

Hence, though there are still gaps in the research literature with respect to the enduring effects of early political socialization on adults' attitudes in these five domains, the available evidence is fairly convincing. Preadolescent political socialization does leave, in most Americans, rather stable, consistent, and powerful attitudinal residues.

The reasons that these attitudes tend to endure cannot be resolved so easily. Four factors seem the most likely ones: (1) *a primacy effect*—the earliest attitude acquired tends to be the strongest; (2) *duration of opinion holding*—long-held opinions gain a special strength from practice; (3) *persistence of the original socializing environment*—the original socializing environment tends to remain constant, providing continuing reinforcement for the attitudes springing from early socialization; (4) *constant attitude objects*—the attitude objects in question generally have remained constant and, thus, tend to evoke a constant response.

Unfortunately for analytic purposes, all four factors usually are confounded in the real life attitude domains in question. Thus, it is hard to determine which factor, or which combination of factors, bears the main responsibility for the persistence of early political socialization. It is not currently known how much impact primacy and duration have upon opinion strength over long periods of time. The evidence is clear, however, that early socializing environments tend to remain quite constant over a lifetime (Goldberg, 1966; Lane and Sears, 1964) and thus consistently reinforce the effects of early political socialization by a process of *de facto* selective exposure. Indeed, adult Americans show a considerable talent for surrounding themselves with a social environment that will support their beliefs (Berelson *et al.*, 1954; Newcomb *et al.*, 1967; Sears, 1968b). Finally, the attitude objects in these domains have generally shown impressive continuity. "United States," "democracy," and the "police" (to take a few examples) have all been with us for well over a century, for the entire lifetime of every American living today. Their attributes have varied, their leadership has changed, but these concepts have remained as stimuli to which we react.

Change as well as continuity is a factor in socialization. Socializing environments change and new attitude objects appear from time to time. Migrants change their environments. The Watts Riot and black militant organizations certainly represent novel attitude objects to most blacks. What generally happens when things change?

With a constant social environment, the individual is likely to respond to familiar and novel attitude objects alike in a manner consistent with his early socialization, and this persistent response will be reinforced continually by those around him. Even a changed environment probably will not force very much attitude change, as long as the attitude object itself remains more or less constant, as indicated by the studies cited above on the constancy, despite aging or social or geographic mobility, of party identification. The major breaks with early socialization should occur only when *both* elements change: when the attitude object is novel *and* when the individual's childhood and adult environments differ.

Concretely, what these several observations add up to is that the response to longstanding attitude objects will depend principally upon the individual's *childhood* social environment, while the response to novel attitude objects generally should be predictable from knowledge of the individual's *current* environment. Occasionally, of course, late adolescents or young adults do change regarding familiar attitude objects, as in Newcomb's classic case study of Bennington college graduates (1967). This phenomenon can be called "resocialization." The line between resocialization and acquisition of attitudes toward new objects is not a sharp one. It rests upon determining whether a given attitude object is familiar or novel; often the attitude objects combine elements of both. In any case, the key distinction to be made in our discussion below, of a "political socialization" approach to understanding the effects of major demographic changes in the black population, is between (1) persistence of the residues of early political socialization toward stable attitude objects and (2) "resocialization" or the adult acquisition of new attitudes toward new attitude objects.

Modern Urban Northern versus Old-fashioned Rural Southern Political Socialization.   In order to apply this theorizing to the New Urban Blacks, we must be able to specify how their early political socialization differs from that characteristic of the rural South of years gone by. There are, to our knowledge, no systematic data that would permit a definitive answer to this question. However, much has been said and written about the subject, and the gist of it is as follows.

The childhood political socialization of the New Urban Blacks is in some respects conventionally American, emphasizing equality, basic democratic rights, and trust of the political system. The best evidence indicates that, at least initially, northern urban black children accept formal American democratic ideology fully as naively and wholesomely as do white children (Greenberg, 1970b; Laurence, 1970). Presumably this gives them expectations for political rights and power comparable to those of white children. In contrast, blacks reared in the old South were relegated, of course, both socially and legally, to an inferior social caste. They learned in childhood to ride in the backs of buses, to use the back doors of restaurants and separate washrooms, and so on. Hence they learned to expect not to be treated as political equals. Thus as they come to understand the political realities of their situation, the New Urban Blacks understandably are disappointed—more than the older southern migrants—by unchanging levels of political and social inequality.

Another major area of difference is that today northern blacks have much more freedom to express hostility against whites, particularly against whites in positions of power and authority, than did their earlier southern counterparts. In the old South, open hostility, defiance, disobedience, and even disagreement were treated harshly. The most extreme sanction was lynching; indeed, lynchings of blacks in the South occurred at the rate of more than one a week.[4] The somewhat milder threats of beatings and losses of jobs were more frequently applied. It was dangerous to be defiant of whites. While defiance was not necessarily safe in northern cities, the level of threat was not as great. The effect upon the socialization of southern blacks was to emphasize the repression of hostility, according to Pettigrew's analysis (1964). Hostility was expressed only in the very muted and diluted forms he describes as "moving away from the oppressor": aggressive meekness, spiritualism, passivity and withdrawal, passive acquiescence to whites, social insulation, and, in extreme cases, excessive denial of aggression against whites which may have produced "emotional dullness." Contemporary urban northern socialization tends to a greater degree to emphasize direct expression of hostility against white authority, that is, "moving against the oppressor." Of course, this has not been the universal, or even the dominant, pattern of socialization in the urban North. More characteristic has been the assimilation-oriented "moving *toward* the oppressor," which emphasizes self-restraint in the expression of hostility. Nevertheless, even this allows for greater expression of disagreement, assertiveness, ambition, and other related behaviors, than the old South permitted.

Self-derogation on the basis of race is a second consequence of formal relegation to a lower caste. Prejudice and discrimination exist in the North as well as the South, but in the North the social system usually has relegated the black to a lower caste in much less formal and explicit ways. For this reason, one could expect today's northern socialization to result in relatively positive racial self-concepts.

Greater political sophistication and involvement are other likely products of contemporary northern political socialization. Many laws and informal discriminatory practices conspired until quite recently to prevent blacks in the South from achieving even a minimal level of democratic political rights. Poll taxes, literacy tests, "white-only" primaries, gerrymandering, economic threats—the list of ingeniously applied practices is nearly endless. Moreover, in the absence of external constraints, educational level has been the most powerful single determinant of political sophistication and involvement. And the New Urban Blacks, as indicated earlier, are considerably better educated than older southern migrants. Consequently, northern blacks consistently have been more active and more informed about politics than have southern blacks (Campbell *et al.*, 1960; Milbrath, 1965; Matthews and Prothro, 1966).

---

[4]The Tuskegee Institute has documented 4,733 acts of lynching from 1882 to 1959 (Ginzberg, 1962, p. 244).

Finally, the dramatic events of the civil rights struggle during the late 1950s and the early 1960s had a profound influence on the political socialization of the New Urban Blacks. The very visible and salient confrontations between blacks and unsympathetic white authority, such as those represented in the televised civil rights marches, the publicity about court cases, and the confrontations between federal authority and southern obstructionists contributed in all likelihood to an increase in radicalism and militancy among black youth. This atmosphere represented for the young black's political socialization quite a different one than that of his parent's generation. Unlike the other influences we have mentioned, it could be expected mainly to differentiate the generations, rather than the regions, since the media provided full exposure to the movement throughout the country.

These several differences in political socialization lead us to a number of specific predictions about how the New Urban Blacks' political and racial attitudes should differ from those held by older southern migrants.

(1) More open hostility toward whites should be a consequence of northern urban socialization, due to the more relaxed external controls against the expression of anti-white hostility.

(2) Positive black identity should be more common among the New Urban Blacks because in the North the black is not so blatantly assigned to a lower caste position.

(3) Greater political involvement and sophistication should mark the New Urban Blacks, because of their greater educational level and because of their greater freedom to participate politically in the North and their resulting greater political activity.

(4) Greater political disaffection should characterize them because of their more open hostility toward white authorities, higher expectations for equal power and treatment, and increased political awareness. Given the realities of political power in the northern urban centers and the new awareness of these realities in the peer culture of the New Urban Blacks, we would expect generalized political disaffection to be increased not only by northern socialization but also by education and other factors that increase sophistication.

Within any individual's life, we presume the critical socialization of racial attitudes to have taken place prior to adolescence, while in the cases of political sophistication and disaffection, adolescent experiences also should have played an important role.

Resocialization Regarding Novel Events.   Blacks' attitudes toward novel or future attitude objects should, on the other hand, reflect their current environment more than the persisting effects of their early political socialization, as indicated earlier. During the 1950s and 1960s, there were many such novel attitude objects. Indeed, they formed the heart of the black movement in those years; new techniques, rather than old, familiar, tried-and-true practices, were the byword. The black movement in the 1950s and 1960s used astonishingly disparate techniques—the NAACP's moderate and legalistic appeals to the Supreme Court, especially manifest in the 1954 school desegregation decision; Martin Luther King's bus boycott in Montgomery; the mass marches in Birmingham and Selma and many other places; the spell-binding oratory by King, Malcolm X, and others; the great urban insurrections in Watts, Detroit, Newark, and hundreds of other cities; the conventional electioneering of Mayors Hatcher, Stokes, Gibson, and other less successful candidates; the assassinations of police and black leaders by whites and blacks alike; the Panthers' free breakfasts for school children; the lobbying of legislation through Congress and state legislatures; the strikes and protests and demands on multitudes of college campuses; and on and on.

How were blacks to evaluate the relative merits of these wildly varying new approaches? Clearly, early political socialization could not have been applied directly, for it was irrelevant in nearly all cases. No one had learned in childhood about all these new techniques. Rather, new norms had to be developed to deal with radically new events and possibilities. Our central hypothesis is that these norms tended to develop along generational lines, because current experience differed so radically from the experience of the previous generation. That is, we assume the dominating reference group in blacks' current social environment to be their generational group.

The next question is, whose attitudes were to dominate in each generation? The answer is to be found in Table 3.3, we believe; among Los Angeles blacks under 30, the New Urban Blacks were in vast numerical preponderance, while among those over 30, the southern migrants dominated. Thus, we would expect this "resocialization" with respect to novel and future events to enforce throughout the younger age group (even among those originally socialized in the rural South) the more disaffected, politicized, and racially proud approach of the New Urban Blacks. Throughout the older age groups the more conventional and assimilationist views of the older southern migrants should dominate. Concretely, then, we should find strong generational effects, but rather weak socialization effects, in three main areas dealing with novel attitude objects; that is, in matters on which the individual was unlikely to have been directly socialized in childhood:

(1)   Past experience with unconventional techniques of social change. If greater disaffection, and more open hostility toward established authority, represent dominant norms in the younger generation, one could expect them to have influenced quite strongly the younger age group's past choices among types of social action. Thus we should find sharp generational differences in experience with various techniques of political change: the young more experienced in demonstrations and rioting, the old in voting and conventional political campaigning.

(2)   Favorable attitudes toward the riot itself. The riot was a confusing, ambiguous, unprecedented, novel set of wildly disparate events. Attitudes toward the riot, then, had to develop on the spot in the immediate social

environment, rather than being simply deduced from childhood attitudes. The New Urban Blacks' distinctive attitudes should lead the younger generation to more favorable attitudes about the riot, a stronger conviction that it was a symbolic black protest rather than random criminal rampaging, and a greater optimism about its potential beneficial effects.

(3)   Preferences for unconventional political and social action in the future. Again, attitudes toward novel future contingencies are not easily derived from the residues of childhood beliefs about events then current. We would expect the New Urban Blacks' disaffection and politicization to lead the younger generation to prefer more unconventional and more militant actions in the future.

Subjective Status Deprivation

In addition to political socialization, our approach to understanding the rioting makes use of a social-psychological theory which is part of a family known as social evaluation theory. A basic assumption of such theories is that an individual can be motivated to act by an unfavorable evaluation of his ideas, attitudes, abilities, or life situation, one which results from comparing them to the ideas, attitudes, abilities, and life situations of important other people. We wish to propose that one motivating force for the violent upheaval in Watts was an unfavorable comparison between the actual attainments of the New Urban Blacks and the outcomes that they expected or felt they deserved on the basis of what others were receiving and what they had received in the past.[5]

Let us consider a somewhat more formal version of the subjective deprivation hypothesis, deriving from Thibaut and Kelley's notion of "comparison level" (CL). This concept was proposed to account for the manner in which an individual evaluates his or her outcomes (that is, the gains or costs accruing to him) in a given social interaction. According to Thibaut

[5]The basic formulations of social evaluation theory are found in Merton and Kitt (1950); Festinger (1954); Thibaut and Kelley (1959); and Adams (1965). The implications of social evaluation theory for an understanding of American race relations in the mid-1960s have been explored by Pettigrew (1967). The concept of relative deprivation, the particular form of the theory we use here, has been utilized by Gurr and Ruttenberg (1967) in a more formal model of civil violence. While we acknowledge our debt to these earlier works, what we are about to present differs from them with regard to demographic and psychological specifics. Furthermore, while our analysis can be classed with other relative deprivation theories, we are using it more in a psychological (intrapsychic) than in a sociological (intergroup) sense. To maintain this distinction, we refer to the hypothetical drive state of the New Urban Blacks as subjective, rather than relative, deprivation. As will be clearer in Chapters 5 and 6, our measure of deprivation involves the relative gap between the subjective aspiration of an individual and his or her current attainment. Most relative deprivation theorists have utilized aggregate data, comparing large groups of people, rather than estimates based on a given individual's sense of satisfaction or dissatisfaction; see Davies (1969); Gurr (1969); and Feierabend, Feierabend, and Nesvold (1969).

and Kelley "CL is a standard by which the person evaluates the rewards and costs of a given relationship in terms of what he feels he deserves" (1959, p. 21). Yet CL embodies all of the usual features of the sociological concept of relative deprivation: one's life situation is not evaluated in terms of its absolute value but in terms of the way one's present condition compares with the condition of salient others. A classic example of this is Stouffer's (1950) finding that in World War II MP's were very pleased by promotion to corporal, because other MP's rarely got any promotion, while enlisted men in the Air Corps, where promotion tended to be very rapid, were not nearly so pleased by a similar advance.

In addition to this, however, Thibaut and Kelley have proposed that such evaluations also are affected by the outcomes one has experienced in the past. They have defined CL as being "some modal or average value of all outcomes known to the person (by virtue of personal or vicarious experience), each outcome weighted by its salience (or the degree to which it is instigated at the moment)" (Thibaut and Kelley, 1959, p. 81). This modal or average value, CL, is a neutral point on a scale of satisfaction and dissatisfaction. Outcomes falling above CL will be satisfying (regardless of how the "independent observer" may evaluate them) and those falling below will not be satisfying.

Among the variables that Thibaut and Kelley hypothesized to affect CL, two are most important for our understanding of the riots. First, experienced outcomes are expected to be highly salient and hence to carry great weight in the location of CL. Second, perceived extent of control over one's outcomes (subjective power) is proposed to affect the range of groups and other persons whose outcomes vicariously influence an individual's CL.

Comparison Levels of Northern and Southern Blacks. How might this theory predict differences between northern natives and southern migrants? We hypothesize that the joint operation of the experience and perceived control factors would have two effects: (1) northern natives should have a relatively high CL and (2) northern natives should be in a relatively frequent state of subjective deprivation (outcomes below CL).

The first of these expected effects derives from the fact that outcomes are worse for black people in the South than in the North. This is objectively true, as has been documented in numerous studies; for instance, the median income for nonwhites in the western United States in 1966 was $2,500 greater than that of nonwhites in the South, and those in the Northeast and North Central states earned $2,000 and $2,500, respectively, more than those in the South (Bureau of Labor Statistics, 1967, p. 16). It is also subjectively true; that is, there is a consensus in the black community that it is so. When asked, "Do you think that Negroes are generally better off in Los Angeles than in the South?" 67 per cent of our Curfew Zone respondents replied that things were better in Los Angeles, while only 6 per cent thought things were worse in Los Angeles than in the South. The blacks growing up in the South experience only these lesser outcomes and bring a lower CL with them when they migrate to the North. Blacks reared in the North have experienced better outcomes for most of their lives. Thus, their CL's are likely to be higher than those of southern migrants.

Indeed, most empirical studies do show northern blacks to have considerably higher expectations and aspirations than southern blacks. For example, in a large-scale survey in Philadelphia, Parker and Kleiner (1966) found that the northern reared aspired to higher status occupations than did the southern reared. When blacks were offered a hypothetical choice between a low-paying, white-collar job and a high-paying, blue-collar job, 69 per cent of the native-born and 78 per cent of the northern migrants preferred the white-collar job, while only 57 per cent of the southern migrants did.

The second expected effect, a difference in subjective deprivation between northern natives and southern migrants, derives from the difference between the two groups with regard to the social structure of the regions in which they were reared. Thibaut and Kelley proposed that greater perceived control over one's outcomes affects CL by increasing the number of reference groups whose style of living one vicariously experiences. This implies that, in societies with heavy emphasis upon ascribed status, the range of persons and groups whose outcome contribute to an individual's CL is quite restricted, whereas in achieved status systems the range is much greater. In the North, with no history of slavery and much less formal discrimination, the prevailing social ideology always has emphasized achieved status more than has that of the South, where the caste lines have been drawn more sharply.

Both northern natives and southern migrants, then, should compare themselves with other blacks, but northern natives, in addition, will be likely to compare themselves across caste lines with whites whom they perceive as being similar to themselves in relevant aspects. As a result, southern blacks who have migrated to the North will evaluate their new experiences with a lower CL than northern natives use, both because of their poorer past outcomes and because of the narrower range of the people and groups (mostly black) with whom they compared themselves while in the South.

Since the southern migrants' new outcomes are well above their CL, they will (temporarily, at least) be in a state of relative satisfaction. On the other hand, the young northern natives' CL may surpass their own actual outcomes, because they compare themselves with whites as well as blacks. This will, of course, leave them considerably dissatisfied. For example, education is one dimension of perceived similarity which blacks may use in comparing their outcomes with whites. Education is a primary indicator of status in American society and there is a strong tendency to judge one's progress by referring to the achievements of classmates or others of similar educational attainment. However, in 1966, the white person with a grade school education had a median income that was $1,099 above that of the black person with a comparable education. As education increased, the advantage of whites increased, so that the difference between the races was $3,095 for people with a college degree. If a northern black male compared himself with a white male of similar schooling, he had a good chance of finding himself in an unfavorable position, a position that surprisingly enough became increasingly unfavorable as his educational level increased (Bureau of Labor Statistics, 1967, p. 21).

Thus, our analysis would suggest that, though blacks' income was much greater in the North and West than in the South, the New Urban Blacks were not only comparing themselves to other blacks but were looking at their white counterparts and feeling dissatisfied. Though they had high aspirations, these high hopes contributed to their feelings of dissatisfaction in the face of the great distances they had to traverse in order to fulfill their ambitions.[6]

Blocked Grievance Redress Mechanisms

Subjective status deprivation and the residues of early political socialization both constitute predispositions the individual brings with him to his current living situation. Discontent among blacks also might grow from the problems of living in the local community. These reality problems could affect anyone living in the community, irrespective of personal background or predisposition.

A critical area of focus in this respect is the operation of local agencies and institutions (also emphasized in many other studies of ghetto riots; see NACCD, 1968; Campbell and Schuman, 1968; Governor's Commission, 1965). Blacks living in virtually any large city constantly come into contact with, and to some considerable extent are dependent upon, agencies and institutions primarily managed by middle-class whites. Schools, employment agencies, landlords, police forces, hospitals and clinics, welfare agencies, places of employment, local government bureaucracies—all are, in most large American cities, controlled primarily by middle-class whites. This white middle-class control of agencies and institutions with black consumers was almost certain, by its very nature, to create a considerable sense

---

[6]Our theoretical formulation might be construed as a "rising expectations" model, since we have stressed the difference between aspirations and attainments of the New Urban Blacks. However, it is important to note the differences between our formulation and the political scapegoating versions of this theory. For example, Richard M. Nixon in his 1968 campaign oratory stated that he would make no promises to blacks because past promises by Kennedy and Johnson had created expectations that could not be met. According to our theory, optimism and high aspirations emerged from the long-term demographic trends of the entire twentieth century, not merely from the ideals expressed by politicians, social reformers, civil rights leaders, and white liberals in the two or three years just prior to the riot.

of grievance among blacks. This is not the place to analyze in detail the mechanisms by which this occurred; we will take that up in Chapter 8. Here, though, we can briefly rough out the argument.

The fact of white middle-class control meant that the operation of agencies and institutions was bound to be less responsive to blacks than to the needs of middle-class whites. As will be seen, black invisibility to whites in Los Angeles, and the application of conventional middle-class moral values, were much more decisive in biasing these procedures against the interests of blacks than was the relatively mild level of overt racial bigotry manifest in Los Angeles. Thus, "routine procedures" that constituted "business as usual" were designed by middle-class whites with their own values (moral, business, personal convenience, or whatever) foremost in mind, and not with consideration of the interests of the generally "invisible" black population. Hence, work days were set from 9 a.m. to 5 p.m., offices were opened near freeways rather than near blacks' places of residence or employment; and experienced and mature police and teachers were "promoted" to affluent white suburban areas while novices were assigned to the ghetto. All the while, agencies of social control fought drunkenness, gambling, promiscuity, illegitimacy, and irregular work habits, rather than bureaucratic insensitivity, police brutality, tax and legislative favors to the wealthy, sophisticated consumer fraud, and legislative biases against the poor and powerless.

We will analyze all of this in much more detail in Chapter 8. Here it is important only to assert that these "routine procedures" contained elements sure to inconvenience and alienate the poor and the black, not because they were designed out of racism, but because they were designed from a narrowly middle-class white perspective. Blacks reacted with a widespread sense of grievance. The extent of grievance is a matter of some controversy, so it will bear our examination in the next chapter, but its reality is not.

A crucial question, then, is how these grievances normally are dealt with. Most institutions and agencies have some standard procedure for dealing with grievances. The police department has standard bureaucratic procedures for dealing with complaints about police brutality, the small claims court has standard means of dealing with complaints against merchants and landlords, the electoral system provides the citizen standard opportunities to vote out offending politicians.

Our hypothesis is that many blacks in Los Angeles perceived these standard mechanisms of grievance redress to be blocked and ineffective for them. It is not hard to understand why they might feel this way, or why in fact the mechanisms might be largely ineffective for blacks or at least biased against their interests. In each case, control of procedures for grievance redress lay in the aggrieving agency rather than in the aggrieved black citizen. The police controlled mechanisms for handling complaints about police brutality; white politicians controlled redistricting and voter registration and ballot rules; and campaign contributors and business advertisers certainly had more influence over politicians and the media than did poor blacks.

Blacks' grievances about local white-dominated agencies and institutions, and their perceptions that standard mechanisms of grievance redress were blocked, were both potential sources of trouble. We expected, though, that their origins would be quite different from those of the discontents cited earlier. Specifically, early socialization ought to have played a secondary role in generating these grievances and perceptions, which, in most cases, presumably grew less from a conviction based on childhood attitudes than from problems of living experienced broadly throughout the black community. A black who is refused an apartment because of his race, or who is needlessly searched by a policeman, or who cannot get a job, tends to become aggrieved because of the reality he experiences, rather than because of his earlier political socialization. To some extent, institutions do operate selectively upon various segments of the black population: the police have much more contact with the young than with the old; the school system affects children and parents more than others; and so on. But there was no reason to assume that these grievances would be closely related in general to the kinds of background or socialization variables we have been discussing above. Thus we predicted that blacks' grievances with local white-dominated institutions and agencies, and their perceptions of blocked mechanisms of grievance redress, would not be closely related to social background variables.

The "Functional Equivalent" Hypothesis

The final link in our theoretical chain, the "functional equivalent" hypothesis, proposes that these several areas of discontent propelled the violence known as the Watts Riot. Specifically, these were the predispositions born of earlier socialization: subjective status deprivation; positive black identity; anti-white prejudice; generalized political disaffection; and the current reality problems, not particularly dependent upon the individual's background, of local grievances and perceptions that standard mechanisms of grievance redress were blocked. Our "functional equivalent" hypothesis proposes that the riot served as an alternative mechanism of grievance redress, which many blacks resorted to because they believed normal mechanisms had not worked satisfactorily. That is, it served as a functional equivalent to other more conventional techniques for social change.

A second and equally important point to be tested is that the riot was engaged in as a symbolic protest, rather than as a direct instrument for achieving concrete personal goals. For the most part, the discontents we have hypothesized here were not personal problems that a riot could be expected to solve in any direct way. It is unlikely that the riot participants expected the riot immediately to produce for them a better job, or a better teacher, or to force their landlord to make repairs. Their discontents tended not to be concrete but rather to be generalized, abstract, and symbolic in nature. According to our hypothesis, the riot expressed these discontents at a symbolic level rather than through instrumental actions designed to redress them at the concrete personal level.

An Overall Theory

Together, these ideas add up to an overall "politics of violence" theory, centered on a simple two-step causal sequence. First, the massive demographic changes of the twentieth century, with their accompanying effects on blacks' socialization, are hypothesized to have produced a group of New Urban Blacks with greater anti-white hostility, more positive black identity, greater political disaffection (by the political socialization hypothesis), and greater subjective status deprivation (by the subjective deprivation hypothesis) than older and/or migrant blacks. Second, these several residues of early socialization, along with common, reality-based grievances about life in the ghetto and the perception that conventional mechanisms of grievance redress were blocked, produced riot participation (by the functional equivalent hypothesis).

Our empirical analysis of this sequence is the heart of this book. In this chapter we have documented the demographic changes in the black population that suddenly resulted in the presence of large masses of New Urban Blacks in our nation's central cities—young, northern- and urban-bred, and with increasing amounts of education. In Chapter 2 we presented data linking this first element to the last: the New Urban Blacks' demographic characteristics (except for educational level) were indeed found to be related to riot participation. In Chapter 4 we will present a descriptive portrait of the grievances and the racial and political attitudes we have hypothesized to be the mediating links between demographic change and the rioting. In Chapter 5, we will document the first causal step, relating the New Urban Blacks' demographic characteristics to the mediating attitudes and, in Chapter 6, we will document the second, relating these attitudes in turn to riot participation. However, this analysis also must indicate what conceivable grievances were *not* implicated in the rioting. It is not enough to show here that *any conceivable* grievance was related to the rioting, for this would foreclose the possibility that specific grievances were the source of the protest. A second set of analyses related to this must show which institutions, persons, and social attitude objects were *not* involved as causal forces in the rioting. We present these analyses in Chapter 7 as part of the test of the "random outburst" theory.

4 The View from the Ghetto:
Black Grievances and Political Discontent

Blacks in Los Angeles had been angry for a long time, perhaps since the first Negro arrived and the *Los Angeles Times* began printing a column (c. 1880) entitled "News from Nigger Alley." Nevertheless, most whites were unaware of the extent and depth of black grievances until after the rioting of 1965. Since that time a number of official reports (Governor's Commission, 1965), journalistic analyses (Jacobs, 1967; Conot, 1967), and scholarly studies (J. Cohen, 1970; Raine, 1970; Sears, 1969b; Sears and McConahay, 1970b; and Sears and Tomlinson, 1968) have detailed the inadequate treatment of blacks with regard to law enforcement, employment, education, transportation, consumer welfare, health, housing, politics, and racial equality, and the way blacks felt about these inadequacies.

In this chapter, we describe these grievances and discontents. We also provide data countering three common objections to our thesis: (1) that such grievances might be mouthed often by highly politicized black leaders but expressed much less often within the black public as a whole, as suggested by some observers of urban riots (Banfield, 1970), as well as some studies of public opinion on other topics (Converse, Clausen, and Miller, 1965; McClosky, Hoffman, and O'Hara, 1960), (2) that such grievances are merely negativistic response sets, applied indiscriminately to anything mentioned, reflecting more about the respondent's complaining mood than about the realities of society's operation, and (3) that such grievances simply represented post hoc rationalizations for rioting, rather than pre-riot judgments about the realities of black existence (Banfield, 1970).

Local Grievances

Anger, discontent, and despair were most clearly focused upon local rather than national or federal issues and agencies. Contrary to what Chief Parker proclaimed following the riot, blacks in Los Angeles were concerned with local problems and were not dragging in ghosts from southern battlegrounds such as Bogulusa and Americus. Therefore, we present the six most salient local grievances in some detail.

Perceived Police Mistreatment.   Attitudes toward the police revealed particularly raw wounds in the ghetto community, and the police chief represented only part of the problem. Distrust of the police in general was very common. For example, 92 per cent of those in our sample of Los Angeles whites, but only 41 per cent of the Curfew Zone blacks, felt "you generally can trust the police" (6 per cent of the whites and 54 per cent of the blacks felt you could not). Thus, the high levels of generalized trust in the police found so widely in the United States among whites of all ages (Easton and Dennis, 1969) simply did not exist among blacks in Watts.

A majority of the black respondents felt that police mistreatment of a variety of kinds was common in the ghetto. Detailed data on these perceptions are shown in Table 4.1. Indeed a majority felt that each of the offenses mentioned in the interview had happened in the area, except "searching homes for no good reason" (though 42 per cent believed that this, too, had happened). The great strength of these distrusting attitudes toward the police was emphasized by the very high proportion of people who claimed direct or indirect knowledge of such incidents. On the average, about a

TABLE 4.1
Perceived Police Mistreatment

Perceived police offense	"Do you think it happens to people in this area?"	"Has it happened to someone you know?"	"Have you seen it happen?"	"Has it happened to you?"
Lack of respect, insulting language	71%	42%	39%	23%
Roust and frisk without good reason	72	38	41	20
Stop and search cars for no good reason	68	37	40	19
Unnecessary force in arrest	66	32	37	8
Beat up people in custody	65	34	21	4
Search homes for no good reason	42	21	15	5

Note: Data from Raine, 1970, p. 4. Entry is percentage of whole sample ($n = 586$) giving indicated response. Others said it did not happen, and so forth.

TABLE 4.2

Perceived Merchant Exploitation

Question	Often	Sometimes	Rarely or never	Other*	Total†
Do you have trouble with unfair credit policies?	22%	17%	57%	4%	100%
Do you think you are overcharged for goods?	37	32	29	2	100
Do you think you are sold inferior goods?	36	31	31	2	100
In stores are insulting remarks made to you?	10	20	67	4	101
Do you have trouble cashing checks?	17	22	56	5	100
Do you have trouble with quick repossession of goods?	12	10	70	7	99

*"Other" category includes "don't know," "other," and "no answer."
†Each row should add up to 100 per cent. Where it does not, the small deviation is due to rounding.

third said they *personally* had experienced police mistreatment, either seeing it happen or having it happen to them. Even more reported they had secondhand information about it, saying it had happened to people they knew.

Finally, antagonism toward the police was so complete throughout the community that almost everyone supported additional controls upon the police. Of those expressing an opinion on the desirability of a civilian police review board (76 per cent of the sample), almost all (97 per cent) favored it. In 1965, therefore, the people of South Central Los Angeles appear to have been united on the issue of the police.[1]

Merchant Exploitation. Much of the rioting involved attacks upon merchants, such as looting and burning stores. Not surprisingly, then, a great deal of discontent was expressed with respect to merchants' practices in South Central Los Angeles. Table 4.2 shows the proportion of people who expressed various grievances about merchant practices. Complaints about being overcharged or sold inferior goods were expressed by a majority of the respondents. Only a minority were troubled with unfair credit policies,

---

[1]We unfortunately did not have any measure of desire for greater protection by, as well as from, the police. Other surveys at the time showed urban blacks to be aggrieved about this as well. See Campbell and Schuman, 1968.

cashing checks, or the repossession of goods, but, even in these cases, large minorities were aggrieved.

Inadequate Agency Services.   The adequacy of services rendered by public welfare and employment agencies had come under severe attack by black leaders both before and after the riot (Jacobs, 1967; Conot, 1967; and J. Cohen, 1970). These local agencies were alleged to be more concerned with bureaucratic red tape, saving the taxpayers' dollar, efficiency and regulations, and harassing unmarried couples, than with providing jobs and welfare funds for those who needed them. As shown in Table 4.3, these complaints were reflected in unfavorable evaluations by only a minority of our black respondents. Nevertheless, the level of discontent expressed here was high relative to that expressed by whites, or by blacks with regard to federally administered agencies, as will be seen below.

TABLE 4.3

Evaluations of Local Agencies

AGENCY	EVALUATION OF AGENCY PERFORMANCE			
	Favorable (1)	Unfavorable (2)	Net affect (1−2)	No opinion
State Employment Agency	50%	29%	+21%	21%
Bureau of Public Assistance	56	19	+37	24
Aid to Dependent Children	54	15	+39	31
Mean	53%	21%	+32%	

AGENCY	PERCEPTION OF RACIAL DISCRIMINATION IN AGENCIES			
	None (1)	Experienced it (2)	Heard of it (3)	Net affect (1−2, 3)	No opinion
Schools	26%	16%	57%	−47%	1%
Fire department	52	5	41	+ 6	3
Welfare agencies	56	8	32	+16	4
Park department	67	6	24	+37	3
Garbage collection	67	10	19	+38	3
Mean	54%	9%	35%	+10%	

Note: The item used for evaluation was: "Do you think it does a good job [favorable], does nothing, or does harm [both unfavorable]?" The discrimination items read, "Have you heard of or experienced discrimination against Negroes in [e.g.] the schools?"

Racial Discrimination in Public Agencies.   Other evidence of discontent was provided by perceptions of racial discrimination in various public agencies, as also presented in Table 4.3. The most obvious case was the school system, almost a textbook case of *de facto* segregation (Caughey and Caughey, 1966). Seventy-three per cent of the sample indicated that they had heard of, or personally experienced, discrimination by the schools. The fire department had a longstanding reputation for discrimination in hiring, segregation of black firemen, and, after desegregation in 1955, considerable harassment of black firemen (Conot, 1967, pp. 261–267). The welfare agencies also had a broad reputation for racial discrimination; 40 per cent either had experienced it personally or had heard of it. Whites were much less likely to think discrimination against blacks existed in Los Angeles: it was perceived in schools by 25 per cent and in welfare agencies by 6 per cent.

Local White Political Officials.   Pointed hostility was directed at two white political officials, Mayor Sam Yorty, and the late William Parker, then Chief of the Los Angeles Police Department. Both were widely disliked and distrusted, as shown in Table 4.4. Chief Parker's intransigence on the race issue was both longstanding and public. He had been involved in running battles with local civil rights organizations for years. Yorty had firmly supported Parker before, during, and after the riot, when Parker was being attacked for his response to the riot. Their public statements will be examined in detail in Chapter 9. Kenneth Hahn, on the other hand, has for many

TABLE 4.4

Evaluations of Local White Politicians

POLITICIANS	EVALUATIONS			
	Favorable (1)	Unfavorable (2)	Net affect (1—2)	No opinion
Sam Yorty, L.A. Mayor	25%	66%	−41%	9%
William Parker, Chief of L.A.P.D.	10	76	−66	8
John Gibson, L.A. City Council	27	5	+22	67
Kenneth Hahn, L.A. County Supervisor	58	3	+55	39
Mean	40%	38%	+ 2%	

Note: The items used were of a standard evaluation type: "How good a job is Mayor Yorty doing? Is he doing well, doing fairly well [both favorable], doing nothing, or doing harm [both unfavorable]?" The "no opinion" column includes those who "never heard of him," "don't know how he does," and those who failed to answer.

years held an elective seat on the County Board of Supervisors, representing the district containing most of the county's blacks. He has long maintained a high level of support in the black community. Thus, he had only token opposition for reelection in 1972. And John Gibson, a long-time city councilman whose predominantly white district extended to a corner of the riot area, was simply not very well known.

Biased White-Dominated Media.   The final major set of grievances focused on the local communications media. Large minorities felt that each of the major communitywide, white-managed media treated problems of the black community unfairly, as shown in Table 4.5. The contrast with the black-originated media is a sharp one. Only the militant Black Muslim newspaper, *Muhammed Speaks*, was widely thought to treat blacks' problems unfairly. On the average, the white-managed media were twice as likely to draw complaints about unfairness, as shown in Table 4.5.

The strong-unfavorable reaction to the dominant local newspaper, the *Los Angeles Times*, is ironic, in one sense. Throughout the twentieth century, the paper almost invariably had supported conservative candidates

TABLE 4.5

Evaluations of Communications Media

MEDIA	EVALUATIONS			
	Favorable (1)	Unfavorable (2)	Net affect (1−2)	No opinion
White-dominated				
Los Angeles Times	38%	44%	− 6%	19%
Los Angeles Herald-Examiner	54	31	+23	14
Television in general	63	29	+34	8
Radio in general	64	26	+38	11
Mean	55%	32%	+23%	
Black-originated				
Muhammed Speaks	24%	30%	− 6%	47%
Los Angeles Herald Dispatch	35	17	+18	48
Los Angeles Sentinel	48	6	+42	46
Mean	46%	15%	+31%	

Note: The question used read, "How fairly or unfairly do the following cover the problems of the Negro community?"

(such as Nixon and Goldwater) and policies (such as the anti–fair-housing referendum of 1964, Proposition 14). According to our content analysis, it gave little or no coverage of any kind to the black community before the riot (Johnson, Sears, and McConahay, 1971). Nevertheless, it responded more quickly to the rise of the civil rights movement than did its rival, the Hearst *Herald-Examiner*; it won a Pulitzer Prize for its coverage of the riot; it attacked Mayor Yorty on several issues raised by the riot; it supported the black city councilman Thomas Bradley for Mayor in 1969, against Yorty; and it became an outspoken opponent of the war in Vietnam. Thus, its reputation must have reflected its many long years of ultraconservatism and near-total indifference to the blacks of Los Angeles, rather than the sharp changes in editorial policy that were beginning to surface in the mid-1960s.

These six areas of local life evoked core grievances that will recur in our analyses throughout this book. These grievances, more than any other dimensions, reflected the unhappiness of Los Angeles blacks with their situation. In only a few cases (for example, regarding the police, the Mayor, the police chief, and the schools) was a majority aggrieved, but, in a great many cases, large minorities were. Grievances were not simply the invention of ambitious demagogic politicians.

Conventional Mechanisms of Grievance Redress

All societies inevitably produce some grievances (though not usually to this level). Nevertheless, stable (and just) societies usually provide a series of mechanisms by which grievances can be redressed. How did blacks feel about the conventional mechanisms provided by our society? To answer this, we assessed each respondent's trust in the four mechanisms used most often in America: (1) individual striving and mobility, (2) appeals to normal administrative grievance procedures, (3) conventional political action, and (4) nonviolent negotiation and protest.[2]

Individual Striving. Historically, the most conventional mechanism of need satisfaction in American society has been individual striving. When an individual has a problem in life, he is supposed to work harder, get more

---

[2]Some of those items we have identified as "local grievances" are, of course, a mixture of grievance and a lack of faith in conventional grievance redress procedures, especially media fairness and evaluations of local white political officials. That is, normally the political structure itself has been a mechanism by which grievances are redressed and, increasingly in the modern world, the media as well, particularly television, has been a means of grievance redress. The notion is that one can "go to the public" by getting publicity on television and in newspapers and in this way trigger the process of getting one's grievances redressed.

education, or figure out by himself how to solve it. Most blacks, even after the riot, still felt this way. When asked, "What must Negroes do to get what they want?," 56 per cent gave such conventional answers as "get more education," "work hard," or "get jobs," while 30 per cent urged such collective actions as violence (3 per cent), political action (19 per cent), or greater racial solidarity (6 per cent) (for the detailed data, see Sears and Tomlinson, 1968, p. 501).

Administrative Procedures. In extraordinary situations, when the individual cannot obtain relief by virtue of his own efforts, the conventional procedure for Americans has been to turn it over to "the authorities." Virtually all institutions in American society have established standard administrative procedures by which injustices are normally redressed. College students can file petitions, union members can file grievances, insureds can file legal suits. Among the most important of these procedures, in the lives of many blacks in Los Angeles, are the ones for handling cases of police mistreatment. Despite the great mistrust of the police described above, a majority of our black respondents still had faith in the conventional grievance procedure. When asked, "What would you do if you were treated unfairly by the police?," 61 per cent felt that complaints about police mistreatment should be referred to the police, to the courts, or to authorities in general. Only 29 per cent said they would take revenge, or just give up, because nothing would do any good (the exact percentages are given in Table 6.7).

Conventional Electoral Politics. In America, if individuals cannot solve their problems by their own efforts or through institutional procedures, they have been taught from childhood to resort to democratic political action as a means of changing the procedures. When things go wrong, the people should vote out the incumbents and vote in somebody who will change things for the better. Hess and Torney (1967) describe the child's naive faith in "voting" as a mechanism of social change as the "personal clout illusion," but it persists as a prominent feature of most Americans' political thinking throughout adulthood.

Thus, it was quite surprising to discover the high level of generalized political disaffection in our Curfew Zone sample. When asked, "How do you feel about the way you are represented?," 42 per cent responded positively and 42 per cent negatively. Fifty per cent felt that "elected officials can generally be trusted," and 45 per cent felt they could not be. Only 17 per cent of the whites felt they could not be trusted. We have chosen the term "disaffection" advisedly, recognizing it may bear implications we do not wish. The widespread lack of trust in elected officials in general, combined with the widespread feeling of not being represented, suggests more than mere partisan distaste for a current incumbent or two. Yet by itself it does not suggest rejection of the basic framework of our democratic system. "Disaffection," we hope, will connote feelings somewhere between dislike for a few unresponsive local officials and rejection of the political system.[3]

Nor did our respondents feel that their political actions were very effective. Compared to whites they felt much less able to influence public policy, as measured by two "political efficacy" items (Campbell, Gurin, and Miller, 1954). Sixty per cent of the blacks and 27 per cent of the whites agreed that "public officials don't care what people like me think." And 78 per cent of the blacks and only 47 per cent of the whites agreed that "voting is the only way people like me can have any say about how the government runs things" (Sears, 1969b, p. 533). Thus, blacks neither placed much faith in their elected representatives nor felt personally very capable of influencing public policy, beyond the minimal act of voting.

In spite of this, Curfew Zone blacks had engaged in conventional political activity as much as whites, by all standard indicators: political participation, voting, and political contact. Thus, though they had less faith in conventional politics than whites, the majority of blacks had not given up entirely as yet on this mechanism of grievance redress.

Nonviolent Negotiation and Protest. In recent years, those frustrated by the slowness of social change have gone beyond conventional political action, to direct negotiations with officials in recalcitrant institutions and, if need be, to nonviolent protest of various kinds. Insofar as these negotiations and protests follow certain implicit "rules of the game," and so long as they remain nonviolent, they can legitimately in our day be classified as "conventional mechanisms of grievance redress."

Though only 6 per cent had ever participated in sit-ins, picketing, or other civil rights demonstrations before the riot, a large minority (37 per cent) said they would be willing to do so in the future. The majority (57 per cent) said they would *not* be willing to do so, but this did not reflect a despairing preference for violence. Respondents were asked, "What do you think the most effective method is for the Negro to use?," and of the three alternatives offered, 33 per cent chose "negotiations," 42 per cent chose "nonviolent protest," and only 12 per cent chose "violent protest."

Considering all these mechanisms of grievance redress, it is apparent that a very large minority of black respondents, averaging somewhere around 40 per cent, had lost faith in the conventional answer. The size of this minority is important for two reasons. First, it is considerably greater than the minority of whites who had given up on these mechanisms and thus, by the

---

[3]We will discuss these distinctions in more detail in Chapter 12. Some might use the term "alienation" here. We have not been tempted to do so. The concept is too often applied to too wide a variety of manifestly (and statistically demonstrable) heterogeneous psychological phenomena. Thus it is too general and vague in current usage. See Hensler, 1971; Finifter, 1970; and Kraut and McConahay, 1971.

standards of the rest of the society, represents a high level of lost faith. Second, it represents a large mass of people who could have provided social tinder for the spread of the rioting.

It is the aggrieved individuals, of course, for whom society must provide credible channels of grievance redress. Lack of confidence in the normal mechanisms is purely academic for those with little or no grievance. But it will come as no surprise to learn that in our data this was not the case; that, indeed, those who were most aggrieved were also those with the least faith in conventional mechanisms of grievance redress. To test this, we generated scales (see Appendix B for the details) to measure the six dimensions of local grievance described earlier. Greater levels of grievance were significantly ($p < .05$) related to lack of faith in conventional mechanisms of grievance redress—specifically, disenchantment with individual striving, mistrust of normal administrative procedures in the police department, and generalized political disaffection—in 17 of the 18 possible comparisons. In contrast, greater levels of grievance were significantly related to support for more militant and unconventional mechanisms, that is, demonstrations and protest (whether violent or nonviolent) in 9 of 12 cases.[4] Thus, it was those who perceived the black community as being *most in need* of grievance redress who had the *least faith* in the conventional mechanisms and who were most attracted to militant confrontation.

Merely Unselective Negativism?

Our argument is that these local grievances and blocked mechanisms of grievance redress reflected the reality of blacks' treatment in Los Angeles. This interpretation would be much less plausible if they simply reflected the expression of unselective negativism toward anything and everything. This, however, is clearly ruled out by two sources of data. First, the black community as a whole had a quite finely differentiated picture of the various areas of grievance. The level of grievance varied greatly from one agency to another. For example, police mistreatment and racial discrimination in the school system were widely seen as problems, while Supervisor Hahn and garbage collection were not. This does not sound like blanket negativism. Moreover, individual respondents made refined distinctions among the six major dimensions of local grievance. The scales measuring them were not closely related to one another: of the 15 correlations between pairs of grievances, only one exceeded + .10.

Second, the negative attitudes expressed in these local grievances bear a

[4]Several other studies have also reported a strong relationship between grievances and preference for violence as a mechanism for blacks' grievance redress, with data from Los Angeles (Ransford, 1968), Detroit (Aberbach and Walker, 1970), and Waterloo (Muller, 1972). None presents data on riot participation (though each study was conducted following a riot), so they are not relevant to the question we raise in the following chapters about the antecedants of riot participation.

sharp contrast to the overwhelmingly favorable attitudes toward blacks' political allies of the day: the federal government, the white liberal establishment, and almost all types of black leadership.

Blacks' highly favorable attitudes toward the federal government contrast sharply to the high frequency of complaints about local government expressed above. When asked, "Which government does best for your problems?," 58 per cent picked the federal government, while only 4 per cent and 6 per cent chose the city and state governments, respectively. This positive feeling toward the federal government even extended to the federally initiated and financed antipoverty program, whose administration was shared with local government. In our sample, 42 per cent felt the "war on poverty" would "help a lot" and 45 per cent thought it would "help a little," while only 7 per cent felt it would have "no effect." The most dramatic contrast was provided by evaluations of the top federal and local elected officials, the President and the Mayor. Ninety-five per cent were favorable to President Johnson, while only 25 per cent were favorable to Mayor Yorty.

White liberal leaders were regarded very favorably also, whether associated with the federal government or not. Eighty-one per cent were favorable to the liberal Democratic Governor, Edmund G. ("Pat") Brown and 89 per cent were favorable to the Democratic Party, while only 15 per cent were favorable to the conservative Republican Senator, George Murphy, and 30 per cent were favorable to the Republican Party (for complete data throughout this section, see Sears, 1969b, and McConahay, 1970a).

Finally, and most important, blacks in our sample were highly favorable toward almost all black leaders. The generalized political disaffection revealed earlier referred to political officials in general (almost all of whom were white) rather than black leaders in particular. For instance, 62 per cent felt that "Negro elected officials can generally be trusted," while only 50 per cent felt that "elected officials in general" could be. When asked, "Who do you think really represents the Negro?," 58 per cent cited some black leader or black group (most often, Martin Luther King, 24 per cent). Only 24 per cent gave truly disaffected answers, saying "don't know," and only 9 per cent cited white people or white leaders.

Highly favorable attitudes were expressed toward specific black politicians in Los Angeles, as shown in Table 4.6. This contrast with the grievance felt toward prominent local white politicians may be illustrated by comparing Tables 4.4 and 4.6. Similarly, highly favorable attitudes were expressed toward all but the most militant civil rights and protest organizations and their leaders, as shown in Table 4.7. The average attitude toward local white politicians was barely positive (+ 2 per cent), whereas it was highly favorable toward local black politicians (+ 53 per cent), assimilationist civil rights leadership (+ 61 per cent), and protest leadership (+ 74 per cent). Black-originated communications media were also thought to treat black problems more fairly than white-dominated media. This has already been shown in Table 4.5.

TABLE 4.6

Evaluations of Local Black Politicians

POLITICIANS	EVALUATIONS			
	Favorable (1)	Unfavorable (2)	Net affect (1−2)	No opinion
Augustus H. Hawkins, U.S. Congress	67%	3%	+64%	30%
Billy Mills, L.A. City Council	59	5	+54	35
Thomas Bradley, L.A. City Council	54	3	+51	44
Gilbert Lindsay, L.A. City Council	54	6	+48	40
James E. Jones, L.A. City Board of Education	45	1	+44	54
Mervyn Dymally, California State Assembly	44	2	+42	55
F. Douglass Farrell, California State Assembly	35	21	+14	44
Mean	60%	7%	+53%	

Note: A standard evaluation question (see note to Table 4.4) was used in all cases. Proportion "doing well" was 43%, 32%, 30%, 21%, 23%, 22%, and 14%, respectively.

The only element of black leadership not generally favorably regarded was the leading militant group of the day, the Black Muslims, and its leaders (Elijah Muhammed and John Shabazz) and newspaper (*Muhammed Speaks*). This is shown in Tables 4.5 and 4.7. Aside from this one exception, there is in our data little evidence of the cynicism, distrust, and derogation once thought to be characteristic of black evaluations of black politicians. And they indicate beyond any doubt the highly selective nature of black grievances in Los Angeles.

Pre-Riot Grievance Levels

Our theorizing requires measures of pre-riot grievance levels as possible causes of the rioting. Yet our survey measured grievances only after the riot. There is no rigorous and definitive way to determine pre-riot grievance levels from post-riot data. Yet there are numerous indications in the data that these local grievances reflected the pre-riot social realities of Los Angeles life rather than post-riot rationalizations.

TABLE 4.7

Evaluations of Black Leaders and Organizations

LEADERS AND ORGANIZATIONS	EVALUATIONS			
	Favorable (1)	Unfavorable (2)	Net affect (1−2)	No opinion
Assimilationist				
NAACP	91%	2%	+89%	7%
Urban League	83	4	+79	13
Ralph Bunche	70	5	+65	26
United Civil Rights Council	60	6	+54	34
Thurgood Marshall	50	3	+47	47
Reverend H. H. Brookins	42	9	+33	49
Mean	66%	5%	+61%	
Protest				
Martin Luther King	92%	4%	+88%	4%
SCLC	83	2	+81	15
CORE	77	4	+73	18
SNCC	60	8	+52	32
Mean	78%	4%	+74%	
Nationalist				
John Shabazz	22%	23%	− 1%	55%
Elijah Muhammed	22	33	−11	32
Black Muslims	29	54	−25	17
Mean	24%	37%	−13%	

Note: For the Urban League, SCLC, and SNCC, a standard representation item was used: "Do you feel that [e.g.] the Urban League speaks for you or represents you well, a little [both favorable], or doesn't represent you at all [unfavorable]?" In all other cases, a standard evaluation question was used (see note to Table 4.4).

Presumably, post-riot rationalizing would have led to a consistent package of grievances toward all available villains. Certainly this consistency of attitude shows up in attitudes toward the riot itself, which were rather consistent and highly correlated with one another, as will be seen later (see Table 11.1). However, it is hard to imagine how post-riot rationalizing could have generated the refined portrait of Los Angeles political life described in the previous section. Different possible villains were treated quite differently. And the low correlations among different sources of grievance indicate that not all were being seen in the same way.

Post-riot rationalization would be expected steadily to increase reported grievance levels during the period following the riot when our interviewers were in the field. Yet reported grievance levels did not change significantly over this time period. Respondents interviewed in October were more aggrieved than those interviewed in December, January, and February on three dimensions of local grievance, and less on three, but none of the time effects was statistically significant. This suggests that the grievances remained rather unaffected by the growing support for interpretation of the riot as a protest in the post-riot climate of opinion (Chapters 10 and 11). Thus, the grievances reported were more likely to have reflected the realities of blacks' treatment in Los Angeles, long antedating the riot, than to have been fantasies invented later on to justify and rationalize the riot.[5]

Summary

The data presented in this chapter have demonstrated the existence in the black community of serious grievances about police brutality, merchant exploitation, agency discrimination, poor service agency performance, local white political officials, and biases in the white-managed communications media. These varied in intensity but in each case sizable minorities expressed them. Each of the conventional mechanisms provided by our society to redress such grievances—individual striving, normal administrative procedures, conventional politics, and nonviolent protest—appeared blocked to almost half of the community. Most important, those who felt most aggrieved were exactly those who felt the conventional channels of redress were denied to them.

In this description of black attitudes toward political officials and institutions, we have introduced the three central concepts to be used throughout the remainder of the book: (1) local grievances, (2) blocked mechanisms of grievance redress, and (3) generalized political disaffection.

We think that these grievances were longstanding attitudes in the community, predating the riot and based in some measure upon reality (even if only upon the social reality of a community-wide reputation). While the nature of our data precludes definitive proof of this point, the circumstantial evidence is very strong. By this time, in any event, it seems hardly necessary to document grievances among black Americans, following among others Myrdal (1944), Pettigrew (1964), and the Kerner Commission (1968).

[5]Rossi and Berk (1970), in a re-analysis of data collected in 15 major cities following the 1967 rioting (see Campbell and Schuman, 1968), come to a very similar conclusion about allegations of police brutality against blacks. Such charges appear to have been derived ultimately from individual blacks' experiences with the police rather than from ideological preconceptions. Charges of merchant exploitation followed a similar pattern, though publicity by local leaders was also a key factor.

At the time of the riot, then, the community as a whole had not given up hope that redress could be achieved but a sizable minority had. The ghetto smoldered and waited for someone or some group to show it the way. In the next chapter, we shall look at the forces that produced a cadre of those who would be willing to show the way to violence.

5 The New Urban Blacks

In Chapter 3, we documented the tremendous demographic changes which have occurred in the black population during this century. In comparison with the black population of earlier times, that of today is younger, more likely to be native to the north, more likely to have grown up in the cities, and has more education. We suggested that this emerging profile defined a group we called the "New Urban Blacks." In this chapter, we wish to show that the New Urban Blacks are more than a demographic group. They are persons characterized by a distinctive psychology and a common approach to political life.

Our goal here is to test for the effects of the New Urban Blacks' distinctive early political socialization. Thus, our basic analytic strategy is to relate our indicators of this socialization (age, place of origin, urbanization, and education) to those dispositions earlier hypothesized to be products of early political socialization (racial attitudes, political disaffection, and greater political involvement).

Racial Attitudes

We hypothesized that the New Urban Blacks would show more positive racial identity than would their older, less educated, and/or southern migrant counterparts. Our measure of positive black identity was based on an open-ended question: "What do Negroes have that whites don't?" Responses were coded as positive (44 per cent), neutral (29 per cent), negative (17 per cent), or indeterminate (10 per cent). Positive black identity was indeed most common among the young natives of Los Angeles (59 per cent), and age, place of origin, and education generally were related to it in the predicted direction, as shown in Table 5.1. While the findings here do generally support our hypothesis, the relationships are rather weak; for example, the place of origin effect is not significant, even among the young.

This is due in part to our use of too gross an indicator of "native" Los Angeles socialization. We classified as "natives" all those who were born in Los Angeles or arrived before age 17, because political socialization takes place throughout this period of the life cycle. Yet, as indicated above, the literature on the development of group identity, or intergroup prejudice, shows that typically these are acquired earlier, usually prior to adolescence. Hence, this classification includes as "natives" some respondents who lived in the South during preadolescent years, the years presumably crucial to the development of these racial attitudes. To make a more sensitive test of the hypothesis, then, we further distinguished between "true natives," who said they had spent "most of their childhood" in a northern state and arrived in Los Angeles before age 17, and "early southern migrants," who spent most of their childhood in some southern state but still arrived in Los Angeles before age 17.

This distinction greatly clarifies the hypothesized positive black identity among the New Urban Blacks. Among the youngest age group (15–29), 68 per cent of the "true natives" showed positive black identity, and 58 per cent of the "northern migrants" did. Young people socialized in the South lagged far behind, whether they were the "early southern migrants" arriving in Los Angeles before age 17 (39 per cent) or the usual "southern migrants" arriving after age 17 (48 per cent). These data strongly support the hypothesis.

TABLE 5.1

Percentage with Positive Black Identity as a Function of Age, Place of Origin, and Education

	AGE			
	15–29	**30–44**	**45+**	**All ages**
Place of origin				
Los Angeles natives	59	40	31	52
Northern migrants	58	36	44	45
Southern migrants	48	55	42	48
X^2 *(2 df)*	1.73	4.57	0.71	1.32
Education				
High school graduate or more	59	51	47	54
Some high school or less	47	44	39	42
X^2 *(1 df)*	1.73	0.53	0.81	5.98*
All origins	56	48	42	49

*$p < .05$
Note: Age effect: $X^2 = 7.16*$, 2 *df*

Anti-white hostility also was hypothesized to be greater among the New Urban Blacks. But the results did not fit our hypothesis. First of all, the level of anti-white feeling throughout the sample was surprisingly low (considerably lower than the level of anti-black feeling among whites, as measured in comparable terms, as will be seen later). Three items were used. On the first, "As far as white people are concerned, do you feel you can trust most of them, some of them, or none of them?," 18 per cent said they trusted "none." Similar results were obtained from two standard social distance items: "Do you think you would ever find it a little distasteful to go to a party and find most of the people there were white?" (only 21 per cent would) and "Would you find it a little distasteful to have a white person marry someone in your family?" (only 25 per cent would). These items do not indicate a very high level of anti-white prejudice in South Central Los Angeles, even in the aftermath of "Watts."

Further, there was little evidence of any greater prejudice among the New Urban Blacks. Table 5.2 summarizes the data. It shows that on each of the three items, anti-white feeling was sharply higher among the young than the old, but nothing else had any significant or even systematic effect, with or without age controlled. Even subdividing the young natives into "true natives" and "early southern migrants" does not uncover any hidden socialization effect. Thus the findings on anti-white hostility are highly consistent. They yield evidence of the hypothesized generational effect but socialization (place of origin, urbanization, and education) failed in every case (indeed, usually running counter to the hypothesis, though not significantly so).

Yet the New Urban Blacks turn out to be highly suspicious about people in general. On the item, "Do you think people can generally be trusted?," the young natives and the better educated were more distrustful than the older, less educated migrants. This is also shown in Table 5.2. Considering their greater distrust of people in general, the New Urban Blacks were, if anything, actually *less* distrustful of whites than were migrants. Specifically, among those who distrusted people in general, only 22 per cent of the natives, against 35 per cent in each migrant group, also distrusted whites ($X^2 = 3.76$, 2 *df*, $p < .20$).

Thus, the New Urban Blacks had consistently greater black pride than did other blacks but did not differ at all in anti-white prejudice from age mates of different background. Their positive feeling about being black, and their relative lack of anti-white prejudice, seem to us all the more impressive considering their relatively strong mistrust of people in general.

Political Disaffection

The New Urban Blacks also were hypothesized to be more disaffected politically than older, southern-reared, and less educated respondents. We can test this in four areas: generalized political disaffection, approval of white

TABLE 5.2

Anti-White Hostility and Distrust of People as a Function of Age and Socialization

	Age	Place of origin	Place of origin (15–29-year-olds only)	Urban-ization	Education
		DEMOGRAPHIC INDEX			
Anti-white hostility					
Distrust whites	Young†	Southern migrants	Southern migrants	Rural	Less
	12.84	0.41	0.71	5.02	1.47
Discomfort at all-white party	Young*	Southern migrants	Southern migrants	Rural	Less
	10.85	2.24	4.01	1.46	0.61
Discomfort at racial intermarriage	Young	Southern migrants	Northern migrants	Rural	More
	4.87	0.89	0.29	3.24	0.01
Distrust of people in general	Young†	Natives	Southern migrants	Medium	More
	22.2	10.9	1.36	1.7	0.21
df	2	2	2	2	1

*p < .01   †p < .001
Note: Entry is demographic group highest in anti-white hostility or in distrust of people, along with the chi-square for the relationship.

political officials, grievance about local white-dominated agencies and institutions, and approval of black leadership.

Generalized Political Disaffection.   Our scale of generalized political disaffection was based on items measuring trust of elected officials and feelings of being represented adequately. The New Urban Blacks were indeed considerably more disaffected than older, migrant, and/or less educated respondents, as shown in Table 5.3. The most disaffected of all were the young natives; and age, place of origin, urbanization, and education each had a significant effect.

The New Urban Blacks were disaffected specifically from the political process. Their political disaffection was not merely another manifestation of generalized mistrust of people. This was tested by relating place of origin to our item on "trust of elected officials," controlling on "trust of people."

Almost all who distrusted people also distrusted elected officials (over 85 per cent among natives and migrants alike). Among those who trusted people, though, 32 per cent of the natives, 30 per cent of the northern migrants, and only 20 per cent of the southern migrants, distrusted elected officials ($X^2 = 5.49$, 2 *df, p* < .10). So, as we hypothesized, blacks' more open access to the political process in the contemporary urban North was reflected, paradoxically enough, in greater political disaffection; young southern migrants were more trusting of elected officials, and felt more adequately represented.

National and State Political Officials. The New Urban Blacks were somewhat less likely than older and/or migrant respondents to approve of national and state-wide white liberals such as President Johnson and Governor Brown (on our "white liberals" scale). These data are shown in Table 5.4. Yet the relationships were not very strong. Older southern migrants were most strongly positive but the other demographic subgroups were quite similar. And none of our demographic variables related significantly to disapproval of the Republicans. Blacks of all ages and backgrounds, in fact, were highly unfavorable toward the GOP.

TABLE 5.3
Generalized Political Disaffection as a Function of Age,
Place of Origin, and Education

	AGE			
	15–29 ($n = 212$)	30–44 ($n = 172$)	45+ ($n = 171$)	All ages ($n = 571$)
Place of origin				
Los Angeles natives	41%	36%	38%	39%
Northern migrants	24	24	16	21
Southern migrants	30	31	21	27
X^2	4.73	2.75	8.46	14.1
p *(4* df)	n.s.	n.s.	<.10	<.01
Education				
High school graduate or more	34%	38%	24%	33%
Some high school or less	39	20	19	24
X^2	1.48	7.09	1.76	5.52
p *(2* df)	n.s.	<.05	n.s.	<.10
All origins	35%	31%	21%	

Note: Entry is percentage high on the Generalized Political Disaffection scale. Age effect is significant: $X^2 = 23.6$, 4 *df, p* < .001.

TABLE 5.4

Favorable Evaluations of Political Leadership as a Function of Age and Socialization

		DEMOGRAPHIC INDEX			
	Age	Place of origin	Place of origin (15-29-year-olds only)	Urban-ization	Education
White politicians					
White liberals	Old‡	Southern migrants*	Natives	Medium	Less
	18.86	7.89	1.65	1.72	0.00
Republicans	Middle	Northern migrants	Northern migrants*	Urban-medium	More
	0.28	5.13	7.95	0.91	0.08
Black leaders					
Assimilationist	Old†	Northern migrants	Southern migrants	Urban	More‡
	8.68	2.96	3.37	3.55	17.07
Civil rights	Old	Northern migrants	Northern migrants	Urban†	More†
	0.59	3.62	1.78	13.67	10.30
Local black politicians	Old	Natives	Natives†	Urban†	More†
	1.70	5.70	11.39	13.47	10.54
Black Muslims	Young	Natives	Natives	Rural	More
	4.80	0.84	0.80	3.87	0.07
df	2	2	2	2	1

$*p < .05$ $†p < .01$ $‡p < .001$
Note: Entry is demographic subgroup most favorable to type of political leadership cited, along with the chi-square for the relationship. For descriptions of scales used to measure attitudes toward these types of political leadership, see Appendix B.

Older and migrant blacks seem, then, to have been more discriminating than the New Urban Blacks, when it came to white politicians. They evaluated white liberals very positively and conservative Republicans very negatively. The New Urban Blacks also preferred white liberals to conservative Republicans but did not differentiate them so clearly. Apparently their generalized political disaffection tended to infect their attitudes toward white officeholders across the board. Indeed, the New Urban Blacks' greater hostility to white officeholders washed out with generalized political disaffection controlled.

Local Grievances.   As indicated in the previous chapter, the strongest and most general grievances uncovered in our survey focused upon the relationship in six areas between blacks and local white-dominated institutions: perceived police brutality, merchant exploitation, biased white media, local political structure, poor service agency performance, and agency discrimination. While the New Urban Blacks tended to be slightly more aggrieved in each of these respects than the older, rural, southern-socialized, or less educated respondents, only one of the 24 relationships between our socialization measures and our grievance scales was statistically significant (perceived discrimination in service agencies was curvilinearly related to education: $p < .05$). Further, with regard to another generally popular program, the war on poverty, young natives tended to be significantly *more* favorable in their attitudes and evaluations than others in our sample. This adds up to compelling evidence that the New Urban Blacks were no more aggrieved with local agencies than were other black residents of Los Angeles.

Black Leadership.   There was no evidence that the New Urban Blacks had rejected conventional black leadership. We constructed scales measuring approval of assimilationist black leaders, civil rights leaders, and local black politicians. As indicated in the previous chapter, blacks as a whole were highly favorable to all. And, if anything, there was a slight tendency for the New Urban Blacks to be the most favorable, but there is no convincing evidence that they differed very systematically from the rest of the black community. The relationships that did emerge in these data indicated that the strongest supporters of conventional black leadership were the older, northern-bred, better educated respondents. Above and beyond that, civil rights leadership had the most appeal for the young; local black politicians, for Los Angeles natives. But the main point to be emphasized is that the political disaffection of the New Urban Blacks, so evident in their evaluations of white officeholders, did not appear at all with respect to conventional black leadership.[1]

The New Urban Blacks did tend to be somewhat more favorable to militant leadership than were other respondents, as reflected in our scale mea-

---

[1]Additional proof of this point comes from another question we asked: "Can you generally trust Negro elected officials?" At first glance it might appear that the New Urban Blacks did not: 62 per cent of the young, and 74 per cent of the old, trusted them ($X^2 = 7.43$, 2 df, $p < .05$), and natives trusted them less (58 per cent) than did migrants (69 per cent) ($X^2 = 5.31$, 2 df, $p < .10$). However, this merely reflected the young natives' greater generalized political disaffection, rather than rejection of black politicians. When responses to this question were compared with those to the item, "Can you generally trust elected officials?," it became evident that the New Urban Blacks were actually *more* favorable to black elected officials than were older or migrant individuals. The young natives trusted black officials more than they did elected officials in general, by 18 per cent, whereas the old Southern migrants did so by only 7 per cent.

suring evaluations of Black Muslims. However, the trends were not especially strong and none attained statistical significance. All these data on black leadership are summarized in Table 5.4.

Politicization

In this section we consider three areas of politicization: political sophistication, past political experience, and preferred strategies for the future (that is, among various possible mechanisms of grievance redress).

Political Sophistication.   The New Urban Blacks were hypothesized to be more politically sophisticated than others in the black community and to a large degree this was true. On each of our six indexes of political sophistication (four scales measuring various kinds of political information, and two, media exposure), the natives, urban-reared, and better educated were higher than the southern migrants, rural-reared and less educated. Within the youngest age group, the natives were consistently more sophisticated than the southern migrants. (All these data are summarized in Table 5.5.) The hypothesis fails only in that the young were not consistently more sophisticated than the old. Nor were they markedly *less* sophisticated; none of the six age effects was significant. Since young people normally are considerably less informed and politicized than older people (Lane, 1959; Milbrath, 1965; Riley *et al.*, 1970), this indicates a level of sophistication among the young New Urban Blacks that was higher than normal for young people. In this sense the age effects too tend to confirm the hypothesis. Overall, then, the New Urban Blacks are consistently more politically sophisticated than others in the black community.

It is worth noting that the New Urban Blacks' greater sophistication comes through most strongly in the areas of life most uniquely relevant to contemporary blacks. It is clearest in exposure to black-originated media and in familiarity with the great national black leaders, and least apparent in familiarity with white politicians who are largely "irrelevant" to the disaffected New Urban Blacks. Thus, the New Urban Blacks have an unusual interest in blacks throughout America, and particularly in information about the local black community. They seem more oriented in this direction than toward the public life of the nation in general or toward white-dominated local jurisdictions.

Past Political Experience. Younger blacks had experienced a wider *range* of techniques for political and social change than had older blacks. They had been involved in conventional politics slightly less: they were less likely to know someone politically influential (13 per cent did in the youngest age group, and 23 per cent in the oldest), and were a little less likely to have participated in the 1964 election (59 per cent of those age 24-29 had,

TABLE 5.5

Political Sophistication as a Function of Age and Socialization

			DEMOGRAPHIC INDEX		
	Age	**Place of origin**	**Place of origin (15-29-year-olds only)**	**Urban-ization**	**Education**
Familiarity with					
White politicians	Old	Northern migrants	Northern migrants‡	Urban*	More*
	3.9	3.1	13.2	7.1	9.9
Local poverty agencies	Old	Northern migrants	Natives	Urban	More
	1.6	< 1	1.8	2.5	2.0
Black politicians	Old	Natives*	Natives†	Urban‡	More‡
	4.6	6.4	10.5	29.1	34.9
National black leaders	Young, middle	Natives*	Natives*	Urban‡	More‡
	< 1	6.0	8.7	13.0	45.5
Media exposure					
White-dominated media	Middle	Northern migrants*	Natives*	Urban‡	More‡
	3.4	6.0	7.2	13.8	11.5
Black-originated media	Young*	Natives*	Natives*	Urban*	More*
	5.8	6.1	9.1	7.6	8.6
df	2	2	2	2	3

*$p < .05$ †$p < .01$ ‡$p < .001$

Note: Entry is demographic group highest in political familiarity or media exposure, along with the chi-square for the relationship.

against 66 per cent in the 45-and-over age group). On the other hand, they were much more likely to have participated in unconventional change efforts: in protest demonstrations (12 per cent of those under 30 had, against 3 per cent of those over 30) and in witnessing and participating in the riot, as we have seen earlier. All these data are presented in Table 5.6.

TABLE 5.6

Past Political Experience and Strategies for the Future as a Function of Age and Socialization

		DEMOGRAPHIC INDEX			
	Age	Place of origin	Place of origin (15-29-year-olds only)	Urbanization	Education
Past political experience					
Political participation	Middle	Southern migrants‡	Natives	Rural	More
	3.6	24.4	0.2	4.7	1.8
Political contacts	Old*	Northern migrants	Natives	Urban	More
	7.6	0.8	2.3	0.4	2.3
Demonstrations	Young‡	Natives	Northern migrants	Urban	More*
	21.4	2.6	1.1	4.4	6.3
Riot witnessing	Young‡	Natives‡	Natives‡	Urban	More
	15.7	23.5	14.7	5.9	0.0
Riot participation	Young‡	Natives	Natives	Rural	More
	19.6	4.4	5.0	2.0	2.3
Strategies for the future					
Individualistic striving	Middle	Northern migrants	Southern migrants	Rural	More
	0.7	0.1	1.2	0.6	0.0
Standard bureaucratic procedures	Old	Both migrants	Southern migrants	Medium	More
	3.8	2.1	0.6	0.8	0.1
Demonstrations	Young*	Southern migrants	Southern migrants	Medium-rural	More
	7.9	4.8	1.6	0.7	0.7
Violence	Young*	Natives	Northern migrants	Urban	More*
	6.9	2.2	0.0	1.5	0.1
df	2	2	2	2	1

*$p < .05$ †$p < .01$ ‡$p < .001$

Note: Entry is demographic group with most past political experience or most favorable to the future strategy indicated, along with the X^2.

Clearly, the younger generation's experience was much broader than that of the older generation, particularly in relation to open confrontation and even violence.

Data from the socialization variables also emphasize the uniquely broad range of the New Urban Blacks' past political experience, though the relationships were not nearly as strong as those with age. The natives were more likely than migrants to have political contacts (among the young, 16 per cent of the natives, and 8 per cent of the southern migrants, had some contact), and to have participated in or witnessed the riot (see Chapter 2), but no more likely to have participated in conventional politics or to have demonstrated. Education was strongly related to previous experience with demonstrations (among those under 30, 18 per cent of the college educated, and *none* of the others, had demonstrated) but not to the other techniques.

Strategies for the Future. Since the New Urban Blacks were somewhat less practiced in conventional politics and much more disaffected from them, and had considerably more experience with other, more radical techniques, one might reasonably expect them to prefer unconventional strategies for future change.

They did have somewhat less enthusiasm than their predecessors for conventional mechanisms of grievance redress but the effects were not very dramatic. As indicated in the previous chapter, we measured enthusiasm for individualistic striving by dichotomizing responses to the question, "What must Negroes do to get what they want?," into conventional individualistic approaches versus collective tactics. Trust in standard bureaucratic procedures was assessed from responses to the question about what the respondent would do if treated unfairly by the police. In neither case did any of our four demographic variables have any significant effect, as shown in Table 5.6. Still, it is suggestive that the young natives were much less likely to urge conventional individual striving than were natives over 30 (47 per cent to 20 per cent) or young southern migrants (38 per cent). Similarly the New Urban Blacks were consistently less likely (but not significantly so) to express confidence in standard police procedures. Thus, conventional approaches were slightly less unappealing to the New Urban Blacks than to other blacks but the differences were not large and certainly indicate no general rejection of conventional approaches.

However, the young were much more willing than the old to use strategies involving protest and violence. As shown in Table 5.6, there were strong generational effects in willingness to engage in protest demonstrations and to use violence. Consistent with the "resocialization" hypothesis advanced in Chapter 3 for attitudes about current and future events, neither item was related significantly to place of origin, urbanization, or education. The young of all backgrounds appear to have been resocialized to new

TABLE 5.7

Generation Gap in Selected Socialization Groups

	PLACE OF ORIGIN		EDUCATON	
	Natives	Southern migrants	Some college	High school or less
Self-reported riot participation	+28%	+3%	+17%	+13%
Events witnessed	+ 9	−8	−10	+19
Positive black identity	+19	−7	+ 4	+ 9
Willingness to demonstrate	+17	−4	+14	−16
Preference for violence	+ 9	+7	+13	+ 3

Note: Entry is the percentage of difference between age groups 15–29 and 30–44 in selected place of origin and education groups. A positive entry indicates that the under-30 respondents were higher in riot participation, events witnessed, and so forth.

generational norms that favored more active and unconventional political action.[2]

The Political Socialization Hypothesis

So far in this chapter, we have tested whether or not the New Urban Blacks' social and political attitudes differed from those held by other blacks, as we hypothesized in Chapter 3. The analysis proceeded by determining the effects of age, place of origin, urbanization, and education upon a variety of attitudes. Sometimes these demographic variables had conflicting effects but more often they coincided. Let us see how well these data fit our theoretical analysis.

Early Political Socialization. Of the numerous political dispositions distinguishing the New Urban Blacks, four were hypothesized to follow from early political socialization in contemporary northern cities: (1) *positive*

[2]Finally, the sharpness of the New Urban Blacks' radical departure from their elders' thinking can be illustrated by the way in which age interacts with indexes of socialization. The "generation gap" is much greater among the natives, and among better educated blacks than it is among southern migrants or the less educated. Young natives differed much more sharply from older natives than the young southern migrants did from their elders—in riot participation, black identity, willingness to demonstrate, and preference for violence, as shown in Table 5.7. The same generally held for education groups, as also shown in the table. The New Urban Blacks represented a much more radical change in sentiment than did the young southerners who migrated to Los Angeles.

black identity, (2) *anti-white prejudice*, (3) *generalized political disaffection*, and (4) *political sophistication*. The data indicate quite clearly that the New Urban Blacks were higher on each, as hypothesized, with one exception. We obtained age but not socialization effects on anti-white prejudice. In retrospect it appears that we simply underestimated the degree of anti-white feeling socialized among southern blacks, which would be carried by southern migrants to Los Angeles (though again we must note that it was low in all groups relative to anti-black feeling among whites).

Many of our findings in this chapter can be understood as reflecting various combinations of these four basic residues of early political socialization. The New Urban Blacks' less favorable attitude toward white liberals would seem to reflect application of generalized political disaffection to such prominent Democratic liberals as President Johnson and Governor Brown. Older, southern migrant, and/or less educated respondents held such traditional political allies in higher esteem.

On the other hand, blacks of all ages and backgrounds joined in condemning the Republicans (in the aftermath of the Goldwater candidacy and in the beginning stages of a Reagan one, no love was lost), in expressing grievances against those local white authorities and agencies whose actions continuously grated upon Los Angeles blacks, and in perceiving various degrees of blockage in conventional grievance redress mechanisms. Discontent in these cases seems to have stemmed not only from generalized disaffection in the New Urban Blacks but also from more discriminating political judgments by older, migrant, and/or less educated respondents.

Finally, in evaluating conventional black leadership, the New Urban Blacks' positive black identity appears to have over-ridden generalized disaffection. Indeed, the group most explicitly invoking black pride, the Black Muslims, drew more favorable responses from the New Urban Blacks than from anyone else. But even black politicians, civil rights leaders, and prominent spokesmen for integration drew generally favorable evaluations from the New Urban Blacks. This represents an important exception to the more general finding that the New Urban Blacks were the most disaffected from conventional political leadership.

Resocialization.   We hypothesized that the major breaks from early political socialization would occur with respect to novel attitude objects, and then only among respondents whose current social environments were discontinuous with their original backgrounds. With newly emerging attitude objects, such persons would be relatively more influenced by their main reference groups in the current social environment. And for those whose social environments had *not* changed materially since childhood, response to newly emerging attitude objects also should be predictable from knowledge of the current environment, since such knowledge usually would provide an adequate index of early political socialization.

It is easy to distinguish in our study the constant attitude objects from the newly emerging ones. The two main racial groups, the major political parties, the political system, and even the main varieties of black leadership had remained roughly constant in the years before the riot (that is, no new political parties or racial groups, or so forth, had appeared). On the other hand, 1965 suddenly brought with it: (1) the wild and unpredictable moments of the riot itself; (2) then, in the aftermath, the riot events became novel social phenomena to be explained and evaluated; and (3) the future possibilities for blacks, individually and collectively, had to be reevaluated. In all three of these cases, we would explain attitude formation in terms of current reference groups, rather than early socialization.

We hypothesized that generational groups would prove to be the most decisive reference groups in this process. The New Urban Blacks numerically dominated the under-30 age category, so they could be expected to dominate its political norms as well, just as the southern migrants could be expected to dominate the political norms of those over 30.

Consequently, the New Urban Blacks' black pride, disaffection, and political sophistication should have dominated the youngest age group's actions during the riot, attitudes toward the riot, and strategies for the future. The older age group should have been more trusting of the conventional political system and techniques and less oriented to racial protests. Age, rather than socialization, should have been the best predictor in each case.

This analysis fits the data quite closely. Past experience in demonstrations, riot participation, and riot events witnessed all showed strong age effects and weaker or nonexistent socialization effects. We have not yet discussed attitudes toward the riot but we will, in considerable detail, in Chapter 11. Here it is enough to say they too showed age but not socialization effects. And support for future demonstrations and/or violence was closely related to age but not to socialization variables.

Thus, we would expect in the future that the New Urban Blacks' unique political socialization would have not only a strong influence on their own attitudes and behavior but would contribute to the "resocialization" toward newly arising events, programs, or militant groups of those originally socialized to other norms (whether because of rearing in the South, in rural areas, or to the more assimilationist norms of an earlier northern time). The New Urban Blacks' mentality can in this way be expected to come to dominate the thinking of the black community much more broadly. As new problems face black people, their response will be increasingly dominated by the values inherent in the New Urban Blacks' political socialization.

Hope, Optimism, and Subjective Status Deprivation

The second major area of hypothesized effects of early socialization concerned expectations about one's job, occupation, educational attainment, and other matters of adult status. In our theoretical analysis, we speculated that young natives would have higher aspirations, indicating a psychology of hope. Here we wish to document that the psychology of hope also included a sense of optimism but, in the absence of increases in income, status, and the other good things of life, higher aspirations also led to a feeling of deprivation.

Optimism and High Aspirations. Others have shown that the dominant mood of the black population in America during the last decade was characterized by great optimism and rising expectations (Pettigrew, 1967; Brink and Harris, 1966). Their optimism extended into expectations for both improvement in their general life situation and improvement in specific areas, such as income, housing, and education for their children.

The New Urban Blacks were even more optimistic about their own future prospects than were other blacks. For example, when asked if they wished more education, over 90 per cent of the people in every age and socialization category said that they wanted more. But when asked, "Do you think you will be able to get that much more education in the next few years?," the young natives were significantly more optimistic than their southern and/or older counterparts. Eighty-three per cent of the young natives, as opposed to 63 per cent of the young southern migrants and 23 per cent of the old southern migrants expressed confidence about achieving their educational goals.[3]

Our hypothesis was that this greater optimism in the New Urban Blacks did not simply reflect their lower aspirations; rather, we assumed they would have higher aspirations than others in the ghetto. That is, we expected the New Urban Blacks to have higher comparison levels than older and/or southern migrant respondents. To test this, our respondents were asked: "If you could have any job, what would you most like to do?" The young were significantly more likely (90 per cent) than the old (67 per cent) to want a white-collar occupation, as opposed to a lower status blue-collar or service job, and the natives tended to choose a white-collar job (especially a professional or managerial position) more than did the southern migrants. Among the young, the natives expressed the clearest preference for a professional or managerial position. However, neither of these latter differences was statistically significant. Thus, though there is evidence that the New Urban Blacks had higher comparison levels than the recent southern migrants and older blacks, it scarcely represents strong support for the hypothesis.

---

[3]The age, place of origin, and place-of-origin-among-the-young effects were all statistically significant. For age, $X^2 = 99.5$, 2 df, $p < .001$. For place of origin, $X^2 = 46.6$, 2 df, $p < .001$. For place of origin among those aged 15–29, $X^2 = 11.3$, 2 df, $p < .001$. Even the natives who had a chance to complete most of their education (aged 24–29) were more optimistic than all southern migrants below age 30, 78 per cent versus 63 per cent optimistic, respectively.

Subjective Status Deprivation.   The most important feature of our analysis is the prediction that the outcomes of the New Urban Blacks would be below their comparison levels, while those of the older and/or southern migrant respondents would be above CL. Thus, the young natives should be more likely to feel subjectively deprived or dissatisfied than the recent southern migrants and the older ghetto dwellers. In order to test this hypothesis, we needed to construct a measure of subjective deprivation that would reflect each individual's current outcomes or life style relative to his current comparison level.

This was accomplished by subtracting the National Opinion Research Corporation's Socio-Economic Status rating of each respondent's current employment from that for his aspired-to occupation. We felt that these occupational ratings, compiled by a panel of expert judges, would be the best measures of current and aspired-to life outcomes, rewards, or life styles. This is because the type of work one does is a reflection of a combination of factors, including income, prestige, geographic mobility, control over one's destiny, and training or education.[4] Measurement of the discrepancy between aspiration and current attainment allowed us to designate 30 per cent of the sample as subjectively satisfied and the remainder as relatively dissatisfied (see Appendix B for details).

Our hypothesis that the New Urban Blacks would feel most dissatisfied was clearly supported by the data. As shown in Table 5.8, the northern migrants and the Los Angeles natives were significantly more likely to score deprived on our index than the southern migrants (78 per cent and 76 per cent versus 60 per cent respectively). Most important, however, when age was controlled, the differences between northern and southern socialization were largest among the young. As shown in the left-hand column of Table 5.8, the young natives and northern migrants were the most likely of all our respondents to feel relatively deprived while the newly arrived, young southern migrants were the least likely to feel dissatisfied.

Further, as age increased, the natives diverged less and less from the southern migrants, as would be expected from Thibaut and Kelley's treatment of comparison level. The past experience of older natives and older migrants could be expected to be rather similar, since presumably both had resided for many years in Los Angeles. We checked on this by examining the effect of differences in length of residence within each age group. As expected, longer residence in Los Angeles was associated with greater subjective status deprivation within each age group. Among the young, the

---

[4]We recognize that occupation may be a better reflection of these factors within the white middle class than elsewhere in our society. Nevertheless, these factors are reflected in the occupations of blacks to a great extent. Moreover, we are comparing blacks with one another, rather than making comparisons across racial lines. Hence, any distortions are likely to muddy the data rather than to work for or against our hypothesis.

TABLE 5.8

Status Deprivation as a Function of Age and Place of Origin

	AGE			PLACE OF ORIGIN EFFECT
	15–29	**30–44**	**45+**	**All ages**
Place of origin	$(n = 191)$	$(n = 166)$	$(n = 159)$	$(n = 527)$
Los Angeles natives	78%	64%	70% †	76%
Northern migrants	79	74		78
Southern migrants	53	70	66	60
X^2	8.98	2.93	1.0	8.85
df	2	2	1	2
p	<.025	n.s.	n.s.	<.025
Age effect*	68%	74%	68%	

Note: Entry in each cell is percentage deprived on the Status Deprivation Index. See Appendix B for details of this measure.
*For age effect $X^2 = 2.30$, $df = 2$, p is n.s.
†The two northern groups were combined at this age level due to small cell frequencies.

deprivation rate of the natives was 73 per cent; for long-term migrants (those coming from elsewhere, North or South, and living in Los Angeles for more than five years), the rate was 70 per cent; and for those arriving in Los Angeles in the five years immediately preceding the riot, it was 34 per cent. For other age groups and for comparisons of those spending more and less than half of their lives in Los Angeles, the results were the same. Holding age roughly constant, then, the longer one lived in Los Angeles, the greater the dissatisfaction, because the migrants' comparison levels drifted upwards to the natives' level the longer they lived in Los Angeles.

Northern natives have been found to be more subjectively deprived than southern migrants in other recent studies, as well. Kleiner and Parker (1969) found that Philadelphia natives and northern migrants had a significantly larger gap between current achievements and future aspirations than southern migrants. Further, using a measure of occupational deprivation similar to ours, they found that the northern reared were more likely to be deprived than southern reared blacks who moved to Philadelphia. Results replicating and supplementing ours were also obtained by Abeles (1972). He measured general satisfaction, combining questions on job, income, spouse, neighborhood, and "things these days," in a reanalysis of data gathered in 1964 from a national sample of blacks (Marx, 1967). He found that among those under 45 years of age, northern natives were more likely to be dissatisfied (45 per cent) than Southern migrants to the North (37 per cent).

The overall thrust of these data lends strong support to our analysis of the motivational state of the New Urban Blacks, despite the absence of the more sophisticated measures used in more recent studies. The young natives were vastly more likely than older and/or southern migrant respondents to express optimism about being able to meet their own personal goals. Yet their comparison levels were somewhat higher, as well, demanding a higher rate of success to maintain the same level of satisfaction. And that demand had not been met. The northern natives in three different samples and on three different measures were significantly more dissatisfied or subjectively deprived than migrants to the northern cities from the South. Differential early socialization, here resulting in different comparison levels, had led to entirely different evaluations of common adult experiences. Thus the New Urban Blacks were left as the most dissatisfied and subjectively deprived persons (though not the most objectively deprived) in the area.

The fact that these socialization differences were greatest in the youngest age group is of further importance for our theoretical understanding of the effects of socialization upon comparison levels and upon current behavior. The young southern migrants were mostly newcomers to the northern ghetto. Hence, the largest differences in deprivation occurred exactly where our analysis predicted that they would: in that age group where northern blacks knew least about the southern experience and where southern migrants had a fresh, vivid memory of things as they were down South. This emphasizes the role of socialization in the interpretation of current experience. Both northerners and southern newcomers were encountering a similar level of outcomes but they evaluated them quite differently. To the northern socialized, they were not acceptable; to the southern socialized, they were relatively satisfactory.

It should be noted also (Table 5.8) that age had no significant effect on perceived deprivation independent of place of origin. As age increased, the proportion of dissatisfied persons remained fairly constant but the effects of early socialization declined. As they became older, evidently the southern migrants raised their comparison levels and hence became more likely to feel subjectively deprived. Since almost all migrants arrived before the age of 30, the older natives and older migrants had shared a common northern experience over a substantial period of time. And, as Thibaut and Kelley's concept of comparison level would predict, their comparison levels tended to become quite similar over time, as their lengthy shared northern adult experience gradually overrode their divergent early socialization.[5]

[5]The tangled correlations between age, length of residence in Los Angeles, and percentage of lifetime in Los Angeles suggested further data analyses that have been done. The results are not presented here because of space limitations. However, when all of these factors were taken into consideration, the results, in those cells still having more than 10 respondents, were striking. Among the young natives spending more than half their lifetimes in Los Angeles, 87 per cent were dissatisfied. Among the young, southern-socialized migrants who had arrived during the last three years before the riot, only 42 per cent were dissatisfied.

In closing, one paradoxical note should be added. The New Urban Blacks are objectively advantaged relative to older or southern blacks. As we have shown, their income, occupation, and education are superior to that of other blacks. Similarly, their political opportunities and treatment are better and they are more optimistic about their own personal prospects than older and/or migrant blacks.

Yet they feel more subjectively deprived and more politically disaffected. This would seem to betray either a lack of realism or a lack of gratitude for their favored status. Our theoretical analysis points to a contrary interpretation, however. They are not evaluating their status compared to that of previous deprived generations of blacks, nor their political treatment compared to slavery and segregation. They are comparing themselves with whites and with the formal egalitarian ideology of the country.

This we feel is the major reason for the New Urban Blacks' paradoxical combination of anger and pessimism about the status of blacks generally and optimism about their own personal situations.

An Overview of the New Urban Blacks

The basic hypothesis of this chapter was that the New Urban Blacks—those who were under 30, native to Los Angeles, and better educated than most blacks—would have distinctive racial, political, and economic attitudes. This we tested by relating age, place of origin, urbanization, and education to a wide variety of such dispositions.

On the basis of the previous literature on political socialization, we expected the New Urban Blacks to have (1) more positive black identity, (2) more anti-white antagonism, (3) more generalized political disaffection, and (4) more political sophistication than older, southern migrant, rural, or less educated blacks. The data bore this out, except that the New Urban Blacks were not especially anti-white, even though they were more distrustful of people in general than were other respondents.

Consistent with our reasoning in the previous chapter, we expected grievances against local authorities and agencies to be a function of adult experience with them, rather than of early political socialization. Consequently, the New Urban Blacks were not expected to be any more aggrieved, in this sense, than other blacks. Similarly, they were not expected to have especially distinctive attitudes toward black leadership, since in making such evaluations their greater generalized political disaffection would be offset by their more positive black identity. The data again supported both expectations: the New Urban Blacks did not differ from other respondents in local grievances or in evaluations of black leadership.

Large generational differences emerged in past political experiences. The young had been slightly less involved than older blacks in conventional political activity. But they had been vastly more experienced with unconventional activities such as protest demonstrations and rioting. Similarly, they were much more likely than the old to favor protest and violence as future strategies for racial change. In these areas, generational differences were not accompanied by any other socialization effects, which we interpreted as reflecting the "resocialization" in early adulthood of the entire younger generation of urban blacks (irrespective of background) to the more disaffected and confrontation-minded norms of the New Urban Blacks. Resocialization could take place in such cases, we suggested, because the attitude objects being evaluated were novel ones (for example, demonstrations and riots) rather than old, familiar attitude objects toward which people had long-entrenched views deriving from early political socialization.

Finally, the New Urban Blacks were found to have more optimism about their own personal futures, and slightly higher aspirations, than other young blacks. The data suggested that they had higher comparison levels than other blacks, presumably because they tended to compare their own achievements with those of whites, which most southern-reared blacks were not accustomed to doing. Thus, higher comparison levels were a function of socialization in Los Angeles (and indeed varied with length of residence in Los Angeles, everything else being equal). Since their actual occupations were not substantially better, we inferred that the New Urban Blacks experienced higher subjective status deprivation than did other blacks.

6 Rioting as Functional Equivalent

The major hypothesis of the politics of violence theory is that riot participation was a symbolic protest motivated by a variety of socialization residues and reality-based grievances—given the widespread perception that more conventional mechanisms of grievance redress were either blocked or ineffective. We proposed that early socialization contributed more positive black identity, generalized political disaffection, and greater anti-white feeling, while later socialization (along with some resocialization), contributed more subjective status deprivation and greater past experience with unconventional mechanisms of grievance redress. The realities of life in the ghetto apparently resulted in grievances against local white-dominated agencies and institutions and to some degree in a loss of faith in conventional mechanisms. All of these, by the functional equivalent hypothesis, ought to have helped generate riot participation.[1]

[1]The ghetto riots of the 1960s have been so commonly attributed to blacks' legitimate grievances and discontents that it might appear this seemingly straightforward hypothesis would no longer need any documentation. Yet, as will be seen in the next chapter, there are many good and plausible reasons why this hypothesis might not be correct. Moreover, there has been surprisingly little direct evidence, of any systematic kind, on its validity.

Basically the research bearing on it has been of three genres. The simplest and least convincing merely has documented the objective deprivation of the black population, and/or its subjective sense of grievance. The inference has then been made that because blacks are especially deprived, and because the rioters were black, deprivation must have been the cause of their rioting. Typical examples of this kind of work are the Kerner and McCone Commission reports (1968, 1965) and Fogelson's (1971) recent book. This work has made valuable contributions to the description and dissemination of blacks' grievances, but its inference as to the causes of the rioting is clearly unpersuasive.

A second kind of analysis springs from the fact that some cities had riots and others did not. Aggregate-level analyses have been conducted comparing these two sets of cities on a number of demographic, economic, and political dimensions.

This hypothesis is tested empirically in this chapter. The basic plan of analysis is to relate these several sources of black discontent to riot participation. As in Chapter 2, rioters will be compared with nonrioters in three ways: (1) self-reported activity, (2) number of events witnessed, and (3) arrestees versus Curfew Zone respondents.

Residues of Early Socialization

We hypothesized that three residues of early political socialization would be related to riot participation, and, in fact, they were. Disaffection with the conventional political system was unusually strong among the rioters. The item "Can you trust elected officials?" provided the simplest illustration. Among those who trusted officials, 14 per cent said they were active in the riot, while among those who did not trust officials, 31 per cent were active. And in the Curfew Zone sample as a whole, 50 per cent trusted elected

---

Without going into detail on differences among various versions of this basic strategy, mostly they have proven barren of important substantive findings. Larger cities, northern cities, and cities with higher percentages of blacks had more and had more severe riots than smaller, southern, or less black cities, but most such analyses have reported few other differences between riot and nonriot cities, despite some ingenuity in the development of relevant indexes (Ford and Moore, 1970; Jiobu, 1971; Spilerman, 1970; Spilerman, 1971; and Wanderer, 1969; the sole exception is a paper by Downes, 1970). Of course, even if the two sets of cities did differ in dimensions relevant to black discontent, it is a long and hazardous inference to the conclusion that the discontent caused individuals to riot; if a riot city had no black city councilmen, and a nonriot city had several, could one confidently conclude that political disaffection therefore had spurred individual rioters? The absence of systematic findings in these studies has not, it should be noted, inhibited very many of these authors from confident assertions about the causes of the rioting.

Finally, there are studies like our own, looking at individual attributes as causes of individual riot participation. Here there has been surprisingly little research. Caplan (1970) and Paige (1971) have correlated some discontents with riot participation in the Detroit and Newark riots but have not attempted to deal with any of the numerous possible alternative explanations for the correlations they obtained. McPhail (1971) has performed the useful service of collecting and comparing studies of five riots, and indexing correlates of riot participation in comparable form. His hypothesis is that dispositional individual variables were trivial contributors to riot participation relative to such situational variables as availability, proximity, and "the assembling process." Lumping all dispositions together (irrespective of what possible theoretical sense they might or might not make), he notes that most correlations with riot participation fall below the .30 level. He thus discards all dispositional variables (on which he did have data) in favor of asserting that the key factor is "the assembling process" (on which he had no data).

Having theoretical reasons for expecting strong relationships in some cases and weak ones in others, we feel that our findings will yield a more meaningful pattern than McPhail's rather undiscriminating treatment of all possible attitudinal and demographic measures. We do not have data on "the assembling process" either. Although our response to this deficiency is not to trumpet its supremacy, "the assembling process" is unquestionably of some importance; hence, we shall consider it in the next chapter.

officials, whereas only 38 per cent did in the arrestee sample. A more general test of the same point was provided by our scale of "generalized political disaffection." This was related strongly to self-reported activity ($X^2 = 23.64$, 2 df, $p < .001$) and events witnessed ($X^2 = 6.85$, 2 df, $p < .05$) and was slightly (but not significantly) greater in the arrestee than in the Curfew Zone sample.

Racial attitudes also were hypothesized to be present. The ostensible pattern of the rioting, of course, strongly suggested that both black pride and anti-white prejudice were at work. Almost all of the rioters were black. The targets were almost all white people, white-owned stores, white-driven patrol cars, and other symbols of white society. Moreover, many blacks interpreted the riot as a protest that struck directly at whites, in retaliation for their treatment of blacks, as we will see in Chapter 11. Thus, it seems almost self-evident that the rioting was an explicit anti-white act for many blacks, who were expressing their antagonism against centuries of oppression by whites in America.

However, on reflection, it is apparent that racial attitudes could well not have played an important causal role. The riot clearly was aimed almost exclusively at targets that were white, but their sins may have been perceived as being related only incidentally to their whiteness. That is, they may have been attacked for being insensitive, selfish, and intransigent, irrespective of their color. Or they may have been attacked just for doing their normal jobs, which brought them into conflict with some blacks. Thus, more direct proof of the role of racial attitudes is required. We can test for their role by relating riot participation to the several items measuring racial attitudes already discussed in the previous chapter.

Riot participation was, in most cases, significantly greater among those with more anti-white feeling, as shown in Table 6.1. The arrestees showed substantially greater anti-white feeling than did the Curfew Zone sample on two of the three items (the difference was slight with regard to attending an all-white party). Within the Curfew Zone sample, self-reported activity and events witnessed were each related significantly to two of the three anti-white prejudice items. Thus, the greater anti-white prejudice of the riot participants does show through rather strongly as an overall pattern.

We also expected a strong relationship between positive black identity and riot participation. As shown in Table 6.1, positive identity was modestly related to self-reported riot participation within the Curfew Zone sample, and it was more common among arrestees (55 per cent) than among Curfew Zone respondents (44 per cent). Here, then, is some evidence for the operation of black identity as a causal variable producing riot participation.

The greatest riot participation should have occurred therefore among respondents who were high both in black pride and in anti-white hostility and the least among those who were low in both categories. To test the joint effects of these two variables, we cross-tabulated two items: trust of

TABLE 6.1

Racial Attitudes as Determinants of Riot Participation

	PERCENTAGE ACTIVE IN CURFEW ZONE SAMPLE BY		PERCENTAGE HOLDING SPECIFIED RACIAL ATTITUDES IN	
	Self-reported activity	Events witnessed	Arrestee sample	Curfew Zone sample
Anti-white prejudice				
Mistrust of whites				
Trust none	33	38	30	17
Trust some	21	30	63	73
Trust most	19	30	6	9
			—	—
			99	99
X^2 (2 df)	7.28*	1.87	4.55*	
All-white party				
Feel distaste	30	39	25	24
Feel no distaste	16	27	75	76
			—	—
			100	100
X^2 (1 df)	4.73*	4.63*	<1.0	
Intermarriage				
Feel distaste	30	43	45	28
Feel no distaste	21	26	55	72
			—	—
			100	100
X^2 (1 df)	3.57	10.77†	11.38†	
Black identity				
Positive	27	30	55	44
Negative or neutral	20	32	45	56
			—	—
			100	100
X^2 (1 df)	3.54	<1.0	4.29*	

$*p < .05$ $†p < .01$

Note: In first two columns, entry is percentage active among those holding specified attitudes (e.g., of those trusting "none," 33% were self-reported active and 67% were self-reported inactive). Last two columns give marginals for racial attitudes in each sample.

whites and black identity. As we would expect, the greatest riot participation occurred among those with both positive black identity and "no" trust of whites (36 per cent active), while the least active were those who both trusted whites and had negative black identity (18 per cent active). Similarly, those who ranked highest in events witnessed were those who distrusted whites but had positive black identity. This combination was also more common among the arrestees (19 per cent) than among the Curfew Zone sample (12 per cent), whereas the opposite combination, trusting whites and having negative black identity, was much less common among the arrestees (29 per cent to 46 per cent). There was no evidence of an interaction between the two items; rather they appeared to have additive effects.

Finally, each of these three dispositions maintained its relationships to self-reported activity and events witnessed within each age group. With age controlled, the strongest relationships were with disaffection. The only generally negative relationship was between black identity and events witnessed, a relationship which remained negative among those under 30 and in the 30–44 age group.

Now let us test more directly the causal role of these residues of early political socialization upon riot participation. Our hypothesis was that the New Urban Blacks' demographic location affected their riot participation because it resulted in greater extents of political disaffection, black pride, and anti-white prejudice during early political socialization. If these attitudes thus mediated all the effects of age, migrancy, education, and urbanization, then one would expect that (1) they would retain their effects upon riot participation with the demographic variables held constant, while (2) the demographic variables would no longer have significant relationships to riot participation with these attitudes controlled. We tested for such effects by cross-tabulation, introducing controls as required. To simplify, we indexed early demographic location with age and place of origin only, ignoring education and urbanization.

These residues of early socialization and the two demographic variables turn out to have contributed about equally to self-reported riot participation. Specifically, these three attitudes continued to relate positively to riot participation, with age and migrancy controlled, in 75 per cent of the 12 possible comparisons.[2] Similarly, the two demographic variables continued to relate positively to riot participation in 75 per cent of the possible 24 com-

[2]All variables were dichotomized in this analysis—age, by pooling all respondents over 30, and migrancy, by disregarding the northern migrants. We did not perform multiple regressions on these data since most of the important independent and dependent variables were nominal or ordinal at best. The 12 comparisons refer to tests of the effects of each of the three attitudinal dimensions in turn, within each of four demographic groups: young natives, old natives, young southern migrants, and old southern migrants. We have not presented significance tests here because the number of cases is so reduced when the total sample is subdivided so many ways. In all of the analyses in this section, we have not considered any comparisons based on cell N's below 10.

parisons with the attitudinal measures controlled.[3] Though the size of the demographic effect was slightly greater, on the average, the differences were minor. So, on balance, the attitudinal variables accounted for about half of the effects of age and place of origin on self-reported activity.

In contrast, the category of events witnessed was almost entirely accounted for by demographic variables. The three attitude scales continued to be related positively to events witnessed, once age or place of origin was controlled, in only 33 per cent of the 12 possible comparisons, while the demographic variables continued to relate positively, with attitudinal variables controlled, in 75 per cent of the 24 comparisons. Place of origin in particular held strong; among those under 30, natives were consistently about three times as likely as southern migrants to be high in events witnessed, regardless of their disaffection, black identity, or prejudice levels. The chi-squares for migrancy, with age and attitudes controlled, ranged from 6.0 to 10.6, with 1 *df,* over the six comparisons, even with the drastic reduction in cell sizes due to the use of two controls.

On balance, then, there is reasonably strong evidence for the causal role of racial attitudes and generalized political disaffection in producing riot participation. And, as we proposed, they do appear to mediate the effects of early social background upon riot participation. However, social background apparently affected riot participation for other reasons as well. We will speculate about this at the end of the chapter.

Aspirations and Subjective Status Deprivation

The second major consequence of socialization, as shown in the previous chapter, was the New Urban Blacks' greater subjective status deprivation. We measured this in terms of the discrepancy between the individual's current occupation and the job he or she would like to have. The deprived were clearly more active in the riot than the satisfied, in terms of both self-reported riot activity and number of events witnessed, as shown in Table 6.2. Most important, the effects of deprivation were strongest among the young. For both self-reported activity and events witnessed, the deprived were more than twice as active as their satisfied counterparts among the young. Indeed, the young who were deprived were by far the most active subgroup by both measures of activity. Thus, the data strongly supported the hypothesis that the relatively deprived would participate to a greater extent than the relatively satisfied, and this relationship was strongest among the young, the age bracket of the New Urban Blacks.[4]

Despite their greater sense of deprivation, the young natives were also

[3]For example, testing the effects of age among disaffected natives, among disaffected southern migrants, nondisaffected natives, nondisaffected southern migrants, and so on.

[4]These results were consistent with the findings reported by others, though their dependent measures differed from ours. See Ransford (1968), Crawford and Naditch (1970), and Parker and Kleiner (1966).

TABLE 6.2

Riot Participation as a Function of Age and Subjective Deprivation

	AGE			
	15–29	30–44	45+	All ages
Self-reported activity				
Deprivation state	(*n* = 182)	(*n* = 165)	(*n* = 158	(*n* = 513)
Satisfied	20%	10%	10%	16%
Deprived	42	21	25	28
X², *1* df	8.45	2.60	4.13	8.40
p	<.005	n.s.	<.05	<.005
Events witnessed				
Deprivation state	(*n* = 151)	(*n* = 139)	(*n* = 131)	(*n* = 435)
Satisfied	22%	30%	23%	23%
Deprived	50	31	20	37
X², *1* df	10.02	<1.0	<1.0	7.07
p	<.005	n.s.	n.s.	<.01

Note: First entry is percentage in each cell reporting themselves somewhat or very active. See Appendix C for a discussion of this measure. Second entry is percentage in each cell reporting having seen four or five important riot events. See Appendixes B and C for discussions of this measure.

more optimistic about their own future situations than others in the community (specifically, about the possibility of getting the further education they wanted), as was shown in the previous chapter. We wanted to explore the possibility that this optimism might dampen the effects of subjective deprivation. For, although the young natives were dissatisfied, the possibility that their lives would improve might make the deprivation bearable and consequently reduce the chances of their getting involved in a riot.

Surprisingly enough, those who were optimistic about acquiring the additional education they wished actually were much *more* likely to participate in the rioting than those who were pessimistic. This is shown in Table 6.3. Among the optimistic, 29 per cent were active, while only 15 per cent of the pessimistic were active. This strong relationship holds both for self-reported activity and for the number of riot events that were witnessed. Because both optimism and activity were strongly related to age, we also present in Table 6.3 the participation levels with age controlled. Again, the optimists were consistently more active than the pessimists. The differences at each age level were somewhat reduced, though still substantial. Optimism about one's own personal prospects evidently did not dampen the other grievances and discontents we have outlined.

TABLE 6.3

Riot Participation as a Function of Age and Personal Optimism

	AGE			
	15–29	30–44	45+	All ages
Self-reported activity				
*Optimism about further education**	(n = 220)	(n = 175)	(n = 166)	(n = 570)
Will get education	34%	15%	26%	29%
Will not get education	23	15	9	15
X^2 (*1* df)	1.3	<1.0	4.5	14.4
p	n.s.	n.s.	<.05	<.001
Events witnessed				
*Optimism about further education**				
Will get education	46%	39%	23%	42%
Will not get education	30	26	18	24
X^2 (*1* df)	2.3	1.7	3.4	14.7
p	n.s.	n.s.	n.s.	<.001

*Based upon responses to the question: "Do you think you will be able to get that much more [education] in the next few years?"

Note: First entry is percentage in each cell reporting themselves somewhat or very active. See Appendix C for a discussion of this measure. Second entry is percentage in each cell reporting having seen four or five important riot events. See Appendixes B and C for discussion of this measure.

Grievances against Local White Authorities

Blacks in Los Angeles felt particularly aggrieved about their treatment by local agencies and institutions operated and controlled primarily by white people, in six areas in particular, as indicated in Chapter 4—in areas involving (1) police, (2) white merchants, (3) community-wide, white-dominated mass media, (4) local white-dominated politics, (5) discrimination in local agencies, and (6) poor service in local agencies.

Riot participation was related more systematically to these local grievances than to any other measure in our study. The data are shown in Table 6.4. The arrestees were more aggrieved than the Curfew Zone sample in all six areas, with the significance levels varying from .05 in the case of the local service agencies to less than .0001 in the case of merchant exploitation. Within the Curfew Zone sample, self-reported activity related significantly to five of these six indexes of grievances, and events witnessed were related significantly to higher levels of grievance in four of the six cases.

TABLE 6.4

Riot Participation as a Function of Grievances Against Local White-Dominated Authorities

TYPE OF GRIEVANCE	MEAN GRIEVANCE LEVEL[1]			PERCENTAGE SELF-REPORTED ACTIVE AMONG THOSE WITH:			PERCENTAGE HIGH IN EVENTS WITNESSED AMONG THOSE WITH:		
	Arrestee sample		Curfew Zone sample	High grievance[2]		Low grievance	High grievance[2]		Low grievance
Police brutality	16.87	$t = 7.07$‡	15.06	26	$X^2 = 12.97$‡	20	38	$X^2 = 4.68$*	26
Merchant exploitation	18.07	$t = 4.68$‡	16.06	30	$X^2 = 12.97$‡	16	37	$X^2 = 4.68$*	27
Local political structure	11.98	$t = 2.19$*	10.84	30	$X^2 = 13.43$‡	16	35	$X^2 = 2.19$	28
Agency discrimination	8.79	$t = 6.28$‡	7.71	28	$X^2 = 5.00$*	19	39	$X^2 = 6.28$*	27
Inadequate service agencies	5.50	$t = 8.45$‡	4.92	27	$X^2 = 7.89$†	16	39	$X^2 = 8.45$†	26
Biased white media	8.31	$t = 3.50$‡	7.12	30	$X^2 = 12.00$†	17	36	$X^2 = 3.50$	28

*$p < .05$ †$p < .01$ ‡$p < .001$

Note: The higher the score, the greater the grievance. The significance of the differences between the means was tested by t's having 600 df or more.

[1]Note: Grievance level based on median splits of each grievance scale, with proportion in high grievance category varying from 45% to 55% across the six scales. The differences were tested by X^2 having 1 df.

Thus all three indexes of riot participation were related positively to all six areas of grievance, attaining statistical significance in almost all cases.

No one set of grievances against the local situation stood out as a particular focus of attention among riot participants. Grievances varied in strength of association with our measures of riot participation but not in any obvious pattern. The same was true of individual items within the several grievance scales. What stood out, rather, were the consistently higher grievance levels among the participants than among nonparticipants, across all six areas of grievances about the local situation.

The relationship between grievance level and riot participation generally held up strongly among all age groups. With age controlled, 33 of the resulting 36 possible associations (6 grievances by self-reported activity and events witnessed, in 3 age groups), were positive. The grievance basis for riot participation actually was strongest among the young, if anything, but the differences across age groups were not very dramatic.

Lost Faith in Normal Mechanisms of Grievance Redress

Riot participation was most common, then, among those with the greatest discontent in the areas of racial hostility, status deprivation, and grievances against local white authorities and agencies. It turns out that the rioters also had less faith than did nonparticipants in the efficacy of conventional mechanisms for redressing such grievances. We have indexed confidence in such conventional mechanisms in a variety of ways—in terms of individual striving, normal administrative grievance procedures, and conventional political activity—as described already in Chapter 4. The arrestees had less confidence or experience in standard procedures than the Curfew Zone sample on three of the four measures shown in Table 6.5, as well as on generalized political disaffection (described above). The difference was largest in the case of the handling of police mistreatment; these data are presented in more detail in Table 6.6. Within the Curfew Zone sample, too, riot participation also was generally related to the perceived ineffectiveness of conventional mechanisms of grievance redress.[5]

On the other hand, the rioters were *more* experienced in and attracted to unconventional strategies. Arrestees, those self-reported active, and those

[5]The strongest effects were on lack of trust in the authorities' handling of police mistreatment, generalized political disaffection (as discussed earlier), and past political participation. This bears noting, since this distrust of bureaucratic procedures and of conventional politics represented discontents of a highly symbolic nature. That is, riot participation was consistently and significantly related to the individual's disenchantment with conventional mechanisms of social change as they related to the position of blacks in general. But it was less strongly related to the two variables most concerned with the individual's personal life—to whether or not he accepted the "individual striving" approach to improvement of the blacks' lot and whether or not he personally had contacts with politically influential persons. We will comment further on this point. Also see Edelman (1971) and Sears and Kinder (1971) for discussions of symbolic politics.

TABLE 6.5

Riot Participation as a Function of Lost Faith in Conventional Mechanisms of Grievance Redress

GRIEVANCE MECHANISMS	PERCENTAGE ACTIVE IN CURFEW ZONE SAMPLE BY		PERCENTAGE HOLDING SPECIFIED ATTITUDE IN	
	Self-reported activity	Events witnessed	Arrestee sample	Curfew Zone sample
"What must Negroes do . . . ?"				
Collective action	26	28	45	43
Individual striving	20	33	55	57
			100	100
X² *(1* df)	2.05	<1.0	<1.0	
Standard administrative procedure:				
Lack of faith	30	41	63	30
Trusting	20	28	37	70
			100	100
X² *(1* df)	5.91*	6.61*	77.02†	
Past political participation:				
Low	28	38	76	44
High	18	28	24	56
			100	100
X² *(1* df)	7.61*	4.31*	42.69†	
Political contacts:				
None	22	32	80	81
Some	26	34	20	19
			100	100
X² *(1* df)	<1.0	<1.0	<1.0	

*p < .05   †p < .001

TABLE 6.6

Riot Participation as a Function of Response to Unfair Treatment by Police

"What would you do if you were treated unfairly by the police?"	PERCENTAGE ACTIVE IN CURFEW ZONE SAMPLE BY		PERCENTAGE HOLDING SPECIFIED ATTITUDE IN	
	Self-reported activity*	Events witnessed†	Arrestee sample	Curfew Zone sample
Lack of faith responses				
Do nothing, not much I could do, don't know, what could you do?	29	42	51	23
Revenge, self-defense	32	38	10	6
	—	—	—	—
	30	41	61	29
Trusting, good citizen responses				
Get outside help; consult political official or civil rights group	29	38	3	8
Trust police: file complaint with police department	20	31	23	29
Vague system trust: report it to the authorities, take it to court	17	24	10	32
	—	—	—	—
	20	28	36	69
No answer			2	2
			—	—
			99	100

*For lack of faith *vs.* trusting, good citizen response X^2 (1 *df*) = 5.91, $p < .05$.
†For lack of faith *vs.* trusting, good citizen response X^2 (1 *df*) = 6.61, $p < .05$.

ranking high in events witnessed were all more likely than inactive respondents to have participated in past protest demonstrations. Further, the arrestees were much more willing than were blacks in general to demonstrate in the future (by 17 per cent), and almost twice as likely to prefer violent protest (26 per cent to 14 per cent). Within the Curfew Zone sample, three of the four comparisons were statistically significant. All these data are shown in Table 6.7. This, then, represents strong evidence that the rioters

TABLE 6.7

Riot Participation as a Function of Preference for Unconventional Mechanisms of Grievance Redress

GRIEVANCE MECHANISMS	PERCENTAGE ACTIVE IN CURFEW ZONE SAMPLE BY		PERCENTAGE HOLDING SPECIFIED ATTITUDE IN	
	Self-reported activity	Events witnessed	Arrestee sample	Curfew Zone sample
Previous participation in demonstrations				
No	22	30	89	93
Yes	39	39	11	7
			100	100
X^2 *(1 df)*	4.26*	<1.0	<1.0	
Willing to demonstrate in future				
No	19	26	44	61
Yes	29	38	56	39
			100	100
X^2 *(1 df)*	6.06*	6.80*	8.63*	
Preference for future				
Violent protest	41	36	26	14
Nonviolent protest	16	28	42	48
Negotiation	22	33	32	38
			100	100
X^2 *(2 df)*	18.10†	1.88	6.04*	

*$p < .05$ †$p < .001$

more than the nonrioters continued to be drawn to unconventional tactics for grievance redress, such as protest and violence.

The Riot as a Symbolic Protest

A final and important aspect of the politics of violence theory is that riot participation represents a symbolic protest, an attempt to communicate grievances to authorities who previously have been regarded as indifferent and intransigent in responding to expressions of need. The participants' despair about white authorities is easily illustrated. Respondents were asked if they had heard of the term "power structure" and, if they had, to what and/or whom it referred. Riot participation was much less common among those who defined it in trusting and conventional terms. Among those who thought the term referred to conventional political roles or offices (that is, to the President, the Mayor, and other elected officials), only 16 per cent reported themselves active in the riot. But 36 per cent were active among those who referred to "financial interests," "businessmen," "white society," "rich white people," or a similar definition ($X^2 = 6.38$, 2 df, $p < .05$). The arrestees and those who were high in events witnessed also were more likely to use such terms in describing the "power structure," but the differences were not significant.

The symbolic protest was aimed at these indifferent and intransigent authorities, not at poor social conditions in the abstract. Within the majority of the black community who perceived the riot as a "Negro protest," the highest participation rates were among those who perceived the riot as a protest directed against people or groups (39 per cent self-reported active), whereas only 19 per cent reported themselves active among those who saw it as a protest directed against bad conditions ($X^2 = 9.60$, 2 df, $p < .05$). Those who were high in events witnessed also more often perceived it as directed against people or groups ($X^2 = 8.17$, 2 df, $p < .05$), although arrestees were somewhat more likely than Curfew Zone respondents to cite conditions (58 per cent versus 49 per cent).

Thus, the riot participants were particularly sensitive to the various grievances of the black community and more likely than nonparticipants to see treatment from local white authorities as unfair, discriminatory, and indifferent. They also saw the political structure as more refractory and unhelpful than nonparticipants did and the riot as aimed specifically at these intransigent authorities. This provides evidence that the riot served as an alternative to blocked mechanisms of grievance redress. It also underscores the great symbolic importance of the public response made by the police, elected officials, public agencies, and the press, which we will discuss in later chapters.

The Antecedents of Riot Participation

In this chapter we have investigated a variety of antecedents of riot participation: residues of early political socialization (positive black identity, anti-white prejudice, and generalized political disaffection), subjective status deprivation, grievances against local white-dominated agencies and institutions, and perceived blockage in conventional mechanisms of grievance redress. Each was generally related to riot participation and consistent with the functional equivalent hypothesis. Their contributions to riot participation were hypothesized to derive from two quite different causal chains, however, and it is appropriate to consider the evidence for each.

Riot participation was related to the generalized psychological dispositions common to the New Urban Blacks: namely, generalized political disaffection, more positive black identity, increased anti-white hostility, and greater dissatisfaction with their own current occupational situation. These dispositions were sufficient to account, in part, for the effects of social background on riot participation, as expected from our political socialization hypothesis. But they did not adequately account for the greater participation of Los Angeles natives.

Thus, we must conclude that there was something about being native to Los Angeles, above and beyond the political and racial attitudes acquired in local political socialization, that drastically increased the likelihood of being in the crowds during the rioting. Perhaps the natives had more friends in the area, were more familiar with the surrounding environment, had a stronger sense of "turf" or territoriality or possession of the area, were more central to a communication net which spread the word regarding where to find the action, and, thus, were more likely to get swept up in the riot activity. All this may have distinguished the natives, whether or not their political and racial attitudes directed them toward a protest of conditions that aggrieved them. In light of these findings, the strongest form of our functional equivalence theory must be modified. Early political socialization was a powerful mediator of the effects of demographic change on riot participation, but it was not the only factor by any means.

The other hypothesized antecedents of the rioting were the feelings among the participants that those whites with power in the local situation were unresponsive and indifferent to the interests of blacks and intransigent about meeting demands for social change. Grievances against the local white-dominated institutions were among the most powerful instigators of riot participation. Whether or not Los Angeles is (or was) unique in this respect remains to be determined by comparative research. Nevertheless, we must underline once again the central contribution to rioting of the blacks' feelings of frustration and grievance about the way they were treated in the local community, feelings quite aside from those acquired in early socialization.

These data suggest, therefore, that responses to the riot by officials and members of the public who said, in effect, "Well, there are problems but we have good ways of dealing with them!," were sadly off the mark. The riot participants had lost faith in the very mechanisms, generated by a white-managed system, for handling grievances. They were disenchanted with individual striving, normal administrative grievance procedures, and conventional political activity. The rioters were moving instead toward nonviolent confrontations and even violence itself. For the riot participants, the functional equivalent of conventional grievance redress mechanisms was indeed the politics of violence.

Finally, we must note the paradox among the riot participants of greater personal optimism coexisting with greater political disaffection, grievance, and hostility; of a psychology of hope coupled with the politics of despair. The rioters' own personal disadvantages apparently were not at issue nor did they assume that the riot would immediately change the circumstances of their own lives. Rather, the system appeared frozen and unresponsive and the riot was a symbolic protest against that system. The politics of violence aimed not so much at personal return, then, as at inducing powerful whites at all levels and in all areas of society to redress blacks' grievances and to open up fairer and more effective routine procedures for grievance redress.

7   Rioting as Random Outburst

The two major perspectives on urban rioting differ mainly in their view as to whether or not these upheavals had any important political significance. Having presented, in the previous four chapters, the evidence for our politics of violence theory, with its socialization, subjective deprivation, and functional equivalent hypotheses, we now consider evidence for its non-political alternative.

This alternative view denies any major political significance to the rioting, holding that legitimate grievances and discontents did not play a large causal role in inducing the individual rioter's participation. The political and policy implications of this assumption are important. If the individual's participation was not due to discontents, then grievance redress is not a necessary means of reducing the chance of violence.

In this chapter, we wish to pose and empirically test this view. We will present it in two forms. We have constructed one form, the random outburst theory, as a composite of several different hypotheses, which have been offered haphazardly by numerous observers but which never before have been brought together into a coherent and systematic theory. In constructing it, we have tried to bend over backwards to develop a plausible and psychologically sound theory, as will be seen. Yet, there is no real substitute for a theory generated by someone who truly believes in it. For that reason, we also present and test the propositions contained in Edward C. Banfield's interpretation, which he has called "rioting mainly for fun and profit" (see Banfield, 1970). This is, to our knowledge, the most coherent theoretical effort[1] by an observer who assigns relatively little political significance to the rioting.

---

[1]As opposed, for example, to the rudimentary single factor theories tested and rejected in Chapter 2.

The Random Outburst Theory

The random outburst theory denies any grievance basis for the riot and reduces riot participation to a random explosion triggered by chance (or conspiracy) and sustained by social contagion. The riot is assigned about as much symbolic political meaning as a drunken brawl in a tavern. To define the theory, we offer six different testable propositions: (1) *conspiracy*—the violence was triggered by small conspiratorial groups of Black Muslims or of communists; (2) *social contagion*—most rioters became involved simply through social contagion, either through their proximity to other rioters or through watching the riot on television; (3) *youthful male animal spirits*—most of the rioters were young males, letting off their exuberance and rebelliousness, just as young males always have done, from the time of Alcibiades' defacing of the temples to modern-day "panty raids"; (4) *post facto rationalization*—post-riot interpretations of the violence as a protest, or as based on legitimate grievances, were simply rationalizations for behavior engaged in for the far more mundane reasons just mentioned; (5) *undifferentiated hostility*—the correlations between grievance levels and riot participation merely reflected the rioters' blanket hostility and rebelliousness against all forms of authority rather than a discriminating response to specific legitimate grievances; and (6) *lack of sophistication*—the rioters' lack of faith in conventional mechanisms of grievance redress reflected their ignorance of these mechanisms, rather than any major faults in the mechanisms themselves.

Although the random outburst theory has not had wide acceptance among liberal academics, it cannot be rejected out of hand. In one version or another it has been the majority view of white Americans and especially of most conservative white leaders, as will be seen in Chapters 9 and 10. Moreover, most of its propositions derive from widely accepted principles of social psychology and political behavior. These principles may well (and in fact do) turn out to be inconsistent with the empirical evidence about the Watts Riot but they are quite plausible hypotheses, a priori. Finally, post facto correlational data such as ours, by their very nature, never can establish a causal role for any set of factors, since they always allow for alternative interpretations. Still, the politics of violence theory will have considerably more credibility if we can reject the several hypotheses posed by this rival random outburst theory.

Black Muslim and Communist Conspirators.   Conspiracy theories have a long history as explanations of civil violence, as Hofstadter (1965) and Rudé (1964) have shown. With respect to Watts, the most popular form of such theories did not hold that all or a majority of the rioters were communists, Black Muslims, or what-have-you. Rather, it assigned responsibility for igniting the spark to conspirators, who then urged others to antisocial acts and watched malevolently as social contagion did the rest of the job. Hence, as in other forms of contagion theories, the rioters were seen principally as having been caught up in the excitement and unaware that the communists, Black Muslims, and others were duping them.

The conspiracy explanation was enthusiastically embraced by political conservatives, as might be expected (see, for instance, the John Birch Society's *American Opinion*, September 1965). The responsible local white authorities, Mayor Yorty and Police Chief Parker, both widely attributed the rioting to communists and outside agitators (see Chapter 9 for the details). But more surprisingly, the conspiracy theory had extremely wide support among the general public. In November 1965, 51 per cent of a nationwide sample told the Gallup interviewers that they thought the communists were involved "a lot" in the riots, while another 27 per cent felt the communists had been involved "to some extent" (Erskine, 1967, p. 664). In fact, in *all* Gallup, Harris, Minnesota, California, and NORC polls published from August 1965 to August 1967, white Americans ranked communists *first* as the source of the racial trouble (Erskine, 1967, pp. 663-665). In our white sample, communists, Black Muslims, and outside agitators were frequently blamed for the trouble (as shown in Table 10.2 below). Southern Democratic and Republican members of the U. S. House of Representatives were especially fond of a conspiracy theory to account for the 1967 riots: 62 per cent of the southern Democrats and 59 per cent of the Republicans blamed "outside agitators" as a prime cause (Lupsha, 1969). Clearly, communists and other conspirators were very convenient and important scapegoats for the mainstream white American.

Our research was not geared to test directly for the existence of a conspiracy. It is very unlikely that a communist or Muslim conspirator would be in our sample group or that he would tell us about it if he were; and outside agitators doubtless would have moved elsewhere by the time we went into the field. However, a number of rather compelling indirect tests would seem to rule out any very central role for a conspiracy. Only 1 per cent of our black respondents cited conspiratorial groups as causes of the riot. Although they were not perfect interpreters of the riot, they were there, which the John Birchers and the Mayor were not, and a great many were anxious to blame it on some convenient scapegoat. Second, the large number of people involved in the riot (Chapter 1) makes it highly improbable that conspirators played anything more than a very minor role. Third, the strength of the relationships between demographic (Chapter 2) and attitudinal (Chapter 6) variables and riot participation argues against any random triggering by conspirators. Finally, both the McCone Commission and J. Edgar Hoover declared that they found no evidence that communists were at fault. As attractive as the conspiracy theories are to many whites, they appear unlikely to contain much truth.

Social Contagion: Proximity and Television. There is ample evidence that social contagion, deindividuation, and social influence are powerful determinants of social behavior, even when the behavior produced is directly contradictory to a person's attitudes, values, and best judgment. Social-psychological experiments conducted by Asch (1952), Festinger, Pepitone, and Newcomb (1952), Milgram (1964), and Zimbardo (1969) have shown that, when confronted with an overwhelming majority, given an order by someone else, or released from normal social restraints by anonymity and reduced responsibility, people will distort their perceptions of a situation, be dishonest, or give painful or possibly lethal electric shocks to a helpless victim, even to one whom they may like very much. These experiments have been truly graphic demonstrations because of the enormity of the contradictions between the individual's unusual behavior, as influenced by other people, and his better judgment.

Apart from these laboratory demonstrations, the social contagion theory of riot behavior has many supporters at both the common sense or folk level and the academic or theoretical level. Police Chief Parker exclaimed that the sight of one black throwing a rock set off a chain of events in which the rest joined in "like monkeys in a zoo." His remark expressed at the folk level a theory of riot participation developed more formally by Gustav LeBon (1903) and refined by Sigmund Freud (1927). In both the common sense and formalized versions of the theory, proximity to the action is the key factor. Persons near the outburst are thought to have been caught up in the excitement and deindividuated (or robbed of their superego controls), which resulted in regression to a more primitive social or psychological state in which they readily imitated or conformed to the primitive actions of others. Another form of the same idea holds that the rioters' normal aggressions and tendencies to rebel simply were disinhibited by extraneous factors such as alcohol and drugs.

If simple social contagion had been the dominant causal factor in producing the riot, we would expect to find demographic and attitudinal factors not significantly related to participation; rather, only proximity or exposure to one of the disinhibiting agents should be significantly related. However, demographic and attitudinal variables were strongly related to riot activity, as shown earlier. Moreover, 43 per cent of those not active in the riot said the people in their neighborhoods had been active in the rioting (Chapter 1). In these cases social contagion had its opportunity but evidently failed. Thus contagion and disinhibition may have played some role, but these findings severely limit the validity of this hypothesis. The riot cannot simply be "explained away" as reflecting such variables.

A further variant of the contagion hypothesis blamed the rioting on television. Since its invention, television has been blamed almost continuously for every ill of American society, from radiation poisoning and poor nutrition to the breakdown of the American family, playground brawls, and the escalating number of rapes. Thus it was not surprising that many blamed television for the outbreak and persistence of the riots. Here, theorists substituted television for proximity or outside agitation in the contagion hypothesis, that is, they claimed that persons were incited to riot by seeing the actions of others in sensational television coverage of the rioting.

Unfortunately, we have no direct test of this hypothesis. The Watts Riot was extensively covered by television (much of it by cameras safely aloft in a helicopter), and no doubt many local citizens, black and white, followed the riot's progress in this way. In contrast, the news media of Detroit imposed a voluntary moratorium upon riot coverage—one which was completely effective for the first eight hours.[2] Yet during that time, news of the violence flashed through the community, and later the level of conflict escalated until Detroit attained the dubious distinction of being the site of more deaths than occurred in any other city during the riots of the 1960s (Levy, 1968). In our data, scales of exposure to white-dominated media and to black-originated media did not relate to riot participation. They were significantly related to self-reported activity or to events witnessed, or they significantly differentiated arrestees from the Curfew Zone sample, in only one of six comparisons. These data will be discussed in more detail below, but on balance, they indicate that the media played at most a subsidiary role in the outbreak and persistence of violence, a view subscribed to by other informed scholars (see Lang and Lang, 1972).

Youthful Animal Spirits. A further variant on the social contagion theory grew out of the observation that in the main the rioters were young. Banfield (1970) put it most directly, claiming that the young always are filled with exuberance and rebelliousness and tend mindlessly to join up with any such action, regardless of time, place, or historical circumstance, because they like to exercise (or perhaps let off) their "animal spirits." This is clearly opposed to our theory that the New Urban Blacks were *not* just like any other group of young people and that the rioting was motivated by discontents arising from the specific and unpleasant conditions of their lives. The Banfield thesis can be tested as a special case of the social contagion type of theory; namely, by determining whether or not discontent played a lessened causal role in the riot participation of the young. Thus, one would not expect to find riot participation among the young related to any attitudinal measures of discontent, although it might be among older people. Of course this is very plausible for other reasons as well; there is ample evidence elsewhere in the literature that the young are generally less involved in public affairs, less informed about them, and are less likely to participate in them (Milbrath, 1965).

We have indicated already that this hypothesis fails in one respect: each of the major attitudinal variables covered in the last chapter (generalized political disaffection, racial attitudes, subjective status deprivation, and local grievances) was related to riot participation among the young, just as

[2] Only 9 per cent of a sample of Detroit arrestees found out about the riot through television (Singer, 1970).

each was in the sample as a whole (Chapter 6). A more stringent test yields even more compelling evidence. Contrary to the "animal spirits" notion, local grievances were more closely related to riot participation among the young than among the middle or older age groups in 15 of 24 possible comparisons (considering our two measures of riot participation, self-reported activity and events witnessed).[3] If anything, then, grievances were *more* related to riot participation among the young than among their elders. This strongly contradicts the "animal spirits" hypothesis, at least in its simplest form.

Thus, all of these various social contagion hypotheses, whether they rely on cabals and conspirators, proximity, alcohol, television, or youthful animal spirits to account for the contagion, fail to account for the basic data in our study. All of these factors may have made some contribution, and we cannot claim great precision in our measures of their effects, but none was sufficiently strong to overcome the effects of political discontents.

Post Facto Rationalization.   One might still assume that social contagion or excitement was primarily responsible for riot participation but that the rioters later invented discontents as rationalizations for their criminal behavior. In retrospect, they could have found their motives for rioting insubstantial and trivial and felt compelled to glamorize them, to rationalize their behavior in terms of a broader cause. This type of interpretation, reversing the causality between grievances and participation, is the bane of all correlational studies. It would interpret the data presented in the last chapter as a mere artifact, thus invalidating it as counterevidence to the social contagion hypotheses. Worse still, this argument had a special initial appeal to us, for three reasons.

First of all, many experimental social psychologists now feel that situational incentives are more important determinants of social behavior than are internal dispositions such as attitudes. Research on conformity (Asch, 1954), obedience (Milgram, 1964; Freedman, Carlsmith, and Sears, 1970), personality dispositions (Mischel, 1969), the links between attitudes and behavior (Wicker, 1969), and behavior modification all bear this implication.

Second, cognitive dissonance theory has yielded much evidence that people adjust their attitudes in order to account for their previous behavior (Abelson et al., 1968; Festinger and Carlsmith, 1959). For example, if one engages in behavior due to rather mundane situational incentives, one often later glamorizes one's reasons for having done it.

Finally, political analysts, like ourselves, commonly err in the direction

---

[3]Similarly, as will be seen in Chapter 10, local grievances were much more closely related to pro-riot attitudes among the young than among the old. Here, the young, if anything, were considerably *more* motivated by their discontents in their views of the rioting than were older age groups. This appears to us to be a far cry from "panty raids."

of too often attributing ideological political motivation to commonplace acts, despite the evidence of empirical studies which are directly contrary. The American public's political information tends to be fragmentary (Sears, 1969a); few can be said to have an abstract and refined political philosophy or political ideology (Campbell et al., 1960); and only a minority can even define the words "liberal" and "conservative" in terms at all comparable to those conventionally used by political activists (Converse, 1964).

Since these possibilities are so compelling, we devote a major portion of this chapter to the question of rationalization, spelling out its implications as we present our empirical checks. In some respects, this is perhaps the most challenging and most original part of our analysis in this book.

If indeed the rioters rationalized their behavior in noble and glamorous terms, they presumably would have done so in the following sequence: (1) riot participation; (2) more favorable attitudes about the riot itself, to justify participation; (3) interpretation of the riot as a symbolic protest with good potential effects, to justify the positive attitudes toward the rioting; and (4) expression of serious local grievances, to justify the need for a protest. We know from the previous chapter that the first and last of these were related: riot participation and local grievances. The question here is whether or not this relationship was principally mediated by this sequence of rationalization.

We cannot test for this directly but we can do a number of indirect tests. Generally, if this sequence of rationalization accounted for the relationship between discontents and riot participation, (1) all of the above mentioned attitudes should be more pro-riot among the rioters than among the non-rioters, (2) they should follow from one another more closely among the rioters, (3) all of these effects should increase with time after the riot, as the rationalization progressed, and (4) all should be greater with greater political sophistication, presuming that sophistication increases the ability to rationalize.

Did the riot participants approve more of the riot and offer more exalted explanations for the riot, as would be expected if they were rationalizing their own behavior? We measured attitudes toward the riot along three main dimensions: evaluation of the riot, interpretation of the riot as a purposeful symbolic protest, and optimism about the effects of the riot. We will present the data on these attitudes in detail in Chapters 10 and 11. For our purposes here we simply need to compare participants and non-participants; this is done in Table 7.1.

The participants were clearly much more favorable toward the riot than were the nonparticipants. Approval of the riot ran two to one among arrestees and the Curfew Zone respondents, respectively, and, among the latter, two to one among participants and nonparticipants, respectively. These differences are highly significant. The participants also perceived a much larger proportion of the black community as involved in the riot than did the nonparticipants. However, these two dimensions were correlated (see

Table 10.1) in our data, just as data from election campaigns (see Benham, 1965; Lazarsfeld et al., 1948) indicate that people with strong candidate preferences frequently overestimate how many other voters share their preference. Thus, it is likely that here we are dealing primarily with a single dimension of positive affect toward the riot.

However, the rioters did not differ so much from nonrioters on the more telling question of whether or not the riot was a directed symbolic protest against legitimate grievances. The arrestees were significantly higher than the Curfew Zone sample on the "protest interpretation" scale and in criticism of the authorities' role in riot control but both dimensions were less strongly related to participation within the Curfew Zone sample. And the attempt to get at the details of a respondent's interpretation of *what* the purposes of the riot had been did not yield great differences. Finally, the participants were somewhat more optimistic about the effects of the riot than were the nonparticipants but the differences were not significant and probes about the details of possible effects yielded no significant differences.

If post-riot self-justification was an important factor in determining the rioters' attitudes toward the riot, then, it was limited mainly to evaluation of the riot: rioters were more likely to approve of the riot and to perceive broad community involvement in it. Their explanations of the meaning or effects of the riot could not have been affected by rationalization to any great extent, since rioters and nonrioters differed little in seeing the riot as a symbolic protest or in being hopeful about its effects. This is a critical point, because if these explanations of the riot's meaning were greatly affected by rationalization, that might "explain away" the greater grievance levels among the rioters reported in Chapter 6.

The finding that optimism about the riot's effects was not related significantly to participation is especially important: such optimism is the least reality-bound dimension of the riot ideology since it deals with a future-oriented subjective feeling. Hence, due to the minimum of cognitive effort involved in changing this element, we might expect it to be the dimension influenced most easily by the cognitive pressures created by dissonance. That this "weakest link" was so little influenced is further evidence that post hoc rationalization was not a terribly potent factor in producing the relationships between discontent and participation reported above.

Local Grievances.   Rationalization should have led the rioters to a tighter consistency than the nonrioters between their local grievances and their attitudes about the riot. Since the rioters were under greater pressure to justify their behavior (it was illegal and inconsistent with their normal behavior and they were in the minority), they should have been more motivated to seek cognitive consistency. By this argument they should have adjusted their grievances and attitudes toward the riot to fit together better than did the nonrioters.

To test this, we related the six local grievances to the riot approval

TABLE 7.1
Participants' and Nonparticipants' Riot Attitudes

	ARRESTEE SAMPLE†	CURFEW ZONE SAMPLE†				
		Total sample	Very or somewhat active	Not active	X^2	p
Riot approval						
Riot approval scale* (percentage favorable)	57	29	50	22	34.23	<.001
Perceived community activity scale (percentage high)	52	25	46	18	29.18	<.001
Protest interpretation of the riot						
Protest interpretation scale (percentage high)	93	69	75	68	1.66	n.s.
Probe: "What was its purpose?"					12.08	<.01
Revenge, express resentment	6	10	9	10		
Call attention	36	31	32	31		
Instrumentality	12	14	23	12		
Nothing	47	45	35	47		
	101	100	99	100		

Authorities' roles (percentage handled badly)	84	70	80	68	5.38	<.05
Optimism about riot's effects						
Riot optimism scale (percentage high)	68	62	70	60	3.75	<.10
Probe: "Why did it help or hurt?"					3.97	n.s.
Call attention	22	18	24	17		
Affect whites	8	13	13	12		
Affect blacks	4	10	9	10		
Utilitarian effect	17	20	19	20		
None, don't know, no answer	49	40	34	41		
	100	101	99	100		

*See Appendix B for the items and reliabilities of these scales.
†Except in the cases of the two probes, the "don't know's," "no answer's," and so on, are excluded from the base. X^2 on 1 df, except in cases of probes (3 df and 4 df, respectively).

scale and to the protest interpretation scale separately for the "active" and "not active" (by self report). Actually, the opposite held. In both cases, four of the six grievances were more strongly and positively related to these pro-riot attitudes among the *nonparticipants* than among the participants. Apparently those *not* active were more likely to develop a consistent "package" of attitudes relating prior discontents to their evaluations of the riot, contrary to the rationalization hypothesis.

Now let us turn to a further and somewhat subtler elaboration of the same point. According to the rationalization hypothesis, riot approval was a necessary intervening step if riot participation and grievances were to be related. The pressure to justify behavior acts directly upon evaluation of the behavior (Abelson et al., 1968; Festinger, 1957). Riot participants who wound up not liking the riot therefore probably would not be evidencing rationalization. Thus, given rationalization, riot participation should be related to local grievances only among those approving of the riot. In fact, however, the opposite again occurred. Self-reported riot participation was more closely related to five of the six local grievances among those disapproving of the riot than among those approving of it. This is evidence against an hypothesis that would view riot approval as a necessary way station in the sequence by which riot participation is rationalized in terms of local grievances.

Finally, if rationalization were the main explanation for the relationship between grievances and reported activity, we would expect it not to occur among those who did not interpret the riot as a directed protest. To test this possibility, we related grievances and activity, controlling on protest interpretation. In three cases the relationship was stronger among those perceiving the riot as a protest, and in three cases, stronger among those seeing it as a random outburst of violence. So the relationship between grievances and activity did not depend on the protest interpretation of the riot.

We conclude, then, that there is little evidence of a tighter consistency (among riot approval, protest interpretation, and local grievances) among riot participants than among nonparticipants, as the rationalization hypothesis would require.

Increasing Rationalization over Time.   If the participants' local grievances and pro-riot attitudes were mainly due to post-riot rationalization of their own behavior, both should be increasingly related to riot participation as time passed after the riot. Presumably cognitive consistency pressures operate spontaneously and increasingly with time (McGuire, 1960). Thus, participants interviewed a month after the riot would not have developed rationalizations as elaborate as those developed by participants interviewed five months after the riot. Over time, then, we would expect participation to be more closely related to pro-riot attitudes and to local grievances. Also, we would find both pro-riot attitudes and local grievances increasing in intensity over time throughout the black community, as the rioters' rationalization increased. To test this, we compared respondents interviewed (1) during October, (2) during November, and (3) in December, January, and February.[4]

Neither riot approval nor protest interpretation became systematically more closely related to riot participation with time, as shown in Table 7.2. On the other hand, there was some tendency for self-reported riot participation to become more closely associated to local grievances over time, as consistency pressures increasingly promoted rationalization of rioting in terms of broader social ills. Five of the six grievances were in fact most closely related to self-reported riot participation in the last (December-February) interviewing, and only one (perceived police brutality) was most closely related to the earliest (October) interviews. There was no

TABLE 7.2

Riot Ideology as a Function of Riot Participation and Time

	TIME OF INTERVIEW		
	Early (October)	**Middle (November)**	**Late (December-February)**
Percentage high in riot approval			
Participants	54	42	67
Nonparticipants	20	25	21
X^2 *(1 df)*	10.14†	4.29*	19.14†
n	121	216	132
Percentage high in protest interpretation			
Participants	79	64	85
Nonparticipants	59	66	75
X^2 *(1 df)*	2.58	0	0.46
n	111	197	120

*$p < .05$ †$p < .001$
Note: Participation is indexed here by self-reported activity (Curfew Zone sample only).

[4]There were no great demographic differences between respondents interviewed early and late. There were no significant differences in sex, education, region of origin, urban-rural origin, self-classified socio-economic status, employment, place of origin, age, or age and place of origin combined. The strongest effects were sex, where the proportion of females interviewed declined from 58 per cent in the first time period to 46 per cent in the third time period ($X^2 = 5.36$, 2 *df*, $p < .10$), place of origin ($X^2 = 7.97$, 4 *df*, $p < .10$), and self-classified socio-economic status ($X^2 = 7.86$, 4 *df*, $p < .10$). Given these rather slight differences, we feel it is valid to treat this variable as reflecting the time of interview, rather than some sampling bias.

general tendency for the relationship to increase from the early to middle interviewing; the big change was the close correlation among those interviewed last. This then does represent some evidence for increasing rationalization with time.

Did the black community as a whole therefore become more convinced with time both that the riot was a useful symbolic protest and that legitimate grievances existed? Both would be expected from increasing rationalization over time. Both sets of data are presented in other contexts in this book. Here it is sufficient to say that some of the dimensions of pro-riot attitude did increase with time, but riot approval (the likeliest candidate for rationalization) did not, nor did the consistency among riot attitudes (see Chapter 11). And we have seen already (Chapter 4) that local grievances did not increase over time.

Thus, riot participants' attitudes toward the riot did not become more approving and justifying with time, though their grievances did (relative to those of nonparticipants). And the black community's attitudes toward the riot and its local grievances did not consistently move in the direction that would be expected from massive rationalization. Post-riot changes over time, then, do not support the rationalization hypothesis very clearly.

Rationalization and Sophistication.   If the relationship between participation and grievance is due to rationalization, it should be more dependent upon political sophistication (as an index of a wider variety of cognitive skills) than if rioting is an angry and crude response to frustration and grievance. Specifically, were participation and grievance related only among the educated and knowledgeable?

To test this, we related the six grievances to self-reported activity, controlling separately on education and on familiarity with white politicians. Grievances proved to be more closely related to activity among the *less* educated and knowledgeable respondents in slightly over half the comparisons, though the differences were not very great. This is further evidence against rationalization: grievances were not *more* related to activity among the more sophisticated.

These data, then, provide little support for the random outburst theory, or for its notion that the rioters simply rationalized their participation by adopting high levels of grievance, long after the riot zone was quiet. It would be foolish to assert that no rationalization occurred. But rationalization cannot be invoked to "explain away" the relationships between discontent and riot participation described in the previous chapter.

Generalized Hostility toward Authority.   Even if the rioters were not chance actors drawn into the drama by social contagion but were individuals personally disposed to converge upon the action, the relevant dispositions may have been so personal and idiosyncratic that they invalidated the riot as a comment upon society. For example, the rioters just may have been paranoid or they may have been acting out hostilities toward their parents. The most plausible hypothesis of this sort is that the rioters simply had a high level of generalized blanket antagonism and mistrust. Such feelings would not be limited to local white authorities but could be elicited by the federal government, black leadership, or conceivably even by people in general. The rioters' grievances then would reflect their own personal ill temper more than any particular wrongdoing on the part of local white authorities. This can be tested by determining whether or not the rioters were also particularly discontented with people in general and with most other institutions and leadership groups. That is, was riot participation systematically related to attitudes in areas other than those discussed in the previous chapter?

Our contention is that the rioters' greater political disaffection reflected a lack of faith in those managing local institutions, rather than mistrust of people in general. This can be tested by comparing two very similar items: "Do you think elected officials can generally be trusted?" and "Do you think people can generally be trusted?" Distrust of elected officials clearly was the item more closely related to riot participation and to attitudes about the riot and to local grievances, as shown in Table 7.3. In *every* one of the 12 comparisons, distrust of elected officials was more closely linked to rioting and grievance than was distrust of people in general. The same is true of comparisons between arrestees and the Curfew Zone sample, not shown in Table 7.3: the arrestees showed greater distrust than did the Curfew Zone sample regarding elected officials (by 11 per cent) than they showed regarding people in general (by 7 per cent). These data very strongly pinpoint the rioters' distress as focusing specifically on the political system rather than on people more generally.

Conceivably, though, the rioters may have been especially discontented with *all* forms of political leadership. Hence we tested the relationship between riot participation and approval of black leadership. As indicated earlier, the latter was indexed with four scales—measuring attitudes toward assimilationists, civil rights groups, local black politicians, and Black Muslims. These were not closely related to riot participation. Of the 12 comparisons involved, only three were statistically significant and they went in contradictory directions. Rioters, in one case, were less favorable than nonrioters to assimilationist leaders but, in two cases, they were more favorable than nonrioters to the militant Muslims.[5] The overall pattern, however, is one of very little difference between rioters and nonrioters.

---

[5]Arrestees were less favorable than Curfew Zone respondents to the assimilationists ($t = 2.11$, $p < .05$) and were more favorable to the Black Muslims ($t = 2.21$, $p < .05$). Approval of Black Muslims was associated with events witnessed ($X^2 = 3.85$, 1 df, $p < .05$).

TABLE 7.3

Comparison of Distrust of People in General versus Distrust of Elected Officials in Relationships wth Riot Participation, Riot Ideology, and Grievances

	Distrust of people	Distrust of elected officials
Riot participation		
Self-reported activity	4.46	23.41*
Events witnessed	0.00	2.21*
Riot ideology		
Riot approval	7.94	17.88*
Perceived community activity	7.34	12.92*
Protest interpretation	0.49	3.81*
Authorities' roles	4.90	9.39*
Grievances		
Police brutality	0.42	11.34*
Merchant exploitation	11.01	23.07*
Biased white media	5.82	18.51*
Local political structure	7.34	35.36*
Agency discrimination	2.26	2.68*
Inadequate service agencies	10.72	11.02*

Note: Entry is X^2 on 1 df. $X^2 = 3.84$ is needed for $p < .05$. Starred entry indicates the stronger relationship (Curfew Zone sample only).

Religious leadership evinced this same mixed pattern of differences between rioters and nonrioters. Within the Curfew Zone sample, as already indicated in Chapter 2, those most and least favorable toward their church were the most active in the riot—this was significantly so in the case of self-reported activity but not in that of events witnessed. Arrestees were more disenchanted with their own church than were Curfew Zone respondents.[6] This mixed pattern of results is inconsistent with the "random outburst" assumption of a generalized rejection of authority by the rioters.

Given that the rioters' greater discontent focused on political authority rather than on people in general but excluded black leadership, the final question is whether or not this was specific to *local* white authorities, as suggested in the previous chapter. Here the appropriate test is to relate riot participation to approval of non-local white authorities.

[6]For these three comparisons, respectively, $X^2 = 7.87$, 3 df, $p < .05$; $X^2 = 3.57$, 3 df, n.s.; $t = 2.95$, $p < .01$.

Discontent about such white leaders evidently was not a significant contributor, as we may see in several ways. Approval of whites in nonlocal partisan politics was measured with two scales, evaluating "white liberals" and the Republican Party. Disapproval of the Republicans was not related to any of our three indexes of riot participation, while disapproval of "white liberals" was greater among the arrestees than among the Curfew Zone respondents ($p < .001$), and among those reporting themselves active ($p < .02$), but was not related to events witnessed. Thus, riot participation was not closely related to discontent with nonlocal partisan politicians, yielding significant differences in but two of six comparisons.

Nor was riot participation related systematically to discontent with the federal poverty program and its local agencies. Our general item asked: "Do you think the federal government's anti-poverty program is going to help the Negro in Los Angeles?" The item was related to self-reported activity ($X^2 = 6.20$, 2 df, $p < .05$), but not to events witnessed, and the arrestees and Curfew Zone respondents differed by only 2 per cent. We also constructed a scale combining evaluations of six local agencies of the federal anti-poverty program. Scores on this scale did not relate significantly to either self-reported activity or events witnessed, though the arrestees were less approving than the Curfew Zone respondents ($t = 2.48$, 640 df, $p < .02$). Thus, there was little relationship between discontent with the poverty program and riot participation, the rioters proving significantly more discontented in only two of the six comparisons.

Finally, a more systematic comparison of local and national white leadership is shown in Table 7.4. The arrestees were consistently more hostile toward local authorities than were the Curfew Zone respondents but the two samples were very similar with respect to national political authorities. These various pieces of evidence suggest, then, that the rioters' special antagonism toward local symbols of white authority was not generalized to the remote federal and state levels.

Thus, it is evident that riot participation was tied rather specifically to discontent with local white political authorities and institutions. It was not closely related to mistrust of people in general, discontent with black political or religious leaders, or national white political authorities. This indicates that the relationship between discontent and riot participation demonstrated in the previous chapter was based upon antagonisms specific to local white authorities, rather than simply reflecting the random outburst of ill-tempered blacks hostile to any and all symbols of authority or human society.

Unsophisticated Rioters.   If each of the foregoing alternative explanations were to be rejected, we might indeed conclude that certain specific discontents did motivate an individual's riot participation. Even then, though, some might argue that the rioting stemmed more from the rioters' lack of political sophistication than from offensive political and social conditions. Perhaps

TABLE 7.4

Comparison of Curfew Zone and Arrestee Samples in Positive Evaluations of Local and National Political Persons and Groups

	LOCAL		NATIONAL		NUMBER OF LEADERS OR GROUPS
	Curfew Zone sample	Arrestee sample	Curfew Zone sample	Arrestee sample	
Agency discrimination	53%	39%	—	—	5
White politicians	37	34	64%	60%	3
Legislative bodies	72	68	76	74	2
Political parties	—	—	62	62	2
Agency evaluations	53	45	—	—	3
Average	54%	46%	67%	65%	

Note: Entry is percentage in each sample expressing a positive evaluation, averaged over the number of political leaders or groups indicated in the right-hand column.

the normal channels of grievance redress are in fact reasonably effective, but the rioters were unsophisticated about them, because of their youth and inexperience and impatience, and thus had given up on them prematurely. If this constituted the explanation for the rioting, our data should show it. We did not directly measure sophistication about grievance redress mechanisms. But we did have four scales of political knowledge (familiarity with white politicians, poverty agencies, black politicians, and national black leaders) and two of media exposure (white-dominated media and black-originated media). According to this hypothesis, the rioters should score lower on them. Indeed, riot participation should be more closely related to these scales than to the discontents cited in the previous chapter.

The data show the contrary, however: the riot participants were *more* sophisticated than the nonrioters. The arrestees were significantly more knowledgeable than the Curfew Zone sample on two scales, and marginally significantly more in two other cases. Within the Curfew Zone sample, the only significant effect was that exposure to black-oriented media was positively related to self-reported activity; otherwise, activity and events witnessed did not relate to these scales.

So, of the 18 possible comparisons between rioters and nonrioters, only three are statistically significant, and in each case sophistication was associated with greater, not less, riot participation. Thus it seems extremely unlikely that the rioters' grievances and their disenchantment with conventional grievance redress procedures were due only to an unusual lack of experience or sophistication.

"Rioting Mainly for Fun and Profit"

Having tested the various elements of a counter theory we have constructed, let us consider briefly one developed with more conviction: Edward C. Banfield's theory of rioting presented in his *Unheavenly City* (1970). Though his "theory" is unsystematically presented, and he offers virtually no supporting empirical data, we can frame its main propositions in testable form, so that it can be evaluated with our data.

Banfield distinguishes four types of riots: "rampages," "forays for pillage," "outbursts of righteous indignation," and "demonstrations." He describes the Watts Riot as mainly a combination of the first two. What does he mean by these? A "rampage" is "an outbreak of animal—usually young, male animal—spirits in search of action and excitement," while in the case of a "foray for pillage," "the motive is theft, and here also boys and young adults of the lower class are the principal offenders" (pp. 187, 189).

Banfield separates into two categories what he designates as the riot's causes. The principal "accelerating causes" were (1) the sensational coverage of riots by television, which lured young men into the streets; (2) the laxity of justice produced by frightened police and permissive courts, which gave the rioters nothing to fear from criminal action; and (3) the noble protest rationales given by leadership elements, which gave legitimacy to "rampaging" and "foraying for pillage."

The main "background cause" that Banfield emphasizes was the existence of a large pool of young, lower-class, southern-reared blacks in the inner city, who were largely cut off from participation in middle-class-dominated institutions that might have given them some stake in society. He concedes that many higher status blacks have remained in the inner city due to residential segregation, but these simply "provide enough politically motivated rioters, however, . . . to escalate a rampage-foray into a major riot" (p. 204). On the basis of this analysis, Banfield concludes, then, "that what requires explanation is not so much rebellion by Negroes (whether against the whites, the slum, their own masochism, police, or something else), as it is outbreaks of animal spirits and of stealing by slum dwellers, mostly boys and young men, and mostly Negro" (pp. 197–198).

How does his theory stand up alongside our data?

Class, Not Race. Banfield's central proposition is that the rioting grew out of a general predisposition to violence on the part of the lower classes, irrespective of racial problems, grievances with authorities, or other such factors. That is, the rioting was a class phenomenon rather than a racial or political one (p. 209). On this point our data are quite explicit and show exactly the opposite. As indicated in Chapter 2, our indexes of social class were unrelated to riot participation except for one instance (mothers' education and self-reported activity) and that instance revealed that the offspring of relatively high status, high-school educated mothers were the most active, not the children of dropouts. On the other hand, racial attitudes were closely related to riot participation. The rioters were more anti-white, and had more positive black identity, than did the nonrioters (Chapter 6). So Banfield has it exactly backwards.

A related contention is that southerners are generally disposed to violence, because of the violent history of that region, so Banfield assumes that the southern born were disproportionately represented among the rioters. Our data clearly refute this notion; indeed, the *opposite* was again true—those native to Los Angeles were the most active (see Chapter 2, as well as the Kerner Commission data from Detroit and Newark).

Not a Meaningful Protest. A second key point is that the riot was mainly a "rampage" or a "foray for pillage." Banfield supports this contention in three ways.

First, he argues that most blacks were content before the riot and supported moderate rather than militant leadership (p. 194). Our data indeed pointed toward strong support for moderate black leadership but they also showed high levels of grievance concerning local white authorities and institutions, especially the police, the local newspapers, the most visible local white political officials, such as the mayor and police chief, and discrimination in the local school system (see Chapter 4). Thus, the deduction of contentment from support for moderates was incorrect.

Second, Banfield implies that the rioters were no more aggrieved than the nonrioters. As we have shown in Chapter 6, this was most definitely not true in Los Angeles; rather, riot participation was closely associated with grievance level.[7]

Banfield's repeated use of the term "animal spirits" to explain "rampaging" among the young would imply that the young were the least motivated by grievance and discontent. Our data in this chapter (see p. 111) indicated precisely the opposite. The correlation between grievance and riot participation was actually *highest* among the youngest age group, thereby refuting a simplistic "animal spirits" interpretation of youthful rioting.

Finally, one of Banfield's variations on this theme is his assumption that only middle-class blacks generated principled demonstrations or riots based on protest, whereas the lower class merely engaged in rampages or forays for pillage. However, as shown above, the correlation between participation and grievance was not in any way limited to the educated or the politically sophisticated. It was highly significant even among the less educated and less sophisticated respondents (though admittedly less strong there).

[7]What is perhaps most surprising about Banfield's book is that it ignores almost entirely (with two exceptions) every descriptive or analytic survey study done on blacks' attitudes in general or on their motives for participating in the ghetto riots. Thus, his argument mainly proceeds on the basis of historical analogy (for example, with the Civil War draft riots) or on the basis of bald assertion.

Rationalization.   Banfield's third main point is that a protest interpretation of the riot was mostly the rioters' post hoc rationalization for rampaging and foraying for pillage rather than a genuine belief growing out of a sense of grievance and accurate perceptions of the course of the riot. We examined this allegation unusually closely above and refuted it to our satisfaction, using a number of quite independent tests.

A Political Basis for Riot Participation

While the support accorded our politics of violence theory in earlier chapters and the empirical refutations of alternative theories in this chapter provide strong evidence for the theory's general validity, we cannot definitively settle the matter. Our data cannot refute all possible contributions of the factors emphasized in the random outburst theory or in Banfield's approach. It is never possible to conclude definitively the direction of causality in correlational studies, and even in panel studies the direction of causality is often ambiguous (see Campbell and Stanley, 1963; Hovland, 1959).

Our analysis here has shown, nevertheless, that rationalization and the other elements of these alternative theories were the exceptions to the general rules indicated by our theoretical propositions. They should not have been interpreted as the dominant explanations for the rioting. Therefore, we think that the reader's confidence in a political basis for riot participation (and thus for the major theory outlined in Chapter 3) ought to be considerably enhanced by this careful consideration of the most salient alternative theories.

8 The Politics of Privatism: The Local White Context

Up to this point, we have largely ignored the role of white people in the drama of "Watts," as our analysis has focused almost exclusively upon blacks. But whites' attitudes and behaviors are pivotal elements in understanding that portion of our politics of violence theory that views the riot as a symbolic protest against local grievances and blocked mechanisms of grievance redress. Why did whites allow the conditions that produced the grievances to accumulate and perpetuate? How could whites have been unaware of the intense feelings and despair smoldering in South Central Los Angeles? And why did the major riots begin in Los Angeles? Were (and are) there not worse conditions festering in Harlem, Chicago, Philadelphia, Cleveland, St. Louis, Newark, and Detroit? Finally, we must consider the whites in Los Angeles in order to understand their responses to the riot, which we will present in Chapters 9 and 10.

The reader should be warned, however, that as we examine the local white citizenry from an historical context, we are moving into a broader field of inquiry—one which we might have abandoned to the historians and social commentators. Here we can no longer rely for guidance upon rather rigorous, quantitative analyses of survey responses. Thus, though much of what follows is based upon data, we must increasingly resort to speculation and intuition in order to fill in the gaps where our knowledge is limited.

Southern California Whites: Bigotry and Right-wing Conservatism?

It would be appealing to write off whites in Los Angeles, and white-dominated social and political institutions, as having been "racist" and/or "ultra-conservative." While these terms are vague, they call up sufficiently repellent connotations to provide easy scapegoats both for the riot itself and for whites' reactions to it.

Alas, the data do not allow us to indulge in such romantic simplicities. The vast majority of Los Angeles whites clearly are not, and most probably were not, either "racists" or hard-line conservatives in any conventional sense. Nor, more generally, are white suburbanites in the North and West. Nevertheless, their lifestyles and social attitudes do provide formidable obstacles to racial harmony. Let us look first at the possibility that bigotry is widespread in the area.

Bigotry.　A variety of indicators show whites in Los Angeles (and Southern California more generally) to be relatively unprejudiced. First of all, their demographic characteristics are not like those of the most prejudiced white Americans. They tend to be relatively well educated, few come from the South, and they are not older, on the average, than other metropolitan dwellers (to mention the three demographic variables most closely related to prejudice; Sears, 1969a; Sheatsley, 1966).[1]

Racial attitudes measured in sample surveys make the same point—and more directly. If anything, whites in Southern California (and indeed white Californians or westerners in general) express more tolerant racial attitudes than those expressed by other nonsouthern whites (Campbell, 1971; Sears and Kinder, 1971; Wolfinger and Greenstein, 1968). For example, a survey in 1969 of whites in Los Angeles revealed 92 per cent supporting school integration and 96 per cent supporting integration of public accommodations, compared to 74 per cent and 86 per cent, respectively, in 1970 national samples (Sears and Kinder, 1971).[2] In their racial attitudes more generally, the great majority of Los Angeles whites seem actually to have anticipated somewhat the general national trend for whites to reject formal discrimination and genetic explanations of blacks' disadvantages (see Campbell, 1971; Greeley and Sheatsley, 1971).

Recent elections also suggest that white Southern Californians are if anything more racially liberal than other white northerners. George Wallace's 1968 campaign for the presidency attracted even less support in Southern California than elsewhere in the state. He received 6.7 per cent of the vote in the state as a whole but only 6.5 per cent in Southern California and 5.7 per cent in Los Angeles County.[3] A year later, in 1969, a black mayoral

[1]See the *1960 U.S. Census* for relevant data.

[2]Our discussion here and throughout this chapter of Southern Californians' racial attitudes relies heavily upon a survey conducted in 1969 in the suburban San Fernando Valley during the Los Angeles mayoralty contest between the white conservative incumbent, Sam Yorty, and a liberal black city councilman, Thomas Bradley (Sears and Kinder, 1971).

[3]Southern California is defined as Los Angeles, Ventura, Riverside, Orange, San Diego, Santa Barbara, Imperial, and San Bernardino Counties. Southern California is frequently compared with the San Francisco Bay Area in this chapter as in previous studies (Wolfinger and Greenstein, 1968, 1969). The Bay Area includes San Francisco, Alameda, Contra Costa, Solano, Marin, San Mateo, and Santa Clara Counties. When San Francisco is compared with Los Angeles, it must be remembered that the

candidate in the City of Los Angeles, Thomas Bradley, ran considerably more strongly among white voters than have black candidates in other major cities of the nation. He received more than a third of the white vote, running against a white incumbent, whereas recent black mayoral candidates in Atlanta, Boston, Cleveland, Detroit, Gary, Philadelphia, and Newark have done much less well among white voters. And a black candidate for State Superintendent of Public Instruction, Wilson Riles, won a majority of the vote in Southern California in 1970 against the white conservative incumbent, Max Rafferty (though Riles did run more strongly in the Bay Area than in Southern California: 53 per cent and 60 per cent, respectively).

The major counter example in recent years was the strong vote against fair housing (for ballot Proposition 14) in November 1964. As shown in Table 8.1, fair housing was supported by 42 per cent in the San Francisco Bay Area and by only 31 per cent in Southern California. However, this issue, interpreted in strictly racial terms by liberal whites who supported fair housing, also involved serious questions of private property and personal freedom (for example, the right to sell one's own property to whomever one pleases). Indeed, opponents of fair housing phrased their opinions in just such terms (Wolfinger and Greenstein, 1968). Thus, the outcome of this referendum is not the unambiguous evidence for conventional bigotry in Southern California that many liberals and blacks assumed, even though its message to blacks may have been just that, as the McCone Commission and many others have asserted.

Finally, despite their considerable local grievances, blacks in Los Angeles seemingly have not themselves felt that overt racial prejudice or discrimination was at epidemic levels in government. As shown earlier, only an average of 9 per cent of our black respondents said they had experienced racial discrimination in various public agencies; most said they had neither heard of nor experienced it (see Table 4.3).[4] We have no exactly comparable data from other cities or regions on perceptions of discrimination. However, our data do not indicate any widespread experience of racial discrimination at the hands of government agencies in Los Angeles. Thus, relative to other northern metropolitan areas, Los Angeles government and politics evidently

---

City and County of San Francisco are coterminous, whereas the City of Los Angeles constitutes only about 40 per cent of the population of Los Angeles County. Most of the rest is incorporated in such middle-sized cities as Long Beach, Pasadena, Downey, and numerous others.

[4]More felt discrimination occurred in the private sector—22 per cent said they had experienced discrimination from landlords; 28 per cent, housing discrimination; 43 per cent, job discrimination. Perceived police brutality (though not experienced) was greater in Los Angeles than in other northern cities (compare Raine, 1970, p. 386, with Campbell, 1971, p. 89). Complaints about merchants were also greater (compare Murphy and Watson, 1970, p. 158, with Campbell, 1971, p. 95). However, in these latter cases racial discrimination was not explicitly at issue in the wording of the item.

were not unusually influenced by bigotry, with the outstanding example of the vote on fair housing in 1964, to which we will return later.

Political Conservatism.   In intellectual circles, Southern California has a widespread reputation for political conservatism. It is known as "Reagan Country" (Wilson, 1967), a place where "the conservative tone of political life . . . is well known" (Wolfinger and Greenstein, 1969, p. 74). Yet a

TABLE 8.1

Regional Differences in California Voting: Three Eras

	Southern California	Bay Area	Difference
Party registration			
1936–1956	n.a.	n.a.	n.a.
1958–1962	55.8%	58.0%	+ 2.2%
1964–1970	54.4	58.4	+ 4.0
Vote for President, Governor, U.S. Senator			
1936–1956	47.7	48.8	+ 1.1
1958–1962	49.8	54.5	+ 4.7
1964–1970	45.2	54.4	+ 9.2
Congressional vote			
1936–1956	51.3	52.4	+ 1.1
1958–1962	53.7	53.5	− 0.2
1964–1970	47.1	50.0	+ 2.9
Miscellaneous votes			
1962: State Superintendent of Public Instruction	46	52	+ 6
Proposition 24	53	69	+16
1964: Proposition 14	31	42	+11
Goldwater/Rockefeller primary	41	62	+21
1968: Wallace presidential	6	7	− 1
Rafferty/Kuchel primary	41	61	+20
1970: State Superintendent of Public Instruction	53	60	+ 7

Note: Entry is percentage of the two-party vote (or two-candidate vote, or yes-no vote on propositions) given the more liberal or Democratic alternative (as opposed to the more conservative or Republican alternative).

close look at the voting returns reveals that Southern Californians had never voted in an especially conservative way until the 1960s. The relative fortunes of Democrats and Republicans have varied considerably in California through the twentieth century; the Republicans reigned supreme until Roosevelt swung the state heavily to the Democrats during the 1930s and 1940s; then the Republican dominance resumed until 1958. During this entire period, however, Southern Californians voted much the same as Bay Area residents, who were supposedly living in "a celebrated center of liberal and radical political action" (Wolfinger and Greenstein, 1969, p. 74), as shown in Table 8.1. The two regions differed by only 1.1 per cent, on the average in partisan voting for President, Governor, U.S. Senators, and Congressmen.

Southern Californians did begin to vote more conservatively in the early 1960s, at least in major state-wide races. Major Democratic candidates averaged 54 per cent of the vote in the Bay Area for the 1958–1962 and 1964–1970 periods alike, but dropped from 50 per cent back to 45 per cent in Southern California. However, there was no comparable change in regional differences in voting for congressional seats, as shown in Table 8.1.

Even this recent conservative trend seems scarcely to have affected the *City* of Los Angeles. For our purposes, of course, the city is the central focus of attention. Most of the region's blacks live within the city limits; most of the rioting occurred within the same limits and was dealt with primarily by the city's police department; the public officials whose comments on the riot attracted most attention were the city's police chief, William S. Parker, and mayor, Sam Yorty.

Yet the City of Los Angeles generally has been just as strong a liberal Democratic bastion as other major American cities. Even during the 1960s, as Southern California as a whole was moving toward greater support of Republicans, the City of Los Angeles supported six of the seven Democratic candidates for President, Governor, and Senator. They ran on the average only 1 per cent better in the supposedly more liberal City of San Francisco.

The growing conservatism of Southern California has, rather, been located in the smaller (mostly white) cities of Los Angeles County, and in other outlying suburban and rural areas, especially Orange and San Diego Counties. Democratic candidates for President, Governor, and Senator during the period 1964–1970 averaged 40 per cent in the main outlying counties of Southern California (Orange, San Diego, Riverside, and San Bernardino) and 44 per cent in the portion of Los Angeles County not in the City of Los Angeles. In contrast, Democrats averaged 58 per cent in the City of Los Angeles, 61 per cent in San Francisco, and 52 per cent in the suburban counties in the Bay Area (Marin, San Mateo, and Santa Clara). The same contrast has held for other indexes of conservative voting during the 1960s: ballot referenda on fair housing, communism, and pornography, races for state superintendent of public instruction; and Republican primaries pitting conservative presidential and senatorial candidates against moderates.

In short, the supposed conservatism of white Southern California voters actually has manifested itself only in the last decade or so and then only in the most visible state-wide contests. Moreover, it was most common in the smaller incorporated cities of Los Angeles County and in the more distant Orange and San Diego Counties, not in the City of Los Angeles, where the riot mostly took place. Since neither old-fashioned bigotry nor hard-line political conservatism seem to have distinguished white Southern Californians from other white Americans, let us look at what *was* distinctive about them.

Southern California Newcomers and Life Styles

Our general theoretical approach leads us to analyse whites' opinions as we did with blacks' opinions in Chapter 3, by looking at their early political socialization. Values and attitudes socialized prior to adulthood are viewed as the dominant influence upon adults' predispositions. Los Angeles poses an unusual problem for such an analysis, in that it always has been composed primarily of in-migrants from other parts of the United States. Consequently, an analysis simply of the political culture of Los Angeles, as socializing agent, is likely to be inadequate.[5] Most evidence on political socialization indicates, moreover, that migration serves to transplant fully socialized adults, rather than extensively resocializing them to any particularly unusual norms of the place of destination (Sears, 1969a). Thus, any historical analysis of Southern California must look not only to the distinctive features of the region's social history, which would have contributed a possibly unique cast to the political socialization of local natives, but also to the distinctive origins of the in-migrants.

In looking for the origins of Los Angeles' political culture, we are led to consider the type of person who settled the area between the two world wars. This was the period of Los Angeles' growth from a medium-sized metropolitan area, with a population of under a million, outstripped by the San Francisco Bay Area, to the fourth largest metropolitan area in the nation, with a population of almost three million, twice as large as its northern rival (Thompson, 1955, p. 4). During this period, the in-migration was almost exclusively white; many government and business institutions became

---

[5]For example, in 1960 only 36 per cent of Los Angeles residents had been born in California, whereas 52 per cent of the residents of San Francisco and 72 per cent of the residents of New York City had been born in California and New York, respectively.

established, and their "routine procedures" and modus operandi developed at this time; most of the prominent public officials of the 1950s and 1960s arrived or grew up; and the characteristic life styles of regions, and their housing patterns, in many ways were set. Postwar arrivals, black and white alike, discovered a relatively settled society.

Those who settled in Southern California between the wars were, to an unusual degree, middle-class, white, Protestant, native-American, midwestern families. This distinctiveness, we maintain, has had some fairly clear consequences for the subsequent political climate of the region.[6] Let us first briefly review some of the demographic evidence on these settlers.

The Newcomers.   American-born whites always have dominated Los Angeles to a degree unusual for northern cities. The immigration of blacks from the South came much later to Los Angeles than to other northern cities. It was only a trickle before World War II; in 1940, only 2.7 per cent of Los Angeles County was black. Los Angeles did not even have the oriental flavor of San Francisco, its sister West Coast metropolis.[7] Furthermore, the whites in Los Angeles were mainly native-born Americans. In the late nineteenth and early twentieth centuries, while most northern cities received great numbers of European immigrants with exotic languages, religions, customs, food preferences, clothing, and life styles, Los Angeles received mainly native-born, white, Protestant Americans. For example, in 1930, 33 per cent of New York City's white population was foreign born, while this was true of only 15 per cent of Los Angeles' white population (Fogelson, 1967, p. 80). The Mexican Americans were the major foreign-born group in Los Angeles, but they tended to be isolated in their *barrios* and played little part in the public life of the region.

Before 1930 the Midwest vastly outstripped any other region in producing migrants to Los Angeles. In 1930, for example, 37 per cent of the native white Americans in Los Angeles had been born in the Midwest (especially Illinois, Missouri, Iowa, and Kansas) and only 13 per cent in the South (Fogelson, 1967, p. 81). During the Great Depression, many whites came to Los Angeles from the border states, especially Texas and Oklahoma. To this day, the Midwest and border states contribute more than their share, and the Northeast and the Deep South less, to the population makeup of Southern California.

There have been many vivid and conflicting impressions about the occupational status of white in-migrants to Los Angeles, some viewing them as penniless Horatio Alger-type entrepreneurs, others as retired shopkeepers

---

[6]See Wilson (1967) and Rogin and Shover (1970) for similar arguments.

[7]In each census from 1920 through 1940, the Los Angeles metropolitan area contained a smaller proportion of the state's Chinese, Japanese, or foreign-born whites than it did of the state's native-born whites. The Bay Area's mix, on the other hand, included a higher proportion of Chinese and foreign-born whites, on each occasion (Thompson, 1955, p. 75).

and farmers or displaced Dust Bowl victims (Steinbeck, 1939; Fogelson, 1967). The census and survey data available on the migrants to Los Angeles indicate that, like migrants throughout the United States, they typically have been more likely to be middle class than the average of the population they joined. The dominant migration was of persons with high school but no college education (Thompson, 1955, p. 175).

Most newly founded western frontier cities have attracted a disproportionate number of young, unmarried men. Los Angeles was an exception, even in its earlier days, tending to draw complete families. Census data illustrate this in several ways. First of all, males in Los Angeles tended to be married rather than single. In 1930, 62 per cent of the males of Los Angeles were married, while only 54 per cent were in San Francisco. Second, Los Angeles had an unusually high proportion of women for a growing western city. At every census in the twentieth century, women outnumbered men in Los Angeles, while the reverse held in other western cities such as San Francisco, Seattle, and Portland (Fogelson, 1967, pp. 82–83). Even in 1960, Los Angeles had a higher proportion of women than did San Francisco. Third, Los Angeles always has had an unusually high proportion of children. In 1940, 19 per cent of the Los Angeles population was age 14 or below, as opposed to only 14 per cent in San Francisco. This dominance of the intact nuclear family actually was a much more marked feature of the Los Angeles population than its supposedly irresistible allure for the elderly. In 1930, 21 per cent of all Los Angeles residents were age 55 and over, compared to 20 per cent in San Francisco.

The dominance of the nuclear family in Los Angeles' formative years meant a large number of dependents relative to the number of wage-earning men. In 1940, for example, for every man in the prime wage-earning years (25–64), there were 2.55 other persons in Los Angeles County (and 2.42 in the City of Los Angeles), compared to only 2.05 in San Francisco. The pattern was the same for suburban and outlying areas; the ratio was 2.97 in neighboring Orange County and 2.73 in San Diego County, against only 2.15 in the Bay Area suburb of San Mateo County.

The Low-Density, Home-Owning Life Style.   The most striking aspect of life in Los Angeles always has been the dispersion of the population over vast areas. In 1930, for example, the density of the population in Los Angeles was approximately one-fifth that of any other major American city (Fogelson, 1967, p. 143). Similarly, the owner-occupied, one-family dwelling persistently has dominated the housing of the area. In the 1920s, the one-family house was much more characteristic of Los Angeles than of any other major American city (Fogelson, 1967, p. 146), and this remains true even today. For example, in 1960, 55 per cent of all occupied dwellings in Los Angeles County were owner occupied, against 19 per cent in New York City or 30 per cent in Chicago.

Thus, from its beginnings Los Angeles has differed markedly from other central cities. It has been the very model of today's burgeoning suburban way of life. In the formative interwar years, it contained no substantial mix of national origins or racial types. It simply did not possess the very visible and insistent heterogeneity of most northern industrial cities. Rather, it was disproportionately comprised of white, native-American, Protestant, middle-class, midwestern families, dispersed widely over a large geographic area in their own private single-family homes. Obviously not all Angelenos fit this description but it seems typical of much of Los Angeles' population, especially when contrasted to the populations of other large northern cities.

Black Invisibility

One consequence of these mild peculiarities of the early settlers, and of the life style they created for themselves, was a profound degree of black invisibility—both before and after the mass immigration of blacks to Los Angeles. By "invisibility" we mean an absence of blacks in the perceptual world of white Southern Californians. Whites were (and are) physically isolated from blacks. As a result, blacks were physically invisible to them, and their few physical contacts with blacks were structured so that blacks were psychologically invisible to them as well. Thus, blacks essentially did not exist in the subjective world of whites. In this section, we wish to document this invisibility and to suggest reasons for its existence.

The Naïve In-migrant.   The white midwesterner who typified the in-migrant to Los Angeles between the world wars most likely had had almost no past personal experience with blacks. There were very few blacks or dark-skinned people of any kind in the small towns of the Midwest. Indeed there were few people who differed from the midwesterner in any important ways. Almost everybody spoke with the same midwestern twang and there were none of the vast gradations in color, language, accent, or life style that the eastern industrial cities contained.

In electing to move to Los Angeles instead of into the diversity of teeming eastern urban life, many of these early settlers must have wanted to maintain the homogeneity of their previous social environments. The western frontier, now converging upon Los Angeles and Southern California, offered a new and better life. It would be more peaceful, cleaner, less crowded, more honest and efficient, uncorrupt, and full of opportunity.

More relevant for our purposes, the ideology of that frontier emphasized freedom from group conflict. The West was thought to be untainted by the ethnic prejudices and rivalries of Europe or the eastern cities, and so there would be no grubby and ignorant immigrant groups battling for money and power. And there would be none of the South's racial problems either, for the West had been "left out" of the Civil War. The North and South had fought to the death over the fate of the blacks, but the West had been a prize of the struggle rather than a participant in it. Thus, it was expected that there would be no "race problem" in Los Angeles. Angelenos genuinely believed that they were going to be spared all of the problems of the rest of the country and of the Old World because here, at last, was a new and better social and physical environment.

So, in Los Angeles there were going to be no swarthy faces or funny accents or prejudices, for everyone would be like everyone else: friendly, white, Protestant, middle class, midwestern, and native-born American. And in reality the white Angeleno *could* move into a neighborhood in which people spoke and thought as he did. This striking homogeneity of the white population, and the vast gulf that separated it from the colored minority, must have added to the white Angeleno's conviction that everybody was just like him, that there *was* nobody else (Fogelson, 1967, p. 83).

Racial Isolation. Whites always have had (and still have) little chance for direct interracial contact in the normal course of their daily lives in Los Angeles because (1) until recently only a small proportion of the Los Angeles population has been black, so there were relatively few blacks with whom to have contact, (2) blacks have been highly segregated residentially, and (3) the paths of blacks and whites rarely have intersected, due to the area's population dispersion. Moreover, (4) the uniquely retreatist or privatistic life style of today's new American suburbs has flourished in Los Angeles for many years, further diminishing the opportunities for interracial contact.

De facto residential segregation has been as complete in Los Angeles as in other major American cities (Taeuber and Taeuber, 1965), and it has isolated Los Angeles blacks particularly seriously because of the low residential density of the Los Angeles area. For example, whites have had little casual contact with minorities when shopping because most buying is done in the many suburban shopping centers scattered throughout the metropolitan area. The central business district is much less important in Los Angeles than in other big cities and so many whites have never entered the inner city where they might have encountered blacks who worked or shopped there. Moreover, there has been very little reliable public transportation into or out of the ghetto since shortly after World War II (that is, when the incoming flow of black migrants became extremely heavy). Hence, both in terms of the normal day-to-day movement patterns within the city, and in terms of residential dispersion, Los Angeles always has encouraged racial isolation to a high degree.[8]

This lack of contact was demonstrated clearly by our survey of whites immediately after the rioting. Only 13 per cent said they had "frequent" contact with blacks in clubs, organizations, and informal groups, and 77

---

[8]It should be noted that, although we are speculating that there is more racial isolation in Los Angeles than in other large American cities, it is not necessary for our overall analysis that Los Angeles rank first in racial isolation. The degree of racial isolation has been high throughout America, contributing to the invisibility of blacks everywhere.

per cent had never been to Watts or had only driven through. These figures are even more astounding when one considers that half of the respondents in this post-riot survey were deliberately drawn from the relatively few integrated residential areas of Los Angeles (Morris and Jeffries, 1970). In the 1969 survey of the northern San Fernando Valley, a middle-class suburban area far from the major black ghetto, we found that 36 per cent of the whites said that they had no contact with blacks at all during an average week and 58 per cent reported that at the most they encountered blacks only once a week (Sears and Kinder, 1971). The average white in Los Angeles had only a trivial amount of face-to-face contact with blacks.

Finally, many observers feel that the dispersion of the population of Los Angeles into low density, suburban residential areas set the stage for privatism to become the social norm. The home owner became more concerned with his lawn, his car, and his family than he did with his public obligations as a citizen (Fogelson, 1967; Wilson, 1967). According to this view, the early settler of Los Angeles mostly was seeking "the legitimate comforts in life" (Fogelson, p. 70), but defined in the traditional small-town American way as "the simple comely life of our fathers, the village ideals" (p. 191), which involved having his own plot of land, his own lawn, his own car, and his own separate, individual, private life in which he could rear his children far from the hubbub, conflict, confusion, and crowding so typical of the teeming eastern industrial cities.[9]

To the early settlers' surprise, according to one historian, in Los Angeles this manner of living produced a rather isolated and lonely life, where people lived amid many strangers and consequently grew increasingly suspicious. The rapid mobility within the area also helped break down neighborly relations. The new in-migrants felt increasingly powerless and isolated but, "instead of turning toward an activism that encourages radical alternatives, they drifted toward a personalism that discouraged involvement *per se*" (Fogelson, 1967, p. 198). And most of all such "personalism" prevented involvement with a distant minority group.

Invisibility in the Media. The mass communications media might have been able to compensate whites to some degree for their lack of either past or current personal interracial experience. However, the media presented very little information about blacks to white Angelenos, from the early settlement of Los Angeles to the time of the riot. To examine the coverage of blacks in the press, we conducted a content analysis of Los Angeles newspapers for the period 1892 to 1968. We found references to blacks to be few and far between (for the complete analysis, see Johnson, Sears, and McConahay, 1971). There was almost no reference to blacks in the long period from 1892 to the Supreme Court's school desegregation case of

---

[9]See Rabinowitz and Lamare, 1971, for an updated version of this desire for serenity and privatism, in a contemporary "new town" in open country beyond the suburbs, far from the smog and hubbub of downtown Los Angeles.

1954 in either of the area's two major newspapers, as shown in Figure 8.1. Less than 1 per cent of the total news space was devoted to blacks (except for a brief period early in the century when considerable racial strife surrounded the imposition of rigid Jim Crow regulations in the South). Even after 1940, when the local black community began to grow rapidly in size, the news space devoted to blacks showed no substantial increase.[10]

FIGURE 8.1

Black Visibility in Los Angeles Newspapers, 1892–1968*

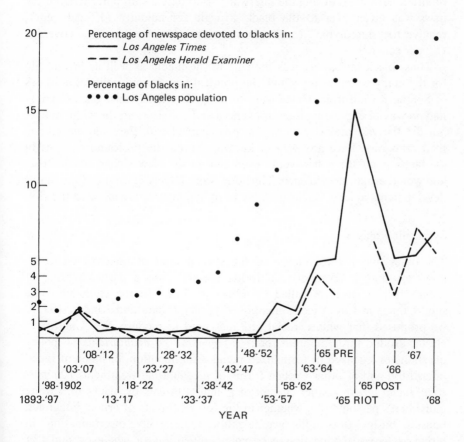

*Although included in the sampling frame, no newspapers from 1892 turned up in the final sample.

[10]This invisibility was partly due to the fact that blacks were not often among the active participants in the public life of the wider community and so only infrequently were "newsworthy." For example, as late as 1962, there was only one black elected official in Los Angeles of any importance, State Assemblyman Augustus Hawkins.

Perhaps it is just as well that media coverage of blacks was so rare for so many years, because the content of it was mostly unflattering. Around the turn of the century, news items dealing with blacks largely recorded acts of crime and other sensational, "yellow journalism" news. As mentioned earlier, the *Los Angeles Times* even ran a column entitled "News from Nigger Alley," which featured mostly details of fights and shootings. The other major category was interracial violence, principally due to anti-black riots on the part of whites in the North and lynchings in the South.

Between the two world wars, some blacks became quite prominent in the entertainment world and received increasing press attention in this role. Crime, sensationalism, and acts of interracial violence were less commonly reported. However, during the interwar period only a slim percentage of the news was given over to the black struggle for equality (17 per cent), relative to "stereotypic" (antisocial, sensational, entertainment) coverage (52 per cent).[11]

Thus, black invisibility was the rule in the media as well as in real life for the many years during which the political culture and political attitudes of Southern California whites were forming. Until the riots, blacks simply had no way of expressing their grievances and anguishes to the white public; nor did the vast majority of whites, preoccupied with their mortgages and their crabgrass, have any way of knowing about the profound changes in the black population that would eventuate in the New Urban Blacks' rise, and would erupt into violence. Thus they were largely ignorant of the major developments among blacks that, we have hypothesized, generated the riot.

Symbolic Racism

The other major consequence of the special kind of interwar white in-migration and the Southern California life style was a particular kind of racial attitude we have called "symbolic racism." In the study of white suburbanites in Los Angeles mentioned earlier (Sears and Kinder, 1971), we proposed that whites' racial attitudes tend in modern-day America to cluster around three different foci: (1) *generalized egalitarianism*—policy questions of legalized or formalized racial discrimination, of inherent racial inferiority, and of other explicit forms of inegalitarian treatment; (2) *personal racial threat*—either current or potential threats by blacks to a white individual's personal life, whether in the formal threats of crime, integrated housing, busing, riots in his own neighborhood, "reverse discrimination" in hiring or access to education, economic competition, or whatever; and (3) *symbolic racism*—abstract moral assertions about blacks' behavior as a group, concerning what blacks deserve, how they ought to act, whether or

---

[11]In the post-riot aftermath, by contrast, stereotypic coverage accounted for only 17 per cent of the items dealing with blacks, while civil rights coverage accounted for 46 per cent. See Johnson et al., 1971.

not they are treated equitably, and so on. These are typically symbolic and abstract, with no tangible consequence for policy legislation, for the white individual's own personal well-being, or for the treatment of any given individual black.[12]

As indicated above, generalized egalitarianism has been the norm in Southern California in recent years. Almost all whites endorse formal and legal racial equality, and there are few who still hold old-fashioned and simple-minded racial stereotypes. We have no data on the point but our suspicion is that this is no sudden modern development. It seems unlikely to us that the prevailing norm was very segregationist in Southern California even as far back as the interwar period.

Moreover, in the Los Angeles suburbs of today (and presumably in Los Angeles more generally, in years gone by), there is little evidence of any very significant reality or experiential basis for perceived *current personal threats*. Personal contact of any kind with blacks seems always to have been rather slight, as indicated above. White suburbanites are quite satisfied with their current economic status relative to blacks' status and with those aspects of their personal lives that can conceivably be threatened by blacks: that is, their children's schools and their family's personal safety in the neighborhood (Sears and Kinder, 1971). And it is understandable that little immediate threat is perceived: concentrations of blacks always have been small or, more recently, far away; housing and school integration in the suburbs always has been negligible; and blacks never have constituted a major potential economic threat to middle-class whites. Thus, the evidence is that immediate personal racial threat, whether objective or purely subjective, was negligible in the white suburbs of Southern California in 1969. And surely in 1965, and 1955, and 1925, the immediate threat must have been even slighter.

Potential racial threats still might be thought to generate much anti-black feeling and action, particularly given whites' manifest concerns, in Los Angeles and nationally, about the future possibilities of busing white children to black neighborhoods, racial violence in white neighborhoods, and residential integration in the suburbs (Campbell, 1971; Sears and Kinder, 1971). Yet these are rather new problems for Los Angeles, and whites' anxieties about them scarcely seem likely to have been responsible for blacks' grievances in the early 1960s. More important, "potential racial threats" are mainly disguised versions of symbolic racism. We have shown this in a variety of ways elsewhere (Sears and Kinder, 1971); for

[12]Items used to measure symbolic racism include these: "Negroes shouldn't push themselves where they're not wanted" (agree or disagree); "Do you think that most Negroes who receive welfare could get along without it if they tried, or do they really need this help?"; "Do Los Angeles city officials pay more, less, or the same attention to a request from a Negro person as from a white person?"; and "Streets aren't safe these days without a policeman around" (agree or disagree) (Sears and Kinder, 1971).

instance, perceived potential racial threats no longer relate to anti-black voting when symbolic racism is controlled (while symbolic racism's relationship to anti-black voting remains strong even with threat controlled).

If *symbolic racism* is the primary and most universal form in which anti-black attitudes are expressed today, what are its origins? It is essentially a blend of strong, traditional American moral values with mild amounts of racial anxiety and antagonism. For example, the best available survey evidence indicates that anti-fair-housing voting in 1964 (on Proposition 14) and voting against the black mayoral candidate, Thomas Bradley, in the 1969 Los Angeles campaign were both based upon symbolic racism. In each case traditionalism and racial anxieties made separate and independent contributions (Wolfinger and Greenstein, 1968; Sears and Kinder, 1971; Jeffries and Ransford, 1972). Most important, the rhetoric of philosophic conservatism used by opponents of fair housing, and of "law and order" by Bradley's opponents, was not exclusively a rationalization for underlying racial antagonisms. It was the expression of the blend of moral traditionalism and racism that symbolic racism constitutes.

We want to argue that the distinctive demographic origins of the old Angelenos made them especially drawn to symbolic racism. Indeed, the distinctive demographic attributes of the early settlers of Los Angeles do resemble the demographic correlates of both traditional political attitudes and mild amounts of racial prejudice. Our recent review of these literatures (Sears, 1969a) shows that general political conservatism (that is, opposition to communism, pornography, generous extensions of civil liberties for political dissenters, and support for conservative candidates and groups), over the past few decades, has been most common among those who are (1) white, native-born Protestants, (2) reared in rural areas or small towns, (3) not college educated, (4) socialized in earlier times, and/or (5) Republican. This matches the particular demographic biases of the early Angeleno, except for Republican Party identification.[13]

Similarly, racial prejudice (or voting against civil rights measures) has been shown to be most common among whites who are (1) socialized in earlier times, (2) not college educated, and/or (3) southern reared. All of these demographic factors were especially characteristic of early Angelenos, as indicated above, except for the southern background. And the forms of prejudice most typical of white southerners—beliefs in racial inferiority and support for official racial discrimination—are relatively uncommon in Los Angeles.

Rather, the old Angelenos seem to have been socialized as what Campbell (1971) has called the "gentle people of prejudice," characteristic of

---

[13]Thus, as long as party identification held sway in California voting, the region's underlying conservatism did not show through at the polls. A notable exception was a prohibition referendum in 1930, in which Southern California voted overwhelmingly dry and the Bay Area wet (Rogin and Shover, 1970).

the pre-World War II North. Northerners brought up before the war lived in an environment in which lynching and discriminatory laws were rare but in which blacks were not allowed to participate in professional sports, serve in integrated units of the army, attend many private northern schools and universities, and so forth. The postwar era quickly brought about some major changes but people socialized before the war were accustomed to an extraordinary degree of racial separation, even in the North. Consequently today they are considerably less modern and progressive in their racial views than whites who have gone to college in the postwar era. It seems plausible then to speculate that it is not southern-bred bigotry and racism, but the milder fears and support for the racial status quo typical of the noncollege-educated white northerner of the pre-World War II era, that have persisted into today's Southern California political culture.

Thus, the political culture recreated in Southern California in the prewar years by the white in-migrants and the political socialization which in all likelihood they passed on to their children probably were dominated by traditional and conventional middle-class values, some hostility toward diversity and deviance, and the mild degrees of racial prejudice and desire for distance from blacks characteristic of the prewar North.

Black invisibility helped perpetuate these parochial and anachronistic racial attitudes. The old Angeleno had been socialized into a mentality that barely admitted of blacks at all, and that applied to them the moralistic standards of a Protestantism of years gone by. Yet as time wore on he had no leavening personal experience with blacks to soften, update, or challenge these archaic attitudes. Nor did the media present any true semblance of blacks and their lives. So, early socialization, always a potent force in an adult's political thinking, was here even more powerful than usual, simply because of an absence of any new informational input in adulthood.[14]

Routine Procedures and Blacks' Grievances

If then the dominant political culture of prewar Los Angeles was especially productive of black invisibility and symbolic racism, how did these in turn contribute to the outbreak of rioting?

The "routine procedures" that these old Angelenos constructed in order

[14]However, the privatistic "lack of community" implied by individualistic values and distance did not by itself produce racial bigotry or malice toward blacks. Measures of "lack of community," whether indexed in terms of lacking close relations with neighbors, lacking relatives in Southern California, or lacking close relations with work partners, have not been found to relate either to racist attitudes or to racist voting (Sears and Kinder, 1971; Seeman et al., 1971). Rather privatism, we suggest, led to a preoccupation with "business as usual," while the invisible black suffered, virtually unnoticed, in Watts.

to run their society in an orderly way were bound to create widespread grievances among blacks because they were constructed out of black invisibility and symbolic racism. The connecting links, we believe, are to be found in the values and life styles of white Southern Californians. We do not have the data to make rigorous observations here but we do wish to make a few speculative suggestions.

In Los Angeles, these midwestern families, mostly middle-class Protestants, owning their own homes, were most likely to share the highly conventional, "middle-class morality" of the 1920s and 1930s, that is the conservative traditional values of the American Protestant ethic. They were attached to property, particularly the value of their own property—their own homes, small plots of land, cars, barbecue pits, and palm trees (Wilson, 1967). They were concerned about success and upward mobility. They revered authority and believed in obedience to it (Sears and Kinder, 1971). They valued "business." And because they came to Los Angeles as nuclear families, rather than as members of extended kinship groups (as did the European immigrants in eastern cities), they did not have a highly developed sense of responsibility for other people.

Even the apparent hedonism and recklessness of the "new" American culture in Southern California did not really change whites' commitment to these Puritan virtues. A day at the beach rarely was followed by a drunken brawl, or mass litters of garbage, or sex orgies, or all-night partying, or offices being closed the next day. The kids were clean and well-mannered, they surfed and played volleyball and football and baseball and tennis, and were polite and friendly to strangers, and always (or almost always) followed the rules. Drivers were courteous and safe, people went to bed early and got to work on time, politics were safe and sane.

The day-to-day institutions of the area were managed by the old Angelenos and their descendants, the good solid folk from "Middle America." In their thinking about government, they valued honesty and efficiency more than human values. The government of Los Angeles has been characterized for many years by exceptional apparent integrity and concern for administrative efficiency. The ideal is a wholly impartial and efficient set of "routine procedures," administered by an honest civil service bureaucracy.[15]

The imposition of these moralistic Protestant virtues upon institutional procedures, we suggest, has caused constant conflict with people of other values and life styles. Success in a white-collar, suburban, middle-class society depends to a large degree upon the socialization of such virtues as thrift, cleanliness, hard work, self-restraint, self-deprivation, obedience to

[15]It has not been noted for its concern about human welfare, however. The Tammany Hall model of using politics as a mechanism for providing for one's fellows, even at the expense of a certain amount of graft and nepotism, never has been very popular in Los Angeles (Fogelson, 1967; Jacobs, 1967).

and identification with authority, punctuality, and so on. To fill out forms, one must pay close attention to instructions. To hold a clerical job, neatness and punctuality are more important than personal warmth or physical strength. To make one's way through a bureaucratized world, one must be prepared to act in a concerted fashion between 8 a.m. and 5 p.m.; hangovers, early drunks, or lazy sex in the morning may mean missing out altogether. Further, when employment is conditional upon prior education, it is, for all practical purposes, contingent on obedience, on being able to sit still, on docile concentration on esoteric and nearly meaningless cognitive tricks, on primness, on careful repression of hostility, and on all of the other socialization residues so prized by meek middle-class teachers and professors.

The relentless application of the individualistic values of the Protestant ethic inevitably would be convenient for the old Angeleno, who lived this way anyhow, and it was to him that the bureaucrats mainly had to answer. But it was equally likely to work against blacks, by building into institutional procedures demands for middle-class, midwestern, small-town, Protestant behavior. This bias surely was not consciously intended by the well-meaning, fair, honest, relatively unprejudiced early Angelenos, most of whom must have rejected overt segregation and most versions of formalized discrimination. Yet it meant inconvenience and blocked opportunities for a great many blacks. "Business as usual" spelled frustration for blacks.

This is most important because it illustrates the one-two punch that overt bigotry and symbolic racism represent. Some whites are overtly prejudiced. But even among those who are not, traditional, middle-class values work to prevent the black person's progress. Such persons place a higher value upon private property, neighborhood schools, "business as usual," merit rather than quota in promotions or admissions to training programs, efficiency and an honest day's work, and the hiring only of those with high school diplomas and without arrest records, than they do upon racial peace or upon de facto as well as de jure equality. But even in the absence of widespread individual bigotry or of hard-line conservatism, neither of which appears to have been epidemic in Los Angeles, traditional American values breed symbolic racism, and thus institutional racism.

The practices of the police department most vividly exemplify this. Chief Parker was an upper-middle-class midwesterner, an intellectual conservative, not an unwashed redneck southerner. His greatest achievements were to clean up the police force and to institute the most "professional" and efficient procedures possible, from highly sophisticated uses of computers to rigorous recruitment standards. And he showed all of the virtues of a good modern manager; among other things, he defended his men from every attack. Morale was high, the force was honest, and it had a worldwide reputation for effectiveness and "professionalism." As we have seen, application of these standard procedures, "business as usual," failed in the

Watts Riot. Police thought they knew how to handle these situations—but their standard operating procedures set off the riot and resulted in mass death and destruction.

Had blacks been more visible, these institutional procedures might well have been corrected and modified with time to fit current reality more closely—but they were not. Whites with responsibility for institutional decisions were shielded from any knowledge of the unhappiness or difficulty their actions created for blacks. Their racial isolation and their naiveté allowed them the comfortable illusion that they were unprejudiced administrators, applying rules and regulations impartially and in line with accepted good practice. Secretaries, distance, suburbia, and the racial homogeneity of their social groups all protected them from any awareness of black discontent. Thus, "routine procedures" were responsive to the needs of middle-class white businessmen and bureaucrats but not very responsive to the more invisible and powerless black clientele. And the routine mechanisms of grievance redress were no different and thus no less likely to create conflict.

Further, blacks' invisibility also prevented whites from becoming aware of the changed black we have called the New Urban Black. Dramatic changes in blacks' educational levels, personalities, aspirations, life styles, discontents, and grievances—all went blithely unnoticed by whites in Los Angeles. Indeed, if the whites had wanted to know about such matters, it is hard to imagine how they could have found out, even with a dedicated effort, so formidable were the barriers of racial isolation.

It is our contention that the embodiment of symbolic racism in local institutional procedures was the vital force behind blacks' grievances, as outlined in Chapter 4. Moralistic rejection, not naked bigotry, lay behind the callousness of the police, the selfishness of shop owners and the impersonal and unresponsive bureaucracy of the school system and welfare agencies. The proudest creations of "good government" in the 1920s and 1930s constituted institutional racism in the 1960s and their legacy was not contented and well-treated citizens but aggrieved and demanding blacks.

Finally, it is this combination of invisibility, indifference, and ignorance, on the one hand, and the moralism of symbolic racism, on the other, that evoked, we believe, one of the oddest and least expected aspects of the riot; namely, the widespread feeling among blacks that the riot was a demand for attention more than an effort to redress specific and concrete deficiencies in their lives. This will be seen in far greater detail in Chapters 9 and 10, in the reactions to the riot of black leaders and the black public. In our interviews, blacks did not complain bitterly about their own personal life situations. Rather, what they wanted was to be heard, to be treated as dignified human beings—and not to be treated as if they were invisible or morally repellent. In this sense, the riot was symbolically *motivated*, as well as having in retrospect a great symbolic *meaning* to blacks and whites alike.

"Why 'Watts'?"—Some Partial Answers

At the start of this chapter, we raised the question of why "Watts" was the first of the major riots. We are now in a position to suggest, tentatively, a few partial answers. To begin with, the riots occurred in Los Angeles first because the city's size and patterns of black migration made it one of the few cities with masses of New Urban Blacks at physical maturity during the 1960s. It was this generation that provided the shock troops. Second, the riots struck Los Angeles first because whites and white leadership there were too self-preoccupied and hence were doing little if anything to head off trouble. This is not to suggest that whites elsewhere were working overtime to anticipate or accommodate blacks' needs. It is simply, we would speculate, that in Los Angeles virtually nothing was being done to clear the tinder conditions or to prevent the spark because Los Angeles "did not have a racial problem." Third, the violence happened in Los Angeles first because Los Angeles and Southern California arrived first at a set of social conditions now just being approached by other cities and their suburban rings.

Here, of course, we have been making our speculations with very broad and bold strokes and so a few qualifications are in order. Obviously, not every Angeleno in the 1920s and 1930s was a white, midwestern, American-born, Protestant home-owner, with conventional middle-class values. What we are arguing, rather, is that such persons were unusually common in Southern California, relative to other rapidly growing western areas (or less rapidly growing northern areas) and relative to the other great cities. Thus, they gave to the political culture of the region a distinctive stamp which has persisted into the present.

The great dominance of the old Angeleno was exerted in the period between the two world wars. Since World War II, immigration to California has given the region a more heterogeneous and cosmopolitan complexion. Los Angeles now has more Jews than anywhere but New York, more Mexican Americans than any other metropolitan area, more blacks than all but five other cities, and vast numbers of homosexuals. It has large numbers of liberal political activists and much of the liberal "big money" of the nation.

Yet these changes had not made their full impact on the prevailing tone of local civic life before the riot (and have not even yet). The "Middle American" suburban home-owner, preoccupied as he is with barbecues, mortgages, and crabgrass, continued to set the dominant tone.

Finally, the unique features of Los Angeles that we have stressed throughout this chapter are unique only in a static sense. In many ways, Los Angeles may be the prototype of where other urban centers (or at least their suburbs) are headed. When a suburban developer in Indiana builds a subdivision with curving streets, single-family dwellings on little plots with barbecue pits in the backyards, and calls the development "Glennaire" or "Glenneagle" or even "Glenndale," what is serving as his prototype? In the near future, at least, it appears that the dominant suburban pattern will be traditional values and privatistic life styles in an ethnically homogeneous retreat from blacks who are isolated in the central city (even when the retreat is homogeneously populated with Roman Catholics espousing Protestant virtues). In this sense, then, Los Angeles differs from the rest of America only in that it is the most American of all.

9 A Confusion of Tongues: Officials' Reactions to the Riot

Most white Angelenos greeted August 1965 safe in their private sanctuaries, far from the ghetto, and largely ignorant of and indifferent to the masses of blacks living there. On the surface, racial peace ruled in Los Angeles. Underneath lay the tensions created by whites' steadfast commitment to their routine procedures, the blacks' frustrations and grievances, and the rising militancy and disaffection of the New Urban Blacks.

The riot was felt as a massive explosion throughout vast areas of Los Angeles, crashing through the barriers of silence and invisibility between whites and blacks. Yet it occurred so far from the worlds inhabited by white Southern Californians, that few of them had any firsthand experience with it. For information about what was happening, they had to rely upon the television and radio stations and the newspapers, which in turn relied upon reporters and police officers and other public officials. And, close as the riot was to the personal lives of blacks living in the Curfew Zone, initially it mystified a great many of them. It must have been experienced as a highly ambiguous, erratic alternation of insane noises, violent movements, fire and flashing lights, with long periods of eerie silence occasionally punctuated by gunfire, shouts, and sirens. In all likelihood, hardly anyone, black or white, could make much sense of the riot on the basis of his own fragmentary personal experience with it.

This confusion created a vacuum, which was partially filled by the interpretations of the events broadcast by public figures in the media during and immediately after the riot. The public's understanding of the riot, among blacks and whites alike, must have been considerably influenced by these initial reactions. We have seen how different were the worlds from which black leaders and white officials came. It should not surprise us then that they were utterly unable to agree even on what had happened or on why— much less on whether it was good or bad or what to do about it.

The tragedy of "Watts" is that these strange, violent, ambiguous, and inscrutable events quickly became the subject of simplistic explanations. These explanations and interpretations of the riot, rather than enlightening the public and contributing to greater mutual understanding between the races, actually helped to create a polarization of the races so severe that it prevented any major consensual response on the part of the community as a whole. In this chapter, we wish to describe how this polarization came about, by looking at the initial responses of public officials to the rioting, and to demonstrate how naturally this polarization grew out of the very conflicts and ignorances that created the riot in the first place. Indeed, as will be seen, responses to the riot may be understood in much the same terms as the causes of the riot, as analyzed in preceding chapters.

The Initial, Bewildered Response of White Officials

Before the rioting, white officialdom was largely unaware of black discontents. They felt themselves unprejudiced and racially liberal and assumed that civil rights progress was made at a reasonable rate, especially in the untroubled West. They knew little about the blacks but assumed that there was no "race problem" in Los Angeles. Thus, initially they were bewildered by the turn of events. Chief William S. Parker of the Los Angeles Police Department had perceived race relations in Los Angeles as being essentially harmonious, even through the early stages of the riot. From riot-control headquarters he remarked, "Los Angeles is quiet as far as racial problems are concerned." The liberal Democratic Governor Edmund G. ("Pat") Brown's first reaction was "Terrible—unbelievable, absolutely beyond my comprehension—it is mob rule at its worst, I cannot understand it. Relations between different races have always been excellent in California." [1] Brown's memory was short. Apparently he had forgotten restrictive covenants, laws against land ownership by Orientals, the "zoot suit" riots, the internment camps of World War II, and the successful statewide referendum against fair-housing laws passed the previous fall. Yet his reactions were spontaneous and genuine. And they apparently expressed the feelings of most whites in California.

Given the consensus among whites that racial problems were absent from the California scene, many attempted first to deny that the rioting had any racial meaning. For example, on August 13th, after two nights of rioting, numerous headlines proclaimed that the authorities all agreed that race was not an issue, that the riot had no racial overtones. The *Los Angeles Times* editorial rejected the idea that it was a race riot, on the grounds that the mob had attacked everyone indiscriminately.

Most white officials then leaped instead to simplistic explanations involv-

---

[1]Quotes in this chapter are taken from the *Los Angeles Times,* the *Los Angeles Herald-Examiner,* and the *New York Times* of the period during and immediately after the riot.

ing conditions they could not possibly have done anything about. One very popular thought was that the weather was responsible. According to the *New York Times* front-page story on August 13th: "Officials called it the worst racial incident in the city's history. . . . Officials were at a loss to explain the cause of the rioting, which started last night after a routine drunken driving arrest. The unusually hot, smoggy weather was doubtless a contributing factor." The local newspapers took the lead in offering these face-saving explanations on behalf of the local establishment. For example, on August 14th, the *Los Angeles Times* carried the amazing front-page headline: "Racial Unrest Laid to Negro Family Failure" (referring to the then unpublished "Moynihan Report" on the Negro family). Presumably if only black women were not so promiscuous, or black men so irresponsible, blacks would be happy and law-abiding rather than burning down the town and stealing everything in sight. Two days later, the *Los Angeles Times* carried a story indicating that Marquette Frye had addressed the local Black Muslims (the Black Muslims and the police had engaged in a highly publicized shoot-out not long before the riot), which presumably helped to explain much about why so many peaceful blacks had been duped into rioting.

The overwhelming dominance of the local establishment by suburban whites, with their limited interests and perspectives, led many into an innocent and naive racism. An August 16th story in the *Los Angeles Times* told about four Minutemen dressed in berets and other paramilitary garb saving two white girls from the ravages of a black mob. (Despite its closeness to Hollywood, the episode was not, as far as anyone knows, a remake of *Birth of a Nation!*) The *New York Times* quoted one white businessman as exclaiming: "The civil rights people keep saying these people are bottled up in the slums. First, their slums aren't all that slummy. Second, they're not bottled up. There are small Negro areas in many parts of Los Angeles and many are very nice." The lead story in the August 14th *Los Angeles Times* began: "A white deputy sheriff and at least seven Negroes were killed . . ."; the death of one deputy sheriff evidently took precedence over those of seven Negroes. Later, the newspapers announced the place and time of funeral services for the fireman and the deputy sheriff who had died in the riot, the only two Anglos to die. Nothing was ever published of the times and places of funeral services for the 32 blacks and Mexican Americans who had been killed, at least some of whom were wholly innocent of wrongdoing.

While puzzled whites innocently pursued comfortable thoughts and familiar explanations, they worked hard at maintaining business as usual. Most obviously, the politicians quickly became preoccupied with saving their own political skins as the riot almost immediately became the prime political issue of the upcoming gubernatorial election. Governor Brown, Lt. Governor Anderson, Mayor Yorty, and Chief Parker vigorously attempted to blame each other for the fact that the riot "got out of hand." The main issue revolved around who was responsible for the so-called delay in calling up the National Guard. The assumption was that if the Guard had been called up five hours earlier, the riot never would have gotten out of control. The order of the day was politicking-as-usual (or perhaps a little more intensely than usual), rather than listening to the blacks.

To a surprising degree, it was business as usual at the newspapers as well. Although the best of them, the *Los Angeles Times,* won the Pulitzer Prize for its coverage of the Watts Riot, one is struck, in looking through the pages of the *Times* during that fateful week, at how little its coverage was affected by the rioting. By our content analysis, about 5 per cent of its news space before the riot had been devoted to items relevant to blacks. During the riot this rose but only to 15 per cent, still slightly under the proportion of blacks in Los Angeles (Johnson, Sears, and McConahay, 1971). Only the front news section carried the rioting; the regional supplements, the opinion section, the sports section, and even the metropolitan news section went on as usual, as if the rioting were a rude noise that the polite could choose to ignore. The sports section's only concessions to the riot were passing mentions of a slight drop in the attendance at Dodger Stadium and a lament for the temporary postponement of a charity professional football game scheduled within the Curfew Zone.

So white authorities in Los Angeles, caught unaware by the violent explosion in Watts, responded with bewilderment and amazement, with a timorous assertion that race was not an issue, and with a preoccupation about returning to business-as-usual, all couched in terms and phrases that revealed a profound lack of comprehension of life in the ghetto. They could not really grasp what was happening.

Intransigence of Local White Authorities

By the second full day of rioting, though, the grim reality began to intrude. Blacks were on the attack and the racial basis of the riot became obvious to all. The *Los Angeles Times* editorial on August 14th acknowledged that race *was* an issue, announced that "race rioting has brought anarchy" and urged support for stronger actions by the police "now that kid glove measures have failed." At this point white authorities began to blame the rioting on various disreputable characters, mainly hoodlums, southern newcomers, and outside agitators, as we have seen earlier. Police Chief Parker on August 14th pictured the riot as "the result of the rebellion of a gang of Negro hoodlums who had no real purpose except rebellion and destruction." Governor Brown blamed the riot not upon local citizens, but upon unadjusted new arrivals. Mayor Yorty acknowledged that blacks had been denied their rights in the South, but said that that was no excuse for terrorizing the innocent citizens of Los Angeles. Parker was more specific. Those responsible were agitators and malcontents who had "dragged ghosts here with reports about Bogalusa and Americus, which is not the situation here."

Most important of all, local white authorities thereafter took an unyielding hard line that allowed no expression of sympathy or understanding for the social conditions of the area, nor any gesture—tangible or symbolic—to the black population and its leaders. Their sole focus was on the prosecution of lawbreakers. The police chief and the Mayor took the lead. The *Los Angeles Times* editorials fell quickly into line. Echoing Parker's definition of the riot as simply an outburst by hoodlums, they said: "The police are doing their job and doing it well." They pleaded for all law-abiding citizens to support the police and concluded that "only after sanity is restored can there be any meaningful talk about long-range cures."

Chief Parker was the most stubborn and outspoken of white officials, and to blacks he soon became the great symbol of white intransigence. During the first days of the riot, black leaders began to express complaints about police brutality and repeatedly requested opportunities to communicate with the police. At the same time, the police had to acknowledge their inability to control the situation and called in the military. Chief Parker, more on the spot than anyone else, grew angrier and angrier. He refused to admit that the police might have overreacted, and he dealt summarily with police brutality charges. It was a "vicious canard" that the police were responsible for the riot; "meddlers" and "preaching politicians" had spread the charge of police brutality. Indeed, Parker felt the police brutality charge was part of a nationwide plot against the police—inspired by leftist elements in order to discredit the forces of law and order.

He chose to attack black leadership, rather than meet with them: "Actually these people have no leaders—nobody's leading the riot and no one can claim to speak for the Negro community. Not even the Muslims, whose anti-white prejudice is well known." He attacked "demagogic attitudes of pseudo-leaders in the Negro community who can't lead at all." He blamed the failure of the initial pullout on the black leadership (even though the decision to remove the police from Watts was made by the police as part of their preliminary battle plan and not at the urging of black leaders; see Conot, 1967). In his anger, Parker went on to goad and derogate the entire black community. On August 15th, he was quoted as saying, "If you think I'm going to go down there and negotiate with a bunch of hoodlums— No!" He went on to compare the rioters to "monkeys in a zoo" and said that "we're on top, they're on the bottom" and announced that he intended to keep it that way.

At the same time, he clearly and unequivocally aligned himself with fearful whites. When Governor Brown said that massive gun buying on the part of whites was dangerous, Parker said that it was the whites' right to do so. He declared that the looters had guns and that what he called "the citizens" were terrified. Parker denied that he had any responsibility to tell whites not to buy guns, since martial law had not been declared. Consequently, he became a minor folk hero to many whites. It was as if he were the symbolic protector of the great investment in property and family so characteristic of Southern California white suburbanites. He began to personify the police, to both blacks and whites. His intransigence thus created an inevitable extreme racial polarization over the issue of the police and the authorities' role in the riot.

Mayor Yorty might have been expected to be more responsive to the diverse interests represented in the nation's third largest city but he was not. He quickly fell into line. He explained the riot as the eruption of lawless elements whose only leadership was criminal. He came no closer to the ravaged area (and the several hundred thousand citizens whose Mayor he was) than to inspect it from a helicopter on August 15th. He expressed no public sympathy or understanding for the people, but stated instead: "We've just got to get more troops in there."

His intransigence never faltered, even after peace was restored. He strongly opposed Martin Luther King's post-riot trip to Los Angeles and expressed outspoken opposition to one of the two blacks (Reverend James Jones, the only black elected to the Los Angeles Board of Education since World War II) appointed by the Governor to the McCone Commission. Yorty felt King did a disservice by coming to Los Angeles and he argued that Jones' critical dissent to the commission's report indicated that his mind had already been made up on the riot's causes.

The Ambivalent Black Leadership Response

Black political and civil rights leaders responded ambivalently from the beginning. They were horrified by the violence but soon began asserting that it called attention to the deep underlying frustrations and angers of the black population. The statement by City Councilman Gilbert Lindsay was typical: "I am ashamed of the vandalism and destruction . . . but my greatest shame is that society has sat blindly by and allowed such terrible situations to develop."

Local black leaders (unlike the white authorities) generally expressed little surprise that the violence had erupted but they were baffled and horrified by its intensity and magnitude. They perceived quickly and accurately that the black community as a whole was in total uproar and was not to be dissuaded by rational means. A reporter described the riot as "a surging sea of hatred directed at police and Caucasians," and a black psychiatrist was quoted in a front-page article as saying that the rioters felt no guilt; rather, "They feel morally right for what they have done." This posed an enormous obstacle to the attempts of black leadership to cope with the riot. Nevertheless, they did continually oppose the violence and made numerous efforts to stop it. The best known attempt is the meeting in Athens Park on August 12th, at which Congressman Hawkins and other black leaders, along with white Councilman Gibson and Supervisor Hahn, called for an end to the violence. The black comedian Dick Gregory was shot in the leg trying to calm the crowd. The local Urban League urged a restoration of law and order before engaging in recriminations, stating that "fixing blame is not a luxury we can afford." On August 14th, black Assemblyman Farrell told the rioters that they had made their point and that the time for violent action was over. He said the riots had already succeeded in drawing public attention to the problems in the community.

At the same time local black leaders could not resist the opportunity to fix blame for the terrible social conditions in the riot area, especially on the police. The Reverend H. H. Brookins, the leader of the local unified civil rights effort, had stated on August 14th that hostility toward the police had caused the rioting and Assemblyman Mervin Dymally called for a civilian police review board as a way of ending the rioting. The next day, Dymally called for Parker's resignation. School board member James E. Jones wrote an editorial in the *Los Angeles Sentinel,* a black-owned paper, decrying police brutality and blaming the riot mainly on the actions of the police. Jones also attributed the riot to years of frustration about rents, housing, unemployment, and the other grievances cited earlier.

National civil rights leaders also responded with the same ambivalent message: they decried the violence and said it could not be condoned, but invariably added that it *did* expose the deep problems that had been given inadequate attention. Roy Wilkins, the leader of the NAACP, stated on August 17th that he was stunned by the violence, appalled by the racist slogans enunciated by the rioters, and that the civil rights cause could not condone this. Still, he added, Los Angeles must realize that deep problems exist, especially with the police. Whitney Young, the national head of the Urban League, also deplored the outbreak but he added that the Urban League had recently warned Los Angeles officials that the city was not immune from violence. Ralph Bunche, Undersecretary of the United Nations, expressed what was probably the reaction of many successful, middle-class blacks when he said that no doubt blacks everywhere would have to pay for what had happened. Yet he prefaced this by saying that only the elimination of every black ghetto in the land would prevent a recurrence of these events.

Despite their feelings, black leaders found that even during the riot, they could not bring blacks' problems to the attention of white authorities or of whites more generally. Blacks remained invisible even in the midst of war. The white authorities wanted to hold their power so tightly in their own hands that they would have nothing at all to do with even the gentlest and best mannered of black spokesmen.

Perhaps the clearest example is black Councilman Billy Mills' attempt to call an open meeting of the City Council during the riot. He expressed the hope that community and indigenous leaders among the blacks would come to the meeting so that the city councilmen could begin getting at the causes of the riot. His request met with great hostility from the Old Angelenos on the council. Councilman Gibson, an elderly white man (who represented a district that, by a fluke of Los Angeles expansionism of the 1920s, included both a part of Watts and also the virtually all-white, seaside San Pedro area many miles away), remarked that law and order should be restored first and that a public meeting would probably attract all types (presumably this is exactly what Mills had in mind). Councilman Holland, another elderly white man, sputtered: "I can imagine the drapes being torn down and the furniture slashed." He warned that the meeting would probably cause a riot in the council chambers. Councilman Cassidy, yet another elderly white, said: "It would cause a parade of people coming down to the center of town and moving in [presumably on City Hall]." To this Councilman Mills said: "I'm willing to run the risk of being told some embarrassing things, and in crude language." Mills had the meeting but none of these gentlemen attended. The drapes and furniture were undisturbed.

Black leaders pleaded for communication between the police and the black community but Chief Parker's response was an emphatic "no," coupled with a slur on both black leaders and the ghetto community. On the 16th, one black said: "How do you expect us to feel when we have a police chief who says he won't bargain with a 'pack of savages'?" Archie Hardwick, a respected black worker at the Westminster Community House, noted that he had been trying desperately to set up communication with the police: "They don't understand the people here. They came into the area like an army of occupation." In the midst of the furor, Senator Robert F. Kennedy (D-N.Y.) perceptively observed that "there is no point in telling Negroes to obey the law when many of them have reason to feel the law is the enemy." Louis Lomax, a local black television commentator, said: "Negro leaders have been predicting about a riot like this for three years. You can't bottle them up and forget about them." He then compared the riot to the French Revolution. He was not the only black thinking in such terms.

The Seeds of Polarization

Faced with utter intransigence from the authorities, angry demands from black leaders, and constant requests for statements from the media, almost every conceivable notable in America soon was found interpreting and explaining the riot. It rapidly became clear that the riot had been so ambiguous, so multifaceted, so beyond anyone's previous experience that it afforded everyone the opportunity to claim, almost completely unhindered by the constraints of reality, that it proved the validity of what he had been saying all along. The populist Congressman from rural Texas, Wright Patman, blamed the Los Angeles loan sharks for the riot. The conservative *Richmond Times-Dispatch* could not pass up the opportunity to taunt self-righteous northern liberals. It pronounced that the riot proved that lots of blacks had actually been better off in Dixie. Social scientists (such as ourselves!) asserted that more research was needed and began to plan elaborate studies of the riot's causes. Sargent Shriver, a Kennedy brother-in-law, blamed intransigent local officials (by which he meant the family *bête noire,* Sam Yorty) for their unwillingness to reach a compromise (with *his* agency, the federal Office of Economic Opportunity) that would release poverty funds for the area. The U. S. Civil Rights Commission let it be known that it had warned Yorty in 1963 that many blacks in Los Angeles felt they were "at the mercy of a bigoted police."

For his part, Mayor Yorty blamed the communists: "For some time there has existed a world-wide subversive campaign to stigmatize all police as brutal. The cry of police brutality has been shouted in cities all over the world by communists, dupes, and demagogues, irrespective of the facts. Such a campaign has been vigorously pushed here in Los Angeles." This had been his most characteristic political theme for almost 30 years. Even Chief Parker managed to turn the riot against his own particular roster of villains. For several years he had been conducting a running battle with civil rights leaders who advocated civil disobedience. The rioting was, to him, the logical fruition of the advocacy of civil disobedience: "You cannot tell the people to disobey the law and not expect them to have a disrespect for law; you cannot keep telling them that they are being abused and mistreated without expecting them to react."

Much of this was simply standard political breast beating, with the familiar message of "I told you so." What paralyzed the broader community was its rapid polarization along conventional ideological lines. Conservatives supported Parker and the local police, while liberals blamed the riot on longstanding conditions and expressed sympathy for the oppressed blacks. Emphasis shifted from an understanding of the real event to the expression of lifelong ideological principles. The possibility of a common understanding of the riot was thus quickly lost and with it the possibility for a broadly based consensus on solutions.

Once Parker and Yorty had become committed to an all-out defense of the police against the rioters, conservatives rushed to support them. Senator George Murphy (R-Calif.) held that the riot had not been caused by ghetto conditions but by disrespect for law and order. He alluded to those who encouraged disrespect for law and order by preaching anarchy, as exemplified in the then current controversy over draft card burning and anti-Vietnam war protests at Berkeley. The president of the California Republican Assembly, an ultra-conservative volunteer organization, said that this was merely a part of an overall plot. Cardinal McIntyre, the highly conservative, elderly local Catholic prelate, "grieved that the splendid spirit and high moral integrity of the Negro is being besmirched by the happenings." (Whereupon a Catholic organization, called "Catholics United for Racial

Equality," urged the Pope to dismiss McIntyre on the ground that he had "contributed to the current racial outbursts.") Former President Dwight D. Eisenhower, too, expressed his feeling that the riots represented the final breakdown of law and order.

Liberal leaders for their part were as bewildered and ambivalent as any set of actors in the drama. They, too, were appalled by the violence but, faced with Parker's hard line and Yorty's familiar red-baiting, they perceived no choice other than to emphasize their instinctive feelings of sympathy for the blacks. Over time, the initial ambivalence of the liberals also gave way and they moved toward their accustomed pole on the spectrum, blaming miserable social and economic conditions for the outbreak of rioting. For example, the *New York Times* editorial of Saturday, August 15th, emphasized that family conditions, discrimination, and housing must be improved. A number of well-known sociologists interviewed by the *New York Times* blamed such things as raised expectations and token middle-class integration and emphasized the symbolism in the attacks upon police and private property. And the newspapers were filled with interviews with the many administrators of federal programs, thinking out loud of ways in which the federal government could be of assistance.

The liberal response was perhaps clearest in President Lyndon B. Johnson's statement on the riot.[2] To be sure, he described the riots as "tragic and shocking," noting that "killing, rioting and looting are contrary to the best traditions of this country." Yet, the striking thing about his response was not his rather ritualistic renunciation of violence but his emphasis upon civil rights and the problems of voting, housing, and discrimination. According to Johnson: "The bitter years that preceded the riots, the death of hope where hope existed, the sense of failure to change the condition of life, these things no doubt lead to these riots but they do not justify them." Then he went on to talk about civil rights acts, about Abraham Lincoln, about how "complex and urgent" the problem was, and in so doing he tied the riots explicitly to civil rights. Later, he told a conference on equal employment: "You are enlisted in what I consider the most important cause of our time [civil rights]." He went on to say that he was "enlisted for the duration" and used the familiar rallying cry of the civil rights movement, "we shall overcome." [3]

Still, most liberals badly miscalculated. As blindly ideological as anyone else, they did not consider the frightening symbolism of a black ghetto rebellion and they did not anticipate the strength of the "law and order" theme

[2] It must be remembered that his administration was at its zenith of popularity, having crushed the presidential campaign of the ultra-conservative Goldwater a few months earlier and having triumphantly led major civil rights legislation through Congress in 1964 and 1965.

[3] He was not above some breast beating, of course. He particularly emphasized the record of his own administration in promoting civil rights and addressing the evil social conditions that breed riots.

that this would later lead to. They really presumed that the civil rights movement would go on and that it would continue to enjoy what appeared to be a national consensus. Johnson's speech is indicative of this misperception. He continued to use the rhetoric of the civil rights movement when that day had abruptly ended.

Governor Brown did anticipate the disaster that would befall his administration at the polls a year later, saying that the riot had greatly damaged community relationships and that it would do irreparable harm to the civil rights movement. Similarly, the *Christian Science Monitor* editorialized that the most lamentable effect of the riot would be the strain on sympathy with or tolerance for the civil rights movement, which hitherto had enjoyed majority support. But few liberals had such foresight, as they reflexively denounced Parker and the police and planned standard liberal programs for blacks.[4]

[4]In the midst of all these preprogrammed responses, simply replaying their old familiar tunes, possibly the most interesting and original one came from Robert F. Kennedy. Rather than patting himself on the back, attacking his enemies, or issuing Pollyanna-ish statements about the future, he expressed a dark, brooding Irish pessimism. Although he agreed with other liberals that the blacks' only real help would come from social programs, he did not expect their results to be seen for many years. He pointed out that securing black voting rights in the South, a triumph of the Kennedy and Johnson Administrations, had been simple compared to the job needed to be done in the North. Nor was he easy on northern mayors, saying that few had effective communication with ghettos or could gauge the emotions felt there, or on civil rights leaders, who had not given appropriate leadership in the North: sit-ins, he said, would not make people literate. His response, a pessimistic one, went far beyond the standard liberal reflex, though its basic sympathies were clear.

10 The Public's Response: Racial Polarization

The racial polarization of local black and white leaders was duplicated almost immediately in the responses of the black and white publics. These descriptions of and feelings about the riot were as different as night and day and they formed the basis for a broad initial polarization over the issue of the riot, with blacks joined by a few liberal whites on one side, against most whites on the other. In this chapter we will describe these responses on the part of the Los Angeles public and then follow the reverberation of this local polarization around the nation.

Blacks' Response: Optimism about a Symbolic Protest

Most blacks perceived the riot as (1) a purposeful symbolic protest (2) against legitimate grievances, (3) designed to call attention to blacks' problems. It was not just a meaningless outburst of hostility directed at random or at whatever target was economically profitable. This perception of the riot as protest can be seen in our data in a variety of ways. When asked directly, a majority felt the riot did have a purpose or a goal, felt that the targets deserved attack, and agreed that the riot constituted a black protest. Also, when given a free choice of descriptive terms, a surprisingly large minority chose to talk about it in revolutionary or insurrectional terms.[1] Official pronouncements in the press and electronic media, almost without

---

[1]The riot label item was the first question dealing with the riot that was asked by our interviewer. After asking questions about Los Angeles and politics, the subject of the riot was introduced in the following manner (exact wording of item): "Now we'd like to talk about what happened here during August, what led up to it, what will happen as a result, and so on.—Various words have been used to describe what happened. What word or term would you use in talking about it? _____ (Interviewer: Use this term in referring to the event from now on.)"

TABLE 10.1

The Riot as Protest

	Black Curfew Zone (n = 586)	Black arrestees (n = 124)	Whites (n = 586)	Mexican Americans (n = 65)
"Was it a Negro Protest?"				
Yes	62%	66%	54%	52%
No	23	16	42	41
Don't know, other	12	15	3	6
No answer	2	3	—	0
	99%‡	100%	99%‡	99%‡
"Did it have a purpose or goal?"*				
Yes	56%	56%	33%	—
No	28	29	62	—
Don't know, other	11	13	4	—
No answer	5	2	—	—
	100%	100%	99%‡	
"Why were they attacked?"†				
Deserved attack	64%	75%	—	36%
Did not deserve attack	14	0	—	43
Ambivalent, don't know	17	21	—	13
No answer	5	4	—	8
	100%	100%		100%
"What word or term would you use in talking about it?"				
Riot	46%	44%	58%	49%
Revolt, revolution, insurrection	38	45	13	6
Other (disaster, tragedy, mess, disgrace, etc.)	8	10	27	43
Don't know, no answer	8	2	2	2
	100%	101%	100%	100%

*Mexican Americans were not asked this question.
†Whites were not asked this question.
‡When entries do not sum up to 100%, rounding is responsible.

TABLE 10.2

What Caused the Riot?

	Black Curfew Zone	Black arrestees	Whites	Mexican Americans
Specific grievances (total)	38%	51%	20%	31%
Discrimination, mistreatment by whites	7	4	5	8
Poverty, economic deprivation, inadequate services	10	5	11	13
Police mistreatment	21	42	4	10
Pent-up hostility, desire for revenge, fed-up	26	34	14	21
Frye incident	11	8	18	8
Undesirable groups (total)	9	2	29	19
Communists, Black Muslims, civil rights groups, organized groups, KKK, agitators	3	0	16	5
Criminals, looters	2	0	8	11
Foolish people, teenagers, southerners	4	2	5	3
Spontaneous explosion, accident, weather	0	0	10	11
Don't know, no answer	17	6	10	11
	101%	101%	101%	101%

exception, had described the disturbance as being a "riot." However, 38 per cent of our black Curfew Zone respondents rejected this official, conventional definition of the situation, selecting "revolt," "insurrection," "rebellion," "uprising" or some other revolutionary term, to characterize it. All these data are shown in Table 10.1. Second, when asked what caused the riot, most blacks cited either specific grievances or generalized pent-up hostility, as shown in Table 10.2. Very few blamed it on the weather, conspiratorial groups, hoodlums, or southern newcomers. In response to the question "What was its purpose?" (asked only of those who said the riot had one), the two most popular responses were (1) to call attention to black problems, 41 per cent, and (2) to express accumulated hostility and resentment, 33 per cent.

Most blacks also were optimistic about the success of this effort. More thought it would "help" the Negro's cause and decrease the gap between the races than thought it would "hurt the Negro's cause" or increase racial hostilities. And most thought whites had become more "aware of Negroes' problems" and more sympathetic to them as a consequence of the riot. All of these data are shown in Table 10.3.

Their optimism about the riot's effects focused largely on a favorable impact on whites. When asked, "What will the main effects of the riot be?," 43 per cent of the black respondents cited help from outside the black

TABLE 10.3

Expected Effects of the Riot

	Black Curfew Zone	Black arrestees	Whites	Mexican Americans
"What will the main effects be?" *				
Very or somewhat favorable	58%	57%	—	—
Neutral, ambivalent, don't know	12	14	—	—
Very or somewhat unfavorable	18	27	—	—
No answer	3	2	—	—
	101%	100%		
"Do you think it helped or hurt the Negro's cause?"				
Helped	38%	54%	19%	22%
No difference, don't know	30	33	5	2
Hurt	24	9	75	75
No answer, other	8	4	1	2
	100%	100%	100%	101%
Are whites more aware of Negro problems? †				
More aware	84%	80%	79%	62%
No change	13	17	18	21
Less aware	2	1	2	11
Other	2	2	1	6
	101%	100%	100%	100%

(continued)

*This question was not asked of white and Mexican American respondents.
†For Mexican American respondents, this question asked whether Mexican Americans had become more aware of Negro problems.

[TABLE 10.3 (continued)]

	Black Curfew Zone	Black arrestees	Whites	Mexican Americans
"Are whites more sympathetic to Negro problems?"‡				
More sympathetic	51%	49%	32%	11%
No change	31	38	27	36
Less sympathetic	12	9	37	46
Other	6	4	4	6
	100%	100%	100%	99%
"Did it increase or decrease the gap between the races?"				
Increase	23%	15%	71%	70%
No change	38	37	11	13
Decrease	24	22	13	6
Other	16	27	4	10
	101%	101%	99%	99%

‡For Mexican American respondents, this question asked whether Mexican Americans had become more sympathetic to Negro problems.

community and another 13 per cent expected better relations between whites and blacks. The main reason given for why it might "help or hurt the Negro's cause" was that it would make whites more attentive and sympathetic to blacks (42 per cent); few expected whites to change for the worse (8 per cent), or thought in terms of change in the black community (15 per cent). Similarly, of those who thought it would increase or decrease the gap between the races, 54 per cent expected some change in whites, 28 per cent change in both races, and only 12 per cent change among blacks themselves. Two possibilities blacks rarely mentioned were "white backlash" and greater black solidarity. Anticipation of greater white hostility or greater racial prejudice was mentioned by only 13 per cent as the most likely effect of the riot and by 8 per cent as the main reason why the riot might help or hurt the black cause. Effects upon blacks aside from effects upon whites were also rarely mentioned. Only 2 per cent saw new self-respect or leadership among blacks as a main effect of the riot, and 15 per cent and 12 per cent respectively, cited change among blacks as the main reason why the riot might help or hurt "the Negro's cause" and "increase or decrease the gap between the races." Ironically, white backlash and more positive self-images among blacks, though cited infrequently by blacks at the time, ultimately proved to be among the riot's most important results, according to the analysis we will present later in this chapter and in Chapter 12.

Finally, most blacks disapproved of the events themselves. When asked, "What did you like or dislike about what was going on?," a majority (67 per cent) expressed disapproval. Further probing revealed that almost as many of the disapprovers were reacting to the killing and bloodshed (43 per cent) as to the property destruction (47 per cent). Since the killed and wounded were mostly blacks, many of them rioters, it is clear that much of the disapproval did not grow out of a concern for white owned property or abstract considerations of law and order.

The blacks' sympathies generally were with the rioters, not with the authorities. Disapproval of the rioters was not as common as it was of the riot itself. When asked, "What kinds of people supported it?" and "What kinds of people were against it?," only 42 per cent were clearly unsympathetic to the participants, while 30 per cent responded in sympathetic terms. Thus, disapproval of the riot focused considerably more upon the violence in the riot than upon the motives and identity of the participants themselves. In distinct contrast, most blacks expressed a great deal of antagonism toward the authorities' role in the riot. Chief Parker was the object of much of this hostility. Among the blacks, 10 per cent evaluated him favorably and 76 per cent unfavorably. Similarly, only 28 per cent thought the authorities had handled the riot "well" and 65 per cent felt it had been handled "badly." The further breakdown of these responses is shown in Table 10.4. Blacks who thought the authorities had done badly were split between those who felt the authorities should have put an end to it earlier and those who felt they had exacerbated the situation. Many ghetto respondents clearly did not like what had happened, but their disposition was to defend and justify the actions of black rioters and to criticize the actions of the white authorities. In this respect their responses paralleled those of black leaders.[2]

Thus the story of "Watts" told by most blacks in its aftermath was that it had been a symbolic black protest, touched off by legitimate grievances,

[2]Since perceptions of police brutality were related to riot activity (Raine, 1970; and Chapter 6), it might be suggested that the riot simply polarized the black community over the issue of the police, leaving the riot participants and other troublemakers embittered, antagonistic, and aggrieved, while the good people of Watts supported their local police and longed for more law and order. Our data contradict such a view, however. First, even among those who did not actively participate in the riot, almost half (46 per cent) felt that four of the six police malpractices shown in Table 4.1 regularly occurred in the riot area. Second, perceptions of a high level of police brutality were distributed evenly through most of the demographic subgroups of the Curfew Zone sample (Chapter 5). Third, antagonism toward Chief Parker was so intense and so general that it did not relate at all to riot activity (48 per cent of the arrestees, 47 per cent of the Curfew Zone sample actives, and 41 per cent of the Curfew Zone inactives *strongly* disapproved of Parker).

TABLE 10.4
Did the Authorities Handle It [the Riot] Well or Badly?

	Black Curfew Zone	Black arrestees	Whites	Mexican Americans
Well	28%	15%	66%	68%
Badly	65	77	32	27
Should have stopped it sooner	*27*	*14*	*26*	*22*
They made it worse, were intransigent	*33*	*56*	*6*	*5*
Other	*5*	*7*	*0*	*0*
Don't know, no answer, other	8	9	2	6
	101%	101%	100%	101%

that it probably would lead to greater white awareness of blacks' problems and to sympathetic corrective action; that the violence and bloodshed were bad but to some extent the participants were justified, while the white authorities were repressive and inept.

Whites' and Mexican Americans' Responses

The story told by whites and Mexican Americans was quite different. Many (especially those close to the Curfew Zone) felt fear for their own safety or for their families' safety during the disturbance. The Mexican American respondents in our sample (all of whom actually lived in the Curfew Zone) were particularly frightened: 52 per cent reported feeling a "great deal" of fear. Fear among whites was greatest in Baldwin Hills and Leimert Park, two integrated communities on the edge of the Curfew Zone (35 per cent reported a "great deal") but, even in affluent Pacific Palisades 20 miles from the riot, 12 per cent reported "a great deal" of fear.

Accompanying the fear was much serious thought about obtaining guns for armed counterviolence. Forty-two per cent of the Mexican Americans and 29 per cent of the whites said "yes" to the question, "Did you at any time consider using firearms to protect yourself or your family?" Also, 5 per cent of the whites and 7 per cent of the Mexican Americans reported that they actually had bought firearms or ammunition as a consequence of the riot. This was a considerable increase in the potential for counterviolence in the Anglo and Mexican American areas, though fortunately it did not materialize at the time.

Almost all whites and Mexican Americans supported the tough, uncompromising stand toward the rioters that Chief Parker and the other California law enforcement authorities established. Both groups almost invariably praised the authorities or criticized them for not being even tougher, as shown in Table 10.4. Only 6 per cent and 5 per cent, respectively, agreed with the contentions of black leaders and most black respondents that the authorities had acted too harshly or had been too difficult to negotiate with. The authorities' response thus became the focus of the sharpest racial polarization. And the racial polarization over Chief Parker was nearly complete. He was evaluated favorably by 79 per cent of the whites and 74 per cent of the Mexican Americans and unfavorably by only 15 per cent in each sample—nearly the mirror image of the blacks' evaluations given above.

Whites and Mexican Americans did agree, in general, that it had been a black protest but they were extremely unlikely to describe the riot in revolutionary terms. They denied that the riot had any purpose and said that the targets attacked had not deserved it. All of these data are shown in Table 10.1. Whites felt the main causes of the riot were the weather, conspiratorial groups, and the accident of the Frye incident itself, rather than more basic grievances and discontents (shown in Table 10.2).[3]

The vast majority of whites and Mexican Americans expressed disapproval of the riot itself. Although no single item measured sympathy completely, this attitude is clear from the pattern of the data in Tables 10.1 to 10.3 (see also data presented by Morris and Jeffries, 1970, p. 485). Mexican Americans, too, were overwhelmingly unsympathetic with the riot. Eighty-nine per cent agreed that "it was too bad that some Negroes were hurt during the riot, but they brought it upon themselves." And when asked, "In general, did Mexican Americans sympathize with what was going on?," 88 per cent replied "very little" or "not at all." Moreover, whites and Mexican Americans were not at all sympathetic toward the participants. They agreed with Chief Parker and Mayor Yorty in describing them as criminals, thugs, hoodlums, and communists.

Finally, then, it should come as no surprise to learn that whites and Mexican Americans thought the riot would have quite unfavorable effects for blacks. As shown in Table 10.3, whites typically expected it to produce increased tensions between the races and a retardation of black progress. Even at the interpersonal level, whites expected greater tension: 17 per cent expected to be less at ease with blacks, against only 2 per cent expecting to be more at ease, after the riot. Similarly, 9 per cent expected to like blacks less, and only 1 per cent expected to like them more; 8 per cent expected

---

[3]The only major divergence between whites and Mexican Americans was over the perceived causes of the riot. The latter, living in the Curfew Zone, saw these more realistically as growing out of blacks' frustrations (see Table 10.2) but still strongly disliked all aspects of the riot.

to trust them less, and only 1 per cent to trust them more (Morris and Jeffries, 1970, p. 491).

Thus, while blacks saw the riot as a protest with two purposes (1) to call attention to black problems and (2) to show whites the depth of their hostility and resentment for past legitimate grievances, whites got only half of this two-pronged message. They had become more aware of black problems but they did not grant that the hostility was legitimate or that the riot was justified. The threat of a massive black rebellion struck real fear in the hearts of many, whether within sight of the Curfew Zone or many miles away. Repression, rather than sympathetic and helpful understanding, was the response most favored.

Toward Nationwide Polarization

As riots broke out in other parts of the nation in the months and years after "Watts," the black and white reactions followed a pattern familiar to those who had observed the aftermath of the violence in Los Angeles.

Fear.   Fear and revulsion against the violence were among the few reactions both races agreed upon throughout the nation. In Detroit, 64 per cent of the whites and 67 per cent of the blacks said they had been personally afraid. When fear for the safety of family and friends was included with personal fear, whites were actually somewhat more afraid, and saw a larger fraction of the black population as being involved, than did blacks (Levy, 1968). And, as in Watts, blacks across the nation did not approve of the rioting and the violence. Beardwood (1968, p. 148) reported that only 14 per cent of a 1967 nationwide sample of blacks favored the rioting, looting, property destruction, and other acts of violence, whereas 58 per cent reacted essentially negatively to these events. Similarly, in Detroit, only 5 per cent of the whites and 6 per cent of the blacks felt that "most of the community" supported the riot.

Sympathy for Participants.   Yet, as with "Watts," blacks everywhere were considerably more sympathetic toward the riot participants than they were toward the violence or than whites were toward the rioters. Campbell and Schuman (1968, p. 55) found that 54 per cent of their sample of blacks in 15 major cities were sympathetic toward the participants and only 24 per cent unsympathetic. Whites, however, were not at all sympathetic toward the participants. The Harris Poll reported that 62 per cent of the whites felt that looters should be shot, while only 28 per cent felt they should not be shot. In this same poll, only 27 per cent of the blacks felt looters should be shot, while 62 per cent felt they should not be (Erskine, 1967). This enormous racial difference revealed how strongly the whites condemned the participants and how eager they were to retaliate against them. It also illustrates the basic empathy blacks had for the rioters and their resistance to harsh and extreme methods of law enforcement.

Causes.   Blacks and whites also differed greatly on the causes of the riots. Most blacks saw the riots as spontaneous protests rather than as conspiratorially planned in advance. Campbell and Schuman discovered in their 15-city study (1968, p. 48) that 48 per cent of the whites (versus 18 per cent of the blacks) thought the riots were planned in advance; 11 per cent of the whites (versus 34 per cent of the blacks) said they were not at all planned in advance.

Blacks tended to see the riots as resulting from legitimate grievances against the police, merchants, and other symbols of white authority; against poor social conditions in education, housing, and jobs; and against prejudice. Whites, on the other hand, were much more likely to attribute the riots to anti-white feeling, to young hoodlums who wanted only to disrupt things, and especially to outside agitation. A most striking demonstration of this polarization over causes emerged in Detroit (Levy, 1968, p. 35). Respondents were asked: "Which of the following is closest to the truth? The riots were caused by bad treatment, or by criminals and people wanting to take things." Whites preferred the second alternative by a two-to-one majority but blacks preferred the first by over two-to-one.

Nevertheless, it is important to note that the white public was not of a single mind, any more than white elites were. Large minorities of whites mentioned bad conditions for blacks as primary causes of the rioting; that is, lack of equal rights and overcrowding (CBS, 1968) or racial discrimination (Campbell and Schuman, 1968).

Thus, a fairly broad consensus existed among blacks that unredressed, legitimate grievances were the root cause of the riots and that outside agitators and police laxity played unimportant roles. Among whites, two clearly differentiated bodies of opinion existed. To the majority of whites, the riots were senseless, meaningless, criminal, and fear-provoking. It is true, though, that a substantial minority did view the riots much as the blacks did and expressed sympathetic understanding of the conditions that forced blacks to turn to violence as a means of protest.

Riot Control.   Whites and blacks, nationwide, also polarized over techniques or actions for riot control. Whites felt that the senseless and fear-provoking rioters should be dealt with harshly. Blacks felt that caution and understanding should temper the actions of riot control forces. The CBS nationwide poll of 1968 presented evidence of these differences. Among whites, 70 per cent felt that the police should be tougher with the rioters and only 5 per cent felt they should be easier with them. The picture was almost exactly the opposite for blacks: 17 per cent felt the police should be tougher and 35 per cent easier. In somewhat diluted form, the blacks' lack of confidence in the police emerged in a second CBS item in which the respondents were asked: "Do people like yourself have to be prepared to defend their homes or can the police take care of the job?" Among whites 40 per cent said the police could take care of it, whereas among blacks 23 per cent felt the police could take care of it. Thus, not only did whites feel that the police were on their side but they had more confidence than did blacks in the ability of the police to look after their personal safety.

Expectations.   As in Los Angeles, blacks elsewhere expressed optimism regarding the effects of the rioting, while whites expected blacks to suffer as a consequence. In 1968, 34 per cent of the blacks in Campbell and Schuman's study thought the riots would help them and 23 per cent thought they would hurt. Whites were of the opposite opinion: 14 per cent felt they would help and 64 per cent felt they would hurt the blacks' cause.

Longer-Term Effects

Blacks expected the riot to turn whites' sympathetic attention to their problems, and hence grievance redress to result. Most whites expected the opposite: less sympathy and help from whites. Who was right?[4]

Surprisingly enough, the greater attention accorded blacks during the riot quickly receded and blacks then lapsed back into near invisibility. For example, in our analysis of Los Angeles newspapers, we found that the amount of post-riot coverage (1965–1968) of blacks was not significantly greater than the amount of pre-riot coverage (Johnson, Sears, and McConahay, 1971). And the content of the coverage actually became somewhat more unfavorable, since racial violence was more newsworthy and attention to civil rights did not increase.

Even though press coverage did not increase, and became less favorable, blacks did become more visible in the media in some other respects. Over the 1965–1969 period they were used increasingly in ads in mass circulation magazines (Colfax and Sternberg, 1972; Cox, 1969; Kassarjian, 1970) and as actors in television dramas (Dominick and Greenberg, 1970). Blacks became much more prominent in the movies in the post-riot era, as well. Thus the advertising, television, and film industries did make some self-conscious effort to improve the visibility of black faces in the media. But such increases in visibility are not unalloyed blessings; for example, there is some evidence that blacks' use in magazine ads has not become any less stereotyped, and indeed that it began to decrease in 1970, after the early post-riot surge had crested (Colfax and Sternberg, 1972). And without an increase in serious coverage of the black community, blacks' hopes for greater attention to their problems will not be met, even in the longer term.

[4]Our research approach is geared to measuring attention and attitudes more than concrete gains in the economic and social realms. Moreover, the kinds of gains blacks expected ought to have been reflected in whites' attention and attitudes. So we will not try to deal with post-riot changes in housing, employment, educational opportunity, police practices, overt racial discrimination, medical care, and so forth. These have been dealt with in follow-up reports from the Kerner and McCone Commissions, and we will leave their evaluation to others.

Whites' predominant initial reactions to the riot, as we have seen, included fear, repressiveness, greater social distance, and severely moralistic rejection of violence as a means of promoting social change. Indeed, whites' and blacks' immediate reactions to the riot were polar opposites on almost every dimension. Our data do not provide any basis for assessing the persistence of this polarization for a longer period after the riot. Fortunately, Campbell's (1971) recent monograph does allow such an assessment, based on national samples of blacks and whites taken in 1964, 1968, and 1970. Among blacks, the riots did leave important attitudinal changes, which we will take up in the next two chapters. But the immediate polarization of the races over the issue of the rioting apparently did not result in a major regression in whites' racial attitudes more generally, Let us review briefly the basis for this assertion.

During the 1960s whites, by an overwhelming margin, felt that blacks were moving too fast and that their activism was dominated by violence and in the main was hurting their cause. The period of the riots (1965–1968) saw increases in this negative response but as the riot era closed (1968–1970), it diminished somewhat. This would indicate some slackening of tension over racial violence after the riots began to lessen.

When we consider attitude changes from before to after the riots, there are very real signs of liberalized racial attitudes on the part of whites. Their feelings toward blacks in general changed little. But they became, as a group, markedly more favorable to school desegregation, open housing, desegregation of public accommodations, and indeed to desegregation as a general concept. Their reported contact with blacks in housing, schools, and friendships increased as well.

Campbell (1971, p. 154) concluded that the riot period of 1965–1968 did not cause the relationships between the races to deteriorate or weaken; it produced no great, lasting polarization. We might put it somewhat differently. The very sharp polarization that did occur immediately over blacks' tactics, and particularly over the rioting, apparently did not generalize into more negative or resistant white attitudes toward blacks and their progress. Indeed, if anything, whites' support for blacks' progress seemed, in the long run, to have increased somewhat. Of course, these are measures of support for blacks in the abstract and not in difficult concrete cases. And, as the issues get closer and closer to home for whites, as they have, we cannot expect whites to react increasingly in a liberal way. But the lesson of these data is that increasingly resistant white behavior may be due to increasingly touchy policy issues and not to increasingly resistant white attitudes. Indeed, it is quite possible that the riots liberalized whites' racial attitudes enough to allow open-minded debate over the most truly difficult issues of all, such as reverse discrimination in hiring and desegregation of the suburbs.

11   The Riot Ideology

One of the most important potential legacies of a mass uprising such as "Watts" can be an ideology about its meaning, in which the events come to symbolize and glorify the rising up of an oppressed people. Such an ideology can serve as a rallying point for collective action. It can help insure solidarity, act as a model for further violence, and justify similar future actions.

The major revolutions of recent history have helped to create such ideologies, in the United States, France, the Soviet Union, China, Cuba, Mexico, and throughout many nations of Africa and South America. The major questions we wish to pose in this chapter are three: Did "Watts" serve as the basis for such an ideology among the blacks of Los Angeles? If so, how general was such an ideology? And how explicable are its origins in terms of the theory we have invoked to understand the origins of rioting itself?

A Coherent Riot Ideology

The first question is whether or not blacks' attitudes about the riot formed, in the aftermath, anything resembling an ideological view of "Watts." An "ideology" should, at a minimum, possess unifying abstract conceptualizations, internal consistency and coherence, and some stability over time.[1] However, the political attitudes held by American mass publics generally lack these characteristics (Campbell et al., 1960; Converse, 1964, 1970;

[1]Our use of the term "ideology" is purely technical and a value judgment is not intended or implied. By an ideology we mean a coherent, interrelated set of beliefs held in common by a group of people. Such beliefs interpret an aspect of life (in this case, racial and political aspects) and include an explicit or implicit guide for action. See Converse (1964) for some empirical criteria by which to define an "ideology."

Sears, 1969a). Rather, coherent ideologies are largely limited to small, politicized, usually well-educated minorities.

Thus, normally we would be surprised to find any widely disseminated political ideology among blacks because their overall educational level is rather low and political apathy and indifference have been common. But the riot was obviously an exceptional event; as we have seen in Chapter 1, it was so massive that it affected almost everyone at a personal level. Hence, one might expect more complex political thinking about an event of the magnitude and impact of "Watts." Did the riot father a coherent ideology?

If such an ideology existed among many blacks, it would obviously center around the content we described in the previous chapter. Among blacks the most common interpretation of the riot was that it was a symbolic protest against legitimate grievances, designed to call attention to blacks' problems; moreover, it was generally expected to be successful in attracting helpful attention from whites. To measure these dimensions, we constructed four scales of attitudes toward the riot on the basis of the individual items discussed in the last chapter.[2]

The protest interpretation scale assessed the extent to which an individual interpreted the riot as a purposeful protest expressing the community's unredressed grievances. The riot optimism scale was designed to assess an individual's optimism regarding the effects of the riot. The riot approval scale measured the degree of approval expressed by an individual toward both the rioters and the violence. The perceived community activity scale was intended to measure perceptions of the extent of participation in and support for the riot throughout the black community.

Consistency of Riot Attitudes. A simple test for the presence of riot ideology is whether or not individual items ostensibly measuring the same dimension of riot attitudes were related to each other. The correlations of individual items with the remainder of their scales give every reason for believing that each scale measures a coherent and internally consistent view of the riot. As shown in Appendix B, these correlations ranged from .53 to .84, with the bulk of the reliabilities clustered around .70. This degree of scale internal consistency is, in itself, some evidence of a coherent riot ideology.

Table 11.1 gives the correlations between different scales of riot attitude. Briefly, riot approval, optimism regarding its effects, and protest interpretation are views of the riot that were rather tightly bound up with one another but perceived community involvement was not included uniformly as part of this ideological package. Among the first three, however, the correlations were sufficiently high to justify regarding them as forming a coherent ideology (at least by comparison with the usual level of internal consistency

[2]The items making up the scales and their reliabilities are given in Appendix B. These scales already have been mentioned briefly in Chapters 1 and 7.

TABLE 11.1

Correlations among Riot Attitude Scales*

	Protest interpretation	Riot optimism	Riot approval
Riot optimism	.35†	—	—
Riot approval	.49	.40	—
Perceived community involvement	.11	.13	.42

*Curfew Zone respondents only. The *n*'s vary from 527 to 549.
†Spearman correlations. All are positive and all are significant, at least at $p < .05$.

in Americans' political attitudes). Hence, in our discussion below, we will define the riot ideology in terms of three dimensions: protest interpretation, riot optimism, and riot approval.

Growth of the Riot Ideology with Time.   If indeed this collection of attitudes was a coherent ideology that grew up following the riot, we ought to be able to trace its development over time. We tested this by comparing respondents interviewed at various intervals after the riot: October versus November versus December-February.[3] Support for the basic elements of the riot ideology generally increased throughout this period. Riot approval increased but only trivially. Protest interpretation advanced significantly over time: 63 per cent fell above the neutral point in the first time period and 77 per cent did so at the end. Optimism about the effects of the riot also increased substantially, from 55 per cent to 69 per cent. The same picture held for increases in coherence of the various riot attitudes. Optimism became increasingly related to protest ideology but both dimensions actually became considerably *less* related to riot approval.[4]

Thus, the nature of the riot ideology changed somewhat as the actual events receded into memory. Initially, interpreting the riot, or foreseeing favorable effects of it, depended more upon approving of the rioters and the events of the riot. As time went on, there was no greater tendency to glorify either the rioters or the events. However, the black community became increasingly convinced that it was an effective protest; perhaps most impor-

[3]As indicated earlier, these respondents did not differ materially in demographic characteristics, so it is plausible to treat the differences in their attitudes as a function of the date of interview. See footnote 4 in Chapter 7.

[4]Increases in protest ideology and optimism over the three interviewing periods were significant: $X^2 = 6.58$, 2 *df*, $p < .05$, and $X^2 = 6.45$, 2 *df*, $p < .05$. These two scales were significantly related in October ($X^2 = 5.71$, 1 *df*, $p < .05$) but even more so in the December-February interviewing ($X^2 = 9.99$, 1 *df*, $p < .01$). Riot approval became less tightly related to protest ideology ($X^2 = 18.83$ *vs.* $X^2 = 7.14$) and optimism ($X^2 = 7.66$ *vs.* 5.99) but the relationship was significant in all time periods (at least $p < .05$, all on 1 *df*).

tant, even those who vigorously condemned the violence began to adopt this protest interpretation of the event. Rather than dividing the black community, then, the riot tended increasingly to unite it ideologically around this protest interpretation.

Origins of the Riot Ideology

Why did the riot ideology arise after the riot? One can easily imagine an outbreak of violence that would *not* lead to this set of interpretations. Murders, wife- or child-beatings, feuds between street gangs, drunken brawls at football games—such violence is around us all the time without being assigned a grand or noble meaning.

Our theoretical analysis points to three sets of possible causal factors: (1) the New Urban Blacks' political socialization, and (2) the grievances and discontents held by blacks more generally, which accounted for large numbers of persons who would be receptive both to becoming involved in a riot *and* to generating an ideology of symbolic protest about it afterwards; and (3) the public responses of black leaders and white liberals, thoroughly publicized in the media from the first days of the riot, made the ideas contained in the riot ideology universally available. We have seen already that almost all blacks had positive attitudes toward the black and/or liberal leaders expressing these ideas, and highly negative attitudes toward those expressing contrary interpretations of the riot (such as Chief Parker, Mayor Yorty, or the police or authorities more generally). Given this great advantage in credibility, these leaders' interpretations should have been much the more persuasive.

Resocialization. Our analysis of the New Urban Blacks certainly would suggest that they had special receptivity to the riot ideology. Our hypothesis presented in Chapter 3 assumed that experiences first and simultaneously encountered by masses of adults would lead to the development of generational norms. As members of each generation compared notes about the riot and influenced each other, we would expect generational norms to emerge that would reflect early socialization differences across but not within generations. The dominant early socialization of each generation would be most influential in this process. Thus, among the young we hypothesized that the generational norms would be dominated by the attitudes of the New Urban Blacks, due to their numerical superiority in that subgroup, whereas in older generations we predicted the emergence of generational norms dominated by the dispositions of the southern, rural migrants. Concretely, then, acquisition of the riot ideology should be determined more by the individual's generation (that is, by his age) than by the circumstances of his early socialization (that is, place of origin, urban-rural, education). In this sense, our theoretical analysis suggests that the riot was an event capable of "resocializing" many in the ghetto to a new set of norms.

An examination of the relationships of age and socialization factors to

TABLE 11.2

Riot Approval and Perceived Community Involvement as a Function of Age and Place of Origin

PLACE OF ORIGIN	AGE			
	15–29	30–44	45+	All ages
Percentage high in riot approval				
Los Angeles natives	40	31	18	36
Northern migrants	46	30	19	30
Southern migrants	40	18	19	23
X^2	<1	3.47	<1	8.66
p (2 df)	n.s.	n.s.	n.s.	<.005
*All origins**	40	24	19	
Percentage high in perceived community involvement				
Los Angeles natives	37	24	40	35
Northern migrants	33	20	21	24
Southern migrants	30	17	13	18
X^2	<1	<1	5.09	11.90
p (2 df)	n.s.	n.s.	<.10	<.005
All origins†	35	19	17	

*Age effect: $X^2 = 11.96$, p (2 df) < .005.
†Age effect: $X^2 = 9.71$, p (2 df) < .005.
Note: Entries are percentages high in riot approval and perceived community involvement, respectively. See Appendix B for details on these scales.

scales measuring reactions to the riot generally supports our hypothesis. As shown in Table 11.2, the young were significantly more likely to react favorably to the riot and to perceive a great deal of community involvement in it. There was also an overall effect for socialization but this disappeared with age controlled, as we would expect. Differences in approval of the riot and perceptions of community involvement were accounted for almost entirely by the respondent's generation, rather than by the locus of his socialization.[5]

The protest interpretation of the riot was not generally affected by age, place of origin, or urbanization; it was accepted throughout most demographic subgroups. Optimism regarding the outcome of the riot also tended

[5]We might add that the generational differences in attitudes toward the riot were not merely the reflection of the greater participation rates of the young. When we controlled for reported participation, the generational effects still obtained. For example, among those not active, the percentages of riot approvers were 32, 20, and 15 for young, middle, and older age groups, respectively. Among riot participants, the percentages were 58, 39, and 20, respectively.

TABLE 11.3

**Protest Interpretation and Optimism about Riot Outcome as a
Function of Age and Place of Origin**

PLACE OF ORIGIN	AGE			
	15–29	**30–44**	**45+**	**All ages**
Percentage high in protest interpretation				
Los Angeles natives	72	64	82	72
Northern migrants	70	66	69	68
Southern migrants	77	68	67	70
X^2	0.56	0.20	0.97	0.37
p (*2* df)	n.s.	n.s.	n.s.	n.s.
*All origins**	73	67	68	
Percentage high in riot optimism				
Los Angeles natives	59	53	67	59
Northern migrants	61	39	53	49
Southern migrants	67	72	60	66
X^2	1.08	11.19	<1	8.03
p (*2* df)	n.s.	<.001	n.s.	<.02
All origins†	62	62	59	

*Age effect: $X^2 = 1.61$, 2 *df,* n.s.
†Age effect: $X^2 < 1$, n.s.

to be quite high in the community, though it too failed to relate to age, place of origin, or urbanization, or to any other demographic variable (Sears and McConahay, 1970b). The data are given in Table 11.3. While these data would seem on the face of it not to support our resocialization hypothesis, they at least are testimony to how widespread were both protest interpretation and riot optimism in the Curfew Zone.

What accounts for the success of our generational prediction with riot approval and perceived community involvement, and its failure with protest ideology ·and riot optimism? It will be recalled from the last chapter that most blacks saw the riot as a protest and that the optimists outnumbered the pessimists—yet only a minority approved of the riot. In our analyses here, we have divided respondents on an absolute basis (that is, separating those who on balance approved more than they disapproved, were more optimistic than pessimistic, and so forth) rather than on a relative statistical basis (by using a median split). This means that we are using a more rigorous relative standard for riot approval than for protest ideology or optimism.

If, however, we consider only those extremely committed to the protest

TABLE 11.4

Residues of Early Socialization as Determinants of the Riot Ideology

	Percentage approving riot	Percentage high in protest interpretation	Percentage optimistic
Black identity			
Positive	39	76	69
Negative, neutral	21	64	55
X^2 *(1 df)*	18.36	7.68	9.83
p	<.001	<.01	<.01
Trust of whites			
Most	12	49	53
None	50	83	71
X^2 *(2 df)*	27.61	16.32	4.78
p	<.001	<.001	<.10
Generalized political disaffection			
High	36	76	63
Low	20	66	62
X^2 *(1 df)*	12.91	4.43	0.05
p	<.001	<.05	n.s.

Note: Entry is percentage holding each riot attitude cited of all those at the given level of socialization residue. For example, 39% of those with positive black identity approved of the riot and 61% disapproved.

ideology (those giving a "protest" response on at least three of the four items in the scale and a neutral response on the fourth), then a strong age effect did emerge. By this criterion, 42 per cent of the young, against 30 per cent of the 30 to 44 year olds and 25 per cent of the older group, strongly endorsed protest ideology ($X^2 = 6.41$, 2 *df*, $p < .05$). And, though socialization also was related to extreme ideology, age again proved to be the most decisive factor, since the socialization effects were eliminated with age controlled.[6] Changing the cutoff point on riot optimism made no real difference, however.

Residues of Early Socialization.   Even if attitudes toward the riot were newly acquired by many, in conformity to generational norms, the residues of early socialization still should influence their acceptance to some extent.

[6]Age also affected criticism of the authorities' role in handling the riot. The young were most likely to feel the authorities handled it badly (78 per cent), followed by the middle (71 per cent) and older (61 per cent) age groups ($X^2 = 13.0$, 2 *df*, $p < .001$). With age controlled, the modest socialization effects proved ephemeral.

That is, generational norms should dominate but not completely override the effects of early socialization. As in earlier analyses, the three main residues we are concerned with are black identity, anti-white prejudice, and generalized political disaffection. As shown in Table 11.4, all three were strongly related to riot approval and protest ideology but not very strongly to optimism about the effects of the riot. Two other indicators of anti-white prejudice, distaste about attending an all-white party and about racial inter-marriage, were also positively related to riot approval and to protest ideology, though the data are not presented here. So, all three of these residues of early political socialization are strongly related to the riot ideology: indeed, they account for the riot ideology even better than they do for riot participation (compare Tables 6.1 and 11.4).

To support our resocialization hypothesis thoroughly, however, three additional tests must succeed. As indicated above, both age and the residues of early socialization should independently generate the riot ideology: early socialization persists into adulthood but the riot presumably "resocialized" many other blacks to the norms characteristic of their generation. However, any effects of place of origin should be accounted for by the attitudinal residues of early socialization. Concretely, then, (1) these additional variables (black identity, distrust of whites, and generalized political disaffection) should continue to relate positively to the riot ideology with age and place of origin controlled—and they do, in 91 per cent of the 22 possible comparisons; (2) age should continue to relate positively to the riot ideology with both place of origin and these attitudes controlled—and it does, in 84 per cent of the 22 possible comparisons; while (3) place of origin should not relate positively to the riot ideology with age and attitudes controlled—and it does not, since only half of the 22 comparisons are positive, which is no greater than chance.[7]

These data strongly support our basic contention, that the riot ideology was a joint function of the residues of early political socialization and of "resocialization" to the norms dominant in each generation. Thus, young blacks adopted the riot ideology so vigorously both because many were New Urban Blacks *and* because the New Urban Blacks' thinking predominated throughout the younger generation, thus resocializing young blacks from southern, rural, migrant backgrounds.[8]

[7]The first of these three analyses was conducted by relating black identity to riot approval within each of the four crucial demographic groups (young natives, old natives, young southern migrants, old southern migrants), then repeating for trust of whites and for generalized political disaffection; then repeating all 12 of these tests for protest interpretation. Cells with $n < 10$ were not considered, which accounts for our base of 22 rather than 24 potential comparisons. The other two analyses were conducted in a parallel way.

[8]Therefore, our political socialization hypothesis received considerably more support in the case of riot ideology than in that of riot participation. It will be remembered from Chapter 6 that the theory was supported for self-reported activity but not for events witnessed.

TABLE 11.5

Local Grievances and Riot Ideology*

	Approval of riot (n = 469–523)	Protest interpretation (n = 435–483)	Optimism about outcome (n = 468–522)
Type of grievance			
Police brutality	.30†	.32	.25
Merchant exploitation	.29	.25	.21
Biased white media	.31	.25	.15
Local political structure	.37	.18	.11
Agency discrimination	.22	.30	.19
Inadequate local service	.20	.12	.11

*Curfew Zone respondents only.
†Spearman correlations. All are positive and all are significant, at least at $p < .05$.

Local Grievances. The riot ideology clearly grew out of the same sense of discontent and frustration as did riot participation. Indeed, if anything, it was founded even more on discontent. To demonstrate this, let us examine briefly the relationships between the local grievances we discussed in Chapter 4 and the riot ideology scales. Each of the six local grievances, as shown in Table 11.5, related consistently to riot approval and protest interpretation. Furthermore, the grievances were related more closely to riot approval than to riot participation in 11 of 12 cases and to protest interpretation in 9 of 12 cases.[9] So, the consistent role of local grievances in determining riot participation here is even magnified in producing riot approval and protest interpretation (though optimism was not so consistently related to local grievances—a point we will take up later).

It might be thought for a variety of reasons that grievances would not be especially important in promoting the younger generation's acceptance of the riot ideology. We found earlier that the young were not unusually high in local grievances. Also it is generally thought that the young are less politically aware and sophisticated than older persons. And, from the data just presented, the young might have been influenced by their age mates to accept the riot ideology without any consideration of grievances against local white-dominated institutions.

However, this turns out not to be true at all; the riot ideology was actually *more* tied to grievances against the police, merchants, agencies, and local white politicians among the young than it was among the old. Considering the six local grievances and the two dimensions of the riot ideology em-

[9]Also grievances were related more closely to protest interpretation than to participation even with education or familiarity with white politicians controlled.

phasized above (riot approval and protest interpretation), 83 per cent of the 12 possible relationships were statistically significant ($p < .05$) among the young (under 30), while only 38 per cent were in the 24 comparisons involving the 30-44 and 45-and-over age groups. So, the grievance basis for the riot ideology emerged *most* clearly of all among the young.

Blocked Mechanisms of Grievance Redress. Riot approval and protest interpretation also sprang from the conviction that conventional mechanisms of grievance redress were inadequate. Rejection of individualized striving as a primary method by which blacks should get what they want was associated with both riot approval and protest interpretation ($X^2 = 15.16$ and 5.49, 1 df, $p < .001$ and $< .05$, respectively). Moreover, riot approval was closely related to distrust of conventional administrative procedures, as illustrated by distrust of the authorities' standard procedures regarding police mistreatment. Of those saying they could "do nothing" or would try self-defense or revenge, 40 per cent approved of the riot. Of those giving trusting responses, only 24 per cent approved of the riot ($X^2 = 12.97$, 1 df, $p < .001$). This is an even closer relationship than that which held with riot participation. However, the relationship with protest interpretation was not significant. Blockages in the area of political redress also tended to be related to riot ideology. Though past political participation and current political contacts were not significantly correlated with the riot scales, generalized political disaffection was, as shown in Table 11.4.

The willingness to adopt *unconventional* strategies for grievance redress in the future was intimately related to the riot ideology. The riot was vastly more popular, and almost universally perceived as a directed protest, among that minority who had decided that violent protest was the best strategy left for blacks. Similarly, willingness to engage in unconventional, though nonviolent, confrontation strategies was closely associated with riot approval and protest interpretation. These data are shown in Table 11.6.

Black Leadership. The interpretations of the riot given by local black leaders tended to correspond to most elements of the riot ideology. They deplored the violence, in general, but noted the legitimate grievances of black people and interpreted the riot as a protest against those conditions. We have no way of testing directly the impact of their statements but we can test the relationship between the riot ideology and (1) exposure to black-originated media and (2) evaluation of these leaders. When this is done, riot approval proves to have been positively related to exposure to black media and to evaluations of the Black Muslims, but negatively related to evaluations of local black politicians.[10] Neither protest interpretation nor riot optimism was related significantly to any of these scales, however. So

[10] The X^2's are 10.20, 12.48, and 6.08, respectively, all on 1 df, $p < .001$, $< .01$, and $< .02$, respectively.

TABLE 11.6
Riot Ideology and Most Effective Method for Blacks to Use

	Percentage approving riot	Percentage high in protest interpretation	Percentage optimistic about effects of riots
"What is the best strategy?"			
Negotiation	24	68	64
Nonviolent protest	18	65	56
Violent protest	65	90	73
X^2 (2 df)	55.60	13.79	7.67
p	<.001	<.001	<.05
"Would you be willing to engage in a demonstration, sit-in, or picketing?"			
Yes	42	77	66
No	19	65	58
X^2 (1 df)	28.64	6.71	3.10
p	<.001	<.01	<.10

Note: Entry is percentage with given riot attitude among those favoring a particular strategy; for example, of those favoring negotiation, 24% approved of the riot, and the remaining 76% disapproved.

militant leaders may have promoted approval of the riot among their followers, and moderate leaders abhorrence for the violence among their special partisans. But the protest interpretation and optimism about the riot's effects seem not to have been directly dependent upon loyalty to any particular set of black leaders.

It was alleged by many whites (foremost among whom were the police chief and the Mayor) that the riot ideology was foisted on gullible black citizens by militant black leaders. This was clearly not so. Acceptance of the riot ideology did not depend on fealty to black leadership, and it spread gradually through the black community over a period of months, as we have seen. Accordingly, black leaders' contributions to widespread acceptance of the riot ideology among black citizens appear to have occurred through the gradual diffusion of the protest interpretation, by informal communication among ordinary citizens, as they gradually found that it fit well with their standing grievances and discontents. Possibly the consensus among black leaders on interpreting the riot as a symbolic protest, presented in Chapter 9, helped to structure this communication. But the evidence strongly opposes the inference that black leaders somehow duped the citizenry into a protest interpretation by their statements during and immediately after the riot. Rather, the protest interpretation seems to have grown more gradually out of black citizens' own grievances.

Thus, the crucial antecedents of the riot ideology appear to have been the attitudinal residues of the New Urban Blacks' early political socialization (positive black identity, anti-white prejudice, and generalized political disaffection), membership in the younger generation (presumably resocialized by the New Urban Blacks), grievances against local white-dominated institutions, perceived blockage in conventional mechanisms of grievance redress, and preferences for unconventional mechanisms.

Broadly Based Acceptance of the Riot Ideology

Although the riot ideology was most enthusiastically accepted by the young and the discontented, it was not limited to such persons. Rather, acceptance of the ideology ran broadly throughout the many layers of the black population. It was *not* limited to any special subgroup or to persons who were deviant in some way. This was an important prerequisite to its long-range impact, since the riot ideology itself therefore would not polarize the black population along preexisting lines. To support this point, we can quickly show that the riot ideology was not limited to those sub-groups that, a priori, might have been thought most receptive to it.

Rioters.   The riot ideology might have been limited to the rioters themselves, possibly in rationalization for their behavior. However, as we have seen in Chapter 7, this was not the case. The riot participants were indeed considerably more likely than the non-participants to approve of the riot and to perceive greater community involvement in it. However, they were only slightly more likely to perceive the riot as a protest, to be optimistic about its effects, and were actually *less* likely to relate their attitudes about the riot to legitimate grievances. On balance, then, there is little evidence that the riot ideology was limited to (or indeed even more prevalent among) the participants themselves.

Supporters.   Another version of the rationalization possibility is that only those who liked and approved of the riot would develop the supporting cognitive apparatus of the riot ideology to rationalize their feelings. Indeed protest interpretation was highly correlated with riot approval (Table 11.1). Yet even those who disapproved of the riot were likely to view it as a symbolic protest (60 per cent of the disapprovers did so). And perception of the riot as a protest was heavily dependent on grievance levels among those who disapproved. Among those who were highly aggrieved, the riot was seen as a symbolic protest, even if a distasteful one. This relationship is documented in Table 11.7.

TABLE 11.7

Protest Interpretation as a Function of Local Grievances, among Riot Approvers and Disapprovers

	Riot approvers	Riot disapprovers
Perceived agency discrimination		
High	93%	75%
Low	89	50
X² *(1 df)*	0.30	19.25
p	n.s.	<.001
Perceived police brutality		
High	94	72
Low	86	52
X² *(1 df)*	1.41	11.91
p	n.s.	<.001
Perceived merchant exploitation		
High	91	69
Low	89	53
X² *(1 df)*	0.02	7.24
p	n.s.	<.01
All levels of grievance	90%	60%

Note: Entry is percentage high on the protest interpretation scale.

Spectators. The riot ideology might have been limited to the spectators; perhaps those experiencing the riot events most vividly would have seen the symbolic protest most clearly, sympathized most with the rioters. On the other hand, the spectators could have been the most frightened, the most likely to see the riot as an irrational drunken outburst with no purpose or meaning, the most pessimistic about any future reconciliation with grim and savagely retaliating white authorities. In fact, our events-witnessed scale correlated highly with perceived community involvement ($r = +.44$) and with riot approval ($r = +.42$); the more of the riot blacks saw, the more they liked it, and the greater numbers of their fellows they perceived as involved in it. But our scale failed to relate very systematically to protest interpretation ($r = +.11$) or riot optimism ($r = +.13$). Thus, there is no evidence that riot ideology was limited to the spectators, or to the non-spectators, either.

Exaggerating Size of Outburst. We have seen that most people in the black community perceived the riot as a massive event in close proximity to their own personal lives. However, variations in the size attributed to it did not seem to determine interpretations of the riot as a black protest. Protest interpretation was not significantly related to the "perceived community involvement" scale ($r = +.11$). Of course, variations in perceived community involvement occurred in a milieu in which virtually everyone knew the outburst to be of unprecedented violence and magnitude. However, these data indicate that the protest interpretation was *not* dependent on exaggerated or unrealistic notions of how many people had in fact been involved.

Sophisticates.   One might expect the riot ideology to be held primarily by the most sophisticated members of the community. Perception of a complex set of events of this kind as a coherent protest against just grievances must depend on some degree of intellectual sophistication. There is certainly much evidence that ideological thinking in general is limited to the highly educated in the American public (Campbell *et al.*, 1960; Converse, 1964). Second, we have seen some evidence already (Chapter 5) that the most discontented citizens were also the most educated. Consequently it might be only among the most educated that the protest ideology would come about. Third, we have indicated that the media were filled with the expressions of the riot ideology almost as soon as the riot broke out (Chapter 9). It could be that only the more literate and attentive respondents, who regularly exposed themselves to the media, would share this view. Finally, there is some evidence that, when attitudes of this kind come to take on a "mainstream" status in a given community, it is primarily the most informed and most educated citizens who hold this "mainstream" set of views (Gamson and Modigliani, 1966; Sears, 1969a). Let us then determine whether or not acceptance of the riot ideology was dependent upon sophistication, by relating it to our indicators of education, political information, and media exposure.

In brief, the riot ideology was *not* more common among the sophisticates. Of 21 possible relationships between our 7 measures of sophistication and our 3 main dimensions of riot attitude (riot approval, protest interpretation, and riot optimism), only 2 were significant. Another possibility, though, is that sophistication was necessary for the riot ideology to be dependent on local grievances, a more exacting cognitive task than merely accepting the riot ideology. In this case sophistication did play a much greater role. To test this, we related the 6 dimensions of local grievance to our protest interpretation scale, controlling on sophistication (here indexed in terms of educational level, familiarity with white politicians, and familiarity with local black politicians). For 14 of the possible 17 comparisons (one of the potential 18 could not be made because of overlapping items in 2 scales), protest was more closely related to grievance level among the more sophisticated. In other words, sophistication level tended to increase the likelihood that a respondent would base an interpretation of the riot as a symbolic protest upon his own grievances. The more sophisticated presumably saw more clearly the connection between local grievances and the riot as an alternative mechanism of grievance redress.

Nevertheless, it is also clear that the relationship between grievance and protest was highly significant even among the less sophisticated. In all cases, high grievance levels were associated with greater protest interpretation, and 9 of the 17 relationships met conventional levels of statistical significance ($p < .05$) among the less sophisticated. Thus, the strong relationship between grievance and protest interpretation was *not* limited to the more sophisticated members of the community (though it was stronger among them). This is further evidence of the broad base of support for the riot ideology.[11]

Resocialization and Future Strategies

One of the major changes wrought by the riot, we hypothesized, was the resocialization of the bulk of the younger generation to the norms typical of the New Urban Blacks—both with respect to the riot itself, as captured in the riot ideology, and, more important, with respect to future strategies of grievance redress. It must be remembered that the New Urban Blacks were both more politically disaffected and more politically sophisticated than other respondents. Thus, our hypothesis was that the junction of the New Urban Blacks and "Watts" would leave the younger generation (irrespective of background) more drawn to imaginative and unconventional strategies, particulary those emphasizing protest and violence.

Participation in the Watts Riot itself was one key indicator of this effect. We have seen in Chapter 2 that youth was a critical factor in riot participation and in Chapters 6 and 7 that it was not merely "animal spirits" that led the young into the fray. Rather, they engaged in the riot from the same sense of grievance as older rioters.

Willingness to engage in future protest demonstrations and preference for the use of violence in the future both showed the same effect. The young were much more drawn to both protest and violence than their elders, while place of origin had no significant effect, as shown in Table 11.8. The differences were clearly across generations and not within them. These results lend themselves readily to the notion that each generation "re-

[11]One important additional point is that the riot ideology was not limited to any one social class. Riot approval, perceptions of community involvement, adoption of the protest interpretation, and optimism regarding its outcome—none showed any statistically significant relationship with education, or a consistent trend, even with age controlled. As we indicated in Chapter 2, *participation* in the Los Angeles, Detroit, Newark, and other riots was *not* related to education. The educated and the uneducated were equally likely to have participated. The riot clearly had no narrow class base, either in participation or riot attitudes, contrary to Banfield's (1970) and Oberschall's (1968) speculations.

socialized" its age mates with respect to the appropriate attitudes toward newly arising events. Of course, each generation's consensus depended very much on its early socialization. The early socialization of the New Urban Blacks very plainly gave them a greater tendency toward political activism, toward positive black identity, and toward cynicism with the conventional mechanisms of grievance redress. The dominance of these attitudes among the young in the black community dictated the norms that resocialized those not brought up in this way (that is, the young southern migrants).

A Meaningful and Purposeful Protest

In sum, as the violence ended, an ideology about the riot sprang up in the black community. It embodied three dominant themes: (1) sympathy for the rioters, coupled with a disavowal of violence; (2) interpretation of the riot as a purposeful protest directed against whites, intended to express the legitimate unredressed grievances of the black population; (3) optimism about the riot's effect, with expectations of drawing more sympathetic atten-

TABLE 11.8

Strategies for the Future as a Function of Age and Place of Origin

PLACE OF ORIGIN	AGE			
	15–29	**30–44**	**45+**	**All ages**
Percentage willing to demonstrate				
Los Angeles natives	45	28	23	39
Northern migrants	32	30	25	29
Southern migrants	47	51	32	42
X^2	1.65	7.76	<1	4.76
p *(2 df)*	n.s.	<.025	n.s.	n.s.
*All origins**	44	42	30	
Percentage willing to use violence				
Los Angeles natives	20	11	8	17
Northern migrants	20	8	3	10
Southern migrants	20	13	12	14
X^2	<1.0	<.14	3.90	4.25
p *(4 df)*	n.s.	n.s.	n.s.	n.s.
All origins†	20	12	10	

*Age effect: $X^2 = 7.93$, p *(2 df)* $< .025$
†Age effect: $X^2 = 9.87$, p *(2 df)* $< .005$
Note: Entries are percentages saying, respectively, they would be willing to engage in demonstrations and responding "violent protest" (as opposed to "negotiation" or "nonviolent protest") to "What must the Negro do to get what he wants?"

tion to the area's problems from whites. These three beliefs were initially closely related but, with time, the protest interpretation became increasingly independent of riot approval; it became increasingly common to disavow the use of violence but to interpret the riot as a meaningful protest.

We have identified several origins of the riot ideology: (1) the distinctive residues of the New Urban Blacks' early political socialization—positive black identity, anti-white prejudice, and generalized political disaffection; (2) resocialization of other young blacks to generational norms dominated by the New Urban Blacks' thinking; and (3) local grievances and perceived ineffectiveness of conventional grievance redress mechanisms. Indeed, these all generated the riot ideology even more powerfully than they did riot participation. Interpretations of the riot by black leaders and white liberals, widely publicized during and immediately after the riot, also presumably played an important formative role, though their impact was indirect and gradual.

Although most widespread in the younger generation, the riot ideology, and its basis in local grievances, was not limited to any particular subgroup within the black community. Rioters and non-rioters alike, spectators and stay-at-homes, those who approved of the riot and those who disapproved of it, sophisticated and unsophisticated, educated and uneducated, young and old alike, all tended to interpret the riot as a purposeful protest against just grievances.

The riot also appears to have helped resocialize the younger generation of blacks to more favorable attitudes toward the future use of protest and violence as strategies of grievance redress.

12 Black Identity and Political Estrangement

Black Americans, since the earliest days of slavery, have suffered under the stigma of being assigned to a lower and inferior caste. This has left its mark upon them in the form of low self-concepts and derogation of themselves and their own efforts. Social scientists and black leaders alike long have believed that if this racial self-hatred could be overcome, blacks would become vastly more effective in promoting their own interests. The Watts Riot helped in exactly that way. Thus, in addition to the riot ideology, a second major enduring legacy of "Watts" was a more positive racial identity for blacks.

Positive Black Identity

Blacks' self-evaluations and evaluations of blacks as a group were mainly quite favorable in our data. The most direct measure of racial identity was the question: "What do Negroes have that whites don't have?" Almost half the sample (44 per cent) cited something desirable, 29 per cent something neutral, and only 17 per cent something undesirable.

Further, black leadership was more positively evaluated than comparable white leadership, as seen in Chapter 4. Blacks felt more positively about black elected officials than about elected officials in general. They almost universally selected a black, rather than a white, leader as the one "who represents" them best. Black leaders and black groups (except for the Black Muslims) were almost universally evaluated more favorably than white leaders and white groups, particularly at the local level; and black-originated media were rated more favorably than were white-dominated, community-wide media. In all of these cases blacks were evaluated more favorably than whites (see Tables 4.4 through 4.7).

Furthermore, ratings of black leaders invariably were highly positive, again with the notable exception of the Black Muslims. It was not a question of the lesser of two evils but of a highly positive evaluation of almost every black leader of every kind. This in itself is not evidence of positive value placed on blackness but it is a far cry from the derogation and shame supposedly characteristic of years gone by.[1]

Increased Black Pride. This positive identity in itself represents an impressive development. Most discussions of racial identity emphasize the long-term psychological change during the twentieth century from the racial self-hatred characteristic of the predominantly southern black population of 1900 to the more positive black identity of today's black militants. We have argued that the change is even more general than that, extending throughout the younger generation of northern natives. And in Chapter 5 we have demonstrated the New Urban Blacks' more positive racial identity, relative to older southern migrants from rural areas. The riot clearly speeded up this process of historical change. Positive black identity increased markedly through our period of post-riot interviewing. During October, only 45 per cent were positive; but among the December-February interviewees, 60 per cent were ($X^2 = 6.53$, 2 df, $p < .05$), as a new and more positive conception of what it meant to be black emerged in the aftermath of the violence.

The riot ideology was intimately involved with this post-riot increase in positive black identity. Specifically, it seems to have occurred as part of the interpretation of the riot as a collective symbolic protest. The relationship between black identity and our protest interpretation scale increased over the period of our interviewing; in October it was not even significant ($X^2 = 1.70$, 1 df) but by the end of the interviewing it was ($X^2 = 5.46$, 1 df, $p < .05$). On the other hand, black identity was not any more related to riot approval or optimism about the riot's effects at the end than at the beginning. We can speculate that post-riot increases in black identity were contingent on viewing the riot as a collective protest but not incompatible with condemnation of the violence or with pessimism about its effects. That is, it meant more to be black after blacks had risen up in protest, even if the protest was put down by force.

[1]These findings resemble the somewhat more direct evidence collected by Caplan and Paige following the Detroit riot (Detroit, Urban League, 1967). Blacks living in Detroit thought blacks "worked harder" than whites by an overwhelming majority, were "smarter" by a two-to-one margin, "braver" by about a nine-to-one margin, and "nicer" by about a seven-to-one margin. They regarded blacks and whites as about equally "well-behaved" and "dependable." Only on the question of happiness did they regard whites more positively; 40 per cent regarded whites as happier than blacks and 25 per cent thought blacks were happier than whites (this, incidentally, was a feature of black life yielding many of the negative responses to our black identity item).

Finally, we want to argue that this post-riot change paralleled changes occurring at the heart of the black community. We have seen repeatedly that local grievances, riot participation, and the riot ideology were not to be found merely in a few deviants, isolates, political "kooks," or half-socialized idiots. They were to be found at least as often (and frequently to an even greater degree) in the best educated, most sophisticated, most completely socialized, most modern blacks in Los Angeles. And the same is true of positive black identity: it was, in the aftermath of "Watts," truly a mainstream value in the black community.

This mainstream characteristic of black pride can be demonstrated empirically in a variety of ways. Positive black identity was significantly related to greater education ($X^2 = 15.99$, 1 df, $p < .001$). By each of our four scales of familiarity with agencies and public persons, the better informed respondents had more positive black identity (though the relationships were not significant). Since positive black identity was generally most characteristic of the New Urban Blacks, it must be considered as in the mainstream of the most important demographic group emerging among blacks. And it was significantly positively related to the other most crucial variables in our analysis: to all local grievances but one (inadequate service agencies), generalized political disaffection,[2] riot participation (Chapter 6), and the riot ideology (Chapter 11). Furthermore, black identity remained related to riot participation and the riot ideology even with demographic variables controlled; that is, within age or migrancy groups.

Thus, positive black identity was at the heart of the historical changes that led to "Watts," at the heart of its impact on the black community, and it quite likely remains at the heart of blacks' thinking today. This is a political and social fact of the utmost importance in that it represents a possibly volatile element in the midst of a complex and interdependent society. Let us then turn to a more precise definition of the limits of the changes wrought by the riot; that is, to assessing possible changes in attitudes that might have been associated with the riot ideology and with more positive black identity.

No Greater Anti-white Hostility. Increased positive black identity did not carry with it increased anti-white feelings. Mistrust of whites in fact did not increase during the time period of our post-riot interviews; distaste for attending an all-white party decreased, while distaste for racial intermarriage increased.[3] These contradictory outcomes describe a picture of no consistent increase in anti-white feeling. This supports Campbell's (1971, p. 141) finding that blacks' feelings toward whites became, if anything, more favorable across the riot span of 1964 to 1970. Thus, blacks were considerably more favorable toward whites than whites were toward blacks

[2]The six significant chi squares ranged from 4.4 to 11.7, each on 1 df.
[3]Chi squares for the changes with time for these three items were 0.04 (1 df), n.s.; 17.02 (4 df), $p < .01$; and 18.81 (4 df), $p < .01$, respectively.

before the riots, immediately afterward, and some years later (Campbell, 1971; Morris and Jeffries, 1970).

Anti-white prejudice quite definitely was not a mainstream value. Our seven indexes of education, political information, and media exposure related to it only weakly and inconsistently in direction. In the only significant case (local black politician familiarity, $X^2 = 9.72$, 1 df, $p < .01$), the more informed respondents were actually *less* prejudiced. And it will be remembered that northern urban socialization did not by itself promote anti-white feeling (Chapter 5).

Support for Militant Leadership.   No simple translation can be made from growing positive black identity to increased preference for militant leadership.[4] Evaluation of the Black Muslims was not significantly related to black identity, did not become more positive over our interview period, and actually became slightly less related to black identity over time.[5] Nor was support for militant leadership (at least as measured with the Black Muslim evaluation scale) closely related to any of the attitudinal variables we have been dealing with. It was related significantly to riot approval but not to protest interpretation, riot optimism, generalized political disaffection, or to five of the six local grievances. From this, we are inclined to think that support for militant leadership was not a particularly crucial element either in the causes or the effects of "Watts." Various militant groups have come and gone but the historical changes we have focused upon, and blacks' reactions to a white-dominated political and social system, are much more fundamental, in our view.

Political Estrangement

Increases in ethnic identity within a multi-ethnic society invariably bring with them questions of how far they will go. To what extent does identification with a subgroup imply estrangement from the institutions and values of the broader society? This has a particular importance here, because in the years after "Watts" some discussions of black power implied that many blacks had come to regard themselves as becoming a separate nation within a nation, owing little loyalty to the conventional political authorities, and preferring to go their own way. Is there any evidence, then, for increasing estrangement among blacks? By "estrangement," we mean a lack of what Easton and Dennis (1969) have termed "diffuse support" for the political system (and here we wish also to include economic and other conventional

---

[4]See Marx (1969) and Sears (1969a) for additional discussion of the more general theoretical position that policy attitudes frequently are not closely related to support for political leaders and groups that support them.

[5]Chi squares for the first two relationships were 2.4 (1 df) and 3.2 (2 df), both n.s.

institutions of American life, not simply focusing upon political institutions and rules).

Traditional American Values.   Blacks in Los Angeles shared with white citizens the major mainstream values of American life. One of these is the value of *hard work* for getting what you want. As we have seen in Chapter 4, over half of the respondents saw either education or hard work as being the primary means by which blacks could get what they want, while another 19 per cent saw the equally conventional (though not conventionally individualistic) political participation as the answer. Only 3 per cent contended that violence was necessary. Marx (1969) also cited post-riot evidence for blacks' retaining the belief that "if you try hard enough, you can get what you want." Seeman, Bishop, and Grigsby (1971) similarly reported evidence that blacks in Los Angeles interviewed after the riot were as willing as whites to move to a new job for a promotion, even if it meant giving up friendship ties in the community.

Another core mainstream American value is the value of the *family*. Seeman et al. (1971) report that blacks did not differ materially from whites of comparable occupational status in choosing the value of being with family over a promotion. Post-riot blacks in Watts were fully as *religious* as whites (McConahay, 1970a) and in that sense adhered as closely to this set of mainstream American values. Finally, blacks have been at least as *optimistic* about the future as have whites, both with respect to their own personal lives and to the advances of the other blacks (Beardwood, 1968; Brink and Harris, 1967; see also our discussion of personal optimism in Chapter 5).

Commitment to the Political System.   Attachment to the political system is acquired in childhood political socialization (see Dawson and Prewitt, 1969; Easton and Dennis, 1969). Studies of black children in various communities (not Los Angeles) following the riot give little evidence that black children have very much less "diffuse support" for the American political system than have white children. Black and white children have not differed markedly in adherence to democratic principles (Laurence, 1970), political trust or disaffection (Greenberg, 1969; Rodgers and Taylor, 1971), support for the government and President (Greenberg, 1970a, 1970b), or tendency to comply with the law (Rodgers and Taylor, 1970; Engstrom, 1970). Black children have consistently been far more negative toward the police than have white children (Laurence, 1970; Greenberg, 1970b; Engstrom, 1970; Rodgers and Taylor, 1971), but this seems to be due more to the reality problems that blacks have with police (as discussed in Chapter 4) rather than to any lack of commitment to the political and authority system per se.

What about indicators of commitment to the political system in adulthood? Perhaps the most extreme test of loyalty to a system is a willingness to give up one's life against a foreign enemy. There is every evidence that blacks consistently have maintained considerable loyalty to the United States in these terms (Brink and Harris, 1966; Marx, 1969).[6]

Similarly, separatism has not found wide favor, even in the urban ghettos. Specific items of separatist ideology attract little black support. In the post-riot era, blacks increasingly supported desegregation in a number of different matters (Campbell, 1971). And separatist advocates have been opposed more often than they have been supported, whereas more moderate leaders typically have received almost universal support from black samples (Brink and Harris, 1966; Campbell and Schuman, 1968; Sears, 1969a). Marx (1969) has presented a particularly careful review of many surveys of blacks conducted between 1966 and 1969, almost all of which found separatist and black power leadership and policy positions to be overwhelmingly rejected. This rejection of separatism does not imply rejection of positive black identity, of course, or even of a more generalized notion of "black power." It simply means that most blacks generally reject the notion of radical changes in the political system.

Grievance Redress Mechanisms.   Similarly, as reported in Chapter 4, the majority of blacks in our survey supported the conventional, not the unconventional, mechanisms for redressing grievances. Most believed in conventional political participation, were willing to resort to the usual administrative mechanism for dealing with police mistreatment, and were much more attracted to negotiation, nonviolent protest, or peaceful demonstrations than they were to the use of violence. Over a large number of surveys, typically only about 10 per cent to 15 per cent of any sample of blacks felt that violence was necessary to achieve their goals (Campbell and Schuman, 1968; Levy, 1968; Beardwood, 1968; Meyer, 1968). Similar percentages typically engaged in rioting itself, though somewhat larger fractions have been supportive of riots per se (Marx, 1969).

Before the riot, northern blacks' conventional political participation was at an all-time high. It had increased sharply in the postwar period. For example, increases in northern black politicization from 1952 to 1964 have been documented by Riley and Sears (unpublished data). They compared northern urban blacks and whites across the 12 years, based on data from the University of Michigan's Survey Research Center. In 1952 blacks were considerably behind whites in political involvement, voter registration, and political participation. Yet, in 1964 the races did not differ at all on any of these three dimensions. This sudden equality was due to very substantial

[6]There are other dimensions of commitment to the system on which post-riot data are not available but on which blacks historically have proven highly supportive. These include viewing the major institutions of American society as helpful to black rights (Brink and Harris, 1966) and belief in democratic principles, such as freedom of speech (Laurence, 1970; Stouffer, 1955), lack of anti-Semitism (Erskine, 1965; Marx, 1969), and racial egalitarianism (Erskine, 1967; 1968).

increases in politicization among blacks—and the largest increases (relative to whites) were among the younger and better-educated blacks, among our New Urban Blacks. Blacks in 1964 were also more partisan than even northern white Democrats: they were more likely to vote a straight ticket, to hold the Democratic Party's liberal positions both on racial and on non-racial issues, and to perceive the party's stands accurately.

Still, there are ominous indications about the course of events since 1965. There is some evidence that the involvement of blacks in conventional political action diminished after the riot, even before the advent of a national administration oriented toward a "(white) southern strategy." The census has estimated that turnout in the 1968 presidential election was down 11 per cent from 1964 among non-southern blacks and down only 3 per cent among whites (U.S. Bureau of the Census, 1969). Similarly, turnout in the 1970 congressional elections was down 1 per cent from 1966, and registration was down 4 per cent (U.S. Bureau of the Census, 1970). Thus, it should by no means be taken for granted that blacks' considerable rise in political sophistication in recent years will continue to be channeled into conventional political activity.

In conclusion, then, it is evident by all these indicators that the riot did not provide the occasion for widespread estrangement from conventional American values and from the American political or economic system among northern urban blacks. During the post-riot period, despite the models of rebellion and insurrection represented in the riot, blacks remained largely loyal to conventional values. They remained basically committed to the American system, and only a relatively small minority felt violence was a necessary mechanism of grievance redress.

Yet it would be exceeding our data to claim the same holds true today or, if it does, that it will continue. The slackened voting rates of northern blacks is ominous. Moreover, the situation is a volatile one and there has been a major change in federal policy. It also would be foolhardy of us to claim we know what is in the minds of blacks today or to try to predict the future. All we can suggest here is that the riot did not itself, and the other urban riots did not in their cumulative impact, precipitate a quick change in blacks to a more estranged view of society.

Dissatisfaction and Optimism about the Future

Much of what we have presented already in this book reveals the very high levels of chronic dissatisfaction within the black population. The grievances described in Chapter 4 have been repeatedly found in other cities as well (Campbell and Schuman, 1968). Almost all official government commission reports on the urban rioting and almost all surveys done on blacks have revealed high levels of dissatisfaction in numerous areas of life, particularly focusing on the police, merchants, schools, employment, service agencies, and housing. Dissatisfaction was there in 1965; it is there today.

This widespread discontent most likely reflects dissatisfaction with current incumbents and their policies rather than a more general loss of attachment to the American political and economic system. First, as indicated above, the polls from 1963 to 1968 revealed that the proportion of blacks endorsing the use of violence as a tactic for advancing their cause has remained consistently low.

Second, there is the blacks' impressive level of discrimination in regard to white Americans. Our data clearly indicate that in 1965 they had not rejected their white liberal allies but were strongly anti-Republican. Similarly, they were much more favorable to the federal than to local government. And in the years since, their voting has been amazingly selective at all levels.

Third, the most dissatisfied blacks were actually the *most* optimistic that the Watts Riot would do some good. We have gone into these data in some detail elsewhere (Sears and McConahay, 1970b) and do not need to examine them in detail again. Briefly, optimism was positively related to agency discrimination, evaluations of service agencies as inadequate, perceived police brutality, and strong disapproval of Chief Parker. However, optimism was *not* related to generalized political disaffection, to disapproval of the local political structure, or to attitudes toward civil rights groups or the white news media. Thus, the major specific grievances associated with optimism grew out of dissatisfaction with treatment at the hands of the most conservative and bureaucratic local administrative agencies, especially the police.

Furthermore, optimism was greatest among those who saw attention seeking as the riot's main purpose and its main effect, rather than among those who saw its purposes and effects in instrumental or merely expressive terms. When asked why it had helped or hurt the black's cause (whichever the respondent indicated), 68 per cent were optimistic among those who felt its effects were attention seeking, 48 per cent optimistic among those responding in terms of effects on whites, but only 37 per cent optimistic of those who foresaw primarily instrumental effects and 23 per cent optimistic of those who responded in terms of effects on blacks (Sears and McConahay, 1970b). Thus, the blacks who were most frustrated were actually the most hopeful, and they were hopeful that these white-dominated agencies would change with sufficient prodding.

That the most frustrated should feel most hopeful about their adversaries' potential for change seems almost miraculous. It could provide a major impetus for positive steps to racial reconciliation, countering the many pressures toward conflict and polarization. But for two reasons we doubt that this hopefulness will last. First, optimism about the riot's effects seems to grow out of the optimism about blacks' progress more characteristic of the integrationist mentality of the early migrants from the South. Most optimistic were those in transition between the old southern migrant and the New Urban Black; that is the young migrants and the older natives. Optimism was also greatest among those most positive toward old-fashioned assimilationist leadership ($X^2 = 5.96$, 1 df, $p < .05$) and among those high in conventional political participation ($X^2 = 4.93$, 1 df, $p < .05$). Second, if white public opinion and major governmental bodies become more flagrantly hostile to blacks and responsive to the symbolic needs of a conservative white constituency, the dissatisfied may no longer feel confident about the ultimately benevolent and caring response of whites. The Nixon Administration's Supreme Court nominations and its Justice Department's civil rights activity represent sufficiently sharp reversals of past liberalism to provide a test of this latter point.

The Riot's Effects

In sum, a second major legacy of the riot, along with the riot ideology, was increased pride in blackness. Blacks' image of blackness became notably more positive over time, following the riot. Black pride was particularly strong among the New Urban Blacks. It appeared to have become a core mainstream value in the contemporary northern urban ghetto, where the best educated and best informed blacks showed the highest levels of black pride.

The riot did not appear to have a number of other commonly assumed effects. It did not increase anti-white prejudice or attraction to militant leadership, and indeed both these dimensions appear to have worked quite independently of black identity. Our evidence also indicated that the riot did not estrange the black community from the American political system or from basic American values. And the most aggrieved blacks were the most hopeful that the riot would awaken whites' social consciousness to sympathetic action.

While a sizable minority had become frustrated with conventional mechanisms of grievance redress, most still clung to them and had not yet concluded that violence was a necessary alternative. There was, however, some evidence of declining conventional political activity, in part reflecting blacks' increased versatility in trying to achieve their aims, though perhaps more recently due to loss of faith in the benevolence of the most important American institutions, particularly the federal government. What that bodes for the future, we shall consider in our final chapter.

13 Politics, Violence, and the Future

In this, our final chapter, we shall attempt to summarize our main line of argument, including our most important empirical findings; to consider the theoretical relevance of those findings; and to look generally at the future of urban violence and race relations in America.

Principal Empirical Findings

We have analyzed the Watts Riot as the collision of a rapidly changing black population with an indifferent white population and the institutions it controlled. As the first of the major confrontations of the races in the North or West, "Watts" was a highly significant historical point of demarcation.

The Historical Context. Demographic data indicated that those who settled Los Angeles in its formative boom years (that is, between the world wars) were disproportionately American-born, white, Protestant families from the Midwest, who lived in owner-occupied, single-family homes in low-density areas. We speculated that due to their early socialization and their middle-class, property-oriented life style, such people would be unusually likely to cling to traditional American values of thrift, hard work, individualism, private property, and a preference for achievement, as opposed to more humanistic values.

To our surprise, and despite their conservative reputations, Los Angeles whites did not have a long history of conservative voting behavior, nor did they express much racial prejudice in the old-fashioned or red-necked form. Much more common was "symbolic racism," a blend of staunch adherence to traditional American moral values with mild degrees of fear or antagonism toward blacks. It dates, we suggested, from childhood social-

196

ization, both of traditional moral values and of the mild stereotyped prejudice common to northern whites throughout the first half of the twentieth century. This perpetuated an archaic and anachronistic view of blacks, essentially unmodified from the attitudes most white adults acquired as children decades earlier.

The persistence of this view over so many years is attributable both to the strength of early socialization on such matters and to white adults' poverty of experience with blacks. We described this lack of reality experience as "black invisibility" and offered three possible reasons for its ubiquity in pre-riot Los Angeles: (1) prewar white in-migrants to Los Angeles were especially naive racially because they came from small midwestern cities or rural areas where they had encountered few blacks or ethnics; (2) great racial isolation in Los Angeles kept direct personal contacts between the races to a minimum; and (3) the media gave little attention to racial minorities. Due to "black invisibility" most whites had little opportunity to test and correct their childhood beliefs about blacks and their lives. Thus, the New Urban Blacks appeared doubly new, surprising, and frightening to whites. We further speculated that symbolic racism had exerted little tangible influence on whites' voting until the 1960s, but had exercised a major impact upon the policies of public and private institutions, which were oriented principally toward the interests and values of the white middle class.

A host of studies have demonstrated, unequivocally, the unfair and unequal treatment that blacks received across the nation and in Los Angeles as a result of these policies. It is now clear that this treatment proved exceptionally irritating to blacks. In Chapter 4, we presented data documenting blacks' high level of grievance and discontent with the operation of local white-dominated authorities and institutions. Moreover, each of the conventional mechanisms for redressing these grievances appeared blocked and ineffective to almost half the black population.

The New Urban Blacks.   The other main historical stream we analyzed was the socio-psychological effects of the massive black population shifts of the twentieth century. Before World War I, the black population was primarily southern, rural, agrarian, and poorly educated. Now, it is nationwide, urbanized, industrialized, considerably better educated, and increasingly youthful. Only in the last years before the riot, however, had these shifts finally managed to produce large numbers of young blacks who had been entirely brought up and educated in northern and western cities. We called this large new generation the "New Urban Blacks."

The socialization of the New Urban Blacks differed from that of older, migrant, rural, and/or less educated blacks, resulting in such distinctive racial and political orientations as more positive black identity, generalized political disaffection, and political sophistication. Also, the New Urban Blacks had greater optimism about their personal futures, slightly higher aspirations, and a significantly greater degree of subjective status deprivation and dissatisfaction than older and southern-reared blacks.

The young of all backgrounds had had greater experience than the old with novel techniques of grievance redress and social change, such as demonstrations and rioting, and only slightly less experience with conventional techniques. Similarly, they were more favorable toward the use of demonstrations and violence in the future. Here, in particular, we felt the resocializing legacy of the civil rights movement could be observed.

However, the New Urban Blacks shared with other blacks their considerable lack of enthusiasm for conservative white political officeholders and their sense of grievance about local conditions and the white authorities' role in them.

Thus, the new generation of blacks questioned the status quo, refusing to adapt fatalistically to it. They felt their elders' grievances against the insensitivity and indifference of white authorities but, rather than placing full faith in the conventional workings of the democratic process, they leaned toward new and emergent techniques of social change, and sometimes toward violence.

The Riot.   The riot was triggered by a clash between the police and a black family. This was a typical "grievance," involving an individual black who felt mistreated by an unsympathetic institution, largely managed and staffed by whites, following its standard operating procedures.[1] However, the outcome of this individual grievance was atypical. Instead of bureaucratic inaction and disregard, the incident mobilized an enormous number of blacks into violent protest.

The event itself was a watershed. After "Watts" and the subsequent riots, American race relations would never be the same. Objectively, the riot was of great magnitude. The riot's subjective magnitude was equally impressive. In an area larger than the city of San Francisco, and half again the size of Manhattan, a majority of the respondents felt the people in their own neighborhoods had been "very" or "somewhat" active in the rioting. Even among the people who themselves had stayed out of the streets, almost half thought their own neighborhood was involved. A majority of the area's residents personally had witnessed the crowds, and the looting and burning of the stores. Indeed, one of the most striking aspects of the riot is how closely it touched the black population throughout this vast area of Los Angeles.

[1]The McCone Commission Report (Governor's Commission, 1966, pp. 11–12) "officially" declared that the handling of the Frye incident was routine and that standard procedures were used. The question of what these standard procedures and practices were doing to produce the explosion that followed was ignored because, in *"Catch 22"* fashion, the "investigators" had determined that the procedures were standard and that was sufficient. This, to us, is crucial to the understanding of white-dominated institutions' production of grievances among blacks before, during and after the riot.

Individual Riot Participation.   The widespread sense of grievance among blacks of all ages and backgrounds about their treatment by local agencies and authorities and the special disaffections and racial attitudes of the New Urban Blacks merged to produce violent protest. Riot participation, we hypothesized, served as the functional equivalent of more conventional grievance redress mechanisms, which blacks perceived as ineffective. This hypothesis was tested in a variety of ways.

The riot participants' demographic characteristics fit this analysis. They were disproportionately composed of young natives to Los Angeles, and the young males were more likely to have been unemployed, but the rioters were not otherwise demographically distinct—not especially uneducated, newcomers from the South, or products of broken homes. Additionally, there is every reason to believe they were not criminals, riffraff, members of the underclass, communists, or Black Muslims, contrary to theories popular among whites (see Chapters 2 and 7).

Riot participation was positively related to the hypothesized dispositions of the New Urban Blacks: (1) generalized political disaffection; (2) positive black identity; (3) anti-white hostility; and (4) optimism about one's own personal future and subjective status deprivation. Additionally, (5) political sophistication was generally positively, but not significantly, related to riot participation. Riot participation was also positively related to grievances against a variety of local white-dominated institutions, to mistrust of conventional mechanisms of grievance redress, and to support for extraordinary mechanisms, such as demonstrations and violent protest.

The Legacy of "Watts."   Whites, their attitudes and behaviors, set the stage for the emergence of conditions that produced the rioting. In addition, many blacks felt that whites were the audience they hoped to impress sympathetically by the violence. In this regard their hopes were mostly ill-founded. White leaders were bewildered at the start of the rioting but quickly moved toward a tough, hardline stance of law enforcement at all costs. Black leaders called for a halt to the violence but coupled this with a message to whites articulating the many black grievances. Black leaders were joined, somewhat meekly, by white liberals who also deplored the violence and called for social reform. The black and white mass publics reacted as did their leaders. Both were frightened, but blacks tended to express understanding for the rioters while whites called for repression. The result was a nationwide polarization over issues surrounding the rioting.

Within the black community, grievances and pride in being black preceded the riot but the articulation and elaboration of them subsequently created the ideology of "Watts" and increased black pride—the two most important long-term products of the rioting.

The riot ideology included three main elements: (1) sympathy for the rioters; (2) interpretation of the riot as a purposeful protest against legitimate grievances; and (3) optimism about the effects of the riot. These spread widely throughout the black community in the months afterwards, particularly the interpretation of the riot as a meaningful protest. The ideology was particularly common among the young but did not depend upon any one socialization background. Apparently, the New Urban Blacks were able to "resocialize" their southern age peers to generational interpretations of this novel event. The elements of the ideology were also closely related to the same attitudes we have identified earlier as generating riot participation: local grievances, lack of faith in conventional mechanisms of grievance redress, generalized political disaffection, positive black identity, and anti-white prejudice.

A second major legacy of the riot, described in Chapter 12, was increased black pride. We have presented evidence that it represented a mainstream value within the black community after the riot. On the other hand, the riot did not increase anti-white hostility, attraction to militant leadership, or estrangement from the American political system or basic American values, and it did not reduce blacks' faith in conventional political action.

Theoretical Analysis

Our main goal has been to understand the origins and immediate effects of recent ghetto riots. First of all, we speculated that a new demographic and social-psychological type, the New Urban Black, had emerged in the ghetto with sufficient numerical strength to influence its norms, values, and attitudes. Basically, the origins of riot participation and the riot ideology were traced in each case to the striking demographic changes that had occurred among the blacks in the last half-century. We proposed that three attitudinal factors mediated the effects of these demographic changes upon riot participation. The *political socialization hypothesis* assumed that the New Urban Blacks had received a new kind of political socialization, resulting in greater political disaffection and a new, emergent orientation to political and social change. The *subjective status deprivation hypothesis* assumed that the New Urban Blacks had been socialized to higher comparison levels, resulting in a greater sense of subjective deprivation. The *functional equivalent hypothesis* assumed that the realities of life in a major northern city had left many black residents (regardless of socialization) with strong grievances against local white authorities and institutions. How well did the data fit these three hypotheses of our politics of violence theory?

The New Urban Blacks' *political socialization* was hypothesized to have made them higher than other blacks in generalized political disaffection, positive black identity, anti-white antagonism, and political sophistication. A variant of the political socialization approach hypothesized that new events (such as the riot) and future political strategies would be evaluated by resocialization to the norms of one's generation, rather than being derived principally from early political socialization. Hence, favorable attitudes toward the riot, and toward future protest and violence in general, were expected to be characteristic of the younger generation regardless of socialization background. The New Urban Blacks' socialization also was expected to leave them with higher aspirations and more optimism but with a greater sense of *subjective status deprivation* about their own personal lives than older southern-socialized blacks. All of these hypotheses were borne out by the data, except that the New Urban Blacks were not especially anti-white, nor was there much evidence of resocialization regarding projected effects of the rioting.

Finally, we tested the notion that the rioting was an attempt to redress grievances by unconventional action because the more conventional mechanisms of grievance redress were blocked. Blacks of all generations and socialization backgrounds shared a common sense of grievance against local white authorities and institutions. We thus predicted that a high level of grievance and disaffection from conventional mechanisms of grievance redress would be associated with riot participation. And this indeed did occur. Relative to nonrioters, the rioters were more subjectively deprived, more politically disaffected, had more positive black identity, had greater anti-white hostility, and were given to preferences for unconventional or violent political strategies (Chapter 6). And these variables related to riot ideology even more strongly than to riot participation (Chapter 11).

Alternative Theories.   We constructed and then rejected empirically one formal nonpolitical alternative to our politics of violence theory, "the random outburst theory" (Chapter 7). We also presented the far less formalized "theories" offered by authorities and by the general public. We described the conspiracy, contagion, riffraff, underclass, family life breakdown, and southern newcomer "theories" and indicated that, with the exception of unemployed males, who were quite active, they did not fit the data (Chapter 2). The most systematic alternative formulation we considered was Banfield's (1970) "fun and profit" theory. We described and refuted empirically his three main propositions: that the rioting simply reflected greater propensity to violence among lower classes, southerners, and the young; that it was merely a rampage or foray for pillage, rather than being motivated by identifiable and genuine discontents; and that the riot ideology merely represented post hoc rationalizations.

All this, however, is simply evidence against the proposition that social contagion or some other nonpolitical motive was the *principal* or primary factor in producing riot participation. It is not logically inconsistent with our data to suspect that many people joined in the riot itself simply because they happened to be in an area where others were throwing stones or looting burning stores. Many others probably joined in simply because a friend already was involved and it looked as if the episode might be convivial. However, we think that the various relationships we found between political attitudes and riot participation provide powerful evidence that most of the participants, especially those who kept the riot going after the first few hours, were people who converged upon the action due to their social, psychological, and *political* predispositions. Hence, we think that our politics of violence theory gives a more complete understanding of the significance of the event than do these nonpolitical alternatives.

Recommendations

Research into policy relevant areas usually concludes with recommendations but we are going to depart from the usual. America does not lack for recommendations concerning urban violence. Following the Chicago riots of 1919, a commission met for three years, investigated the riots thoroughly, and made recommendations. After the Harlem and Detroit riots during World War II, recommendations were made. After "Watts", the McCone Commission made recommendations. After the violent summer of 1967, the Kerner Commission made recommendations. As Kenneth Clark has pointed out, each commission made similar recommendations. Except for purely local references, the recommendations could have been written by the same person.

The recommendations invariably called for a reduction of unemployment, opening of the job structure to blacks, reform of education and of programs to improve the scholastic attainments of blacks, reform of the welfare system (to cut costs) and to give the recipients "who wanted to work" assistance in getting a job, improvement of housing quality and availability, and, finally, suggestions for future police strategies. With the exception of this last, none of the recommendations made since 1919 has been pursued with any vigor and most have remained entombed in the bound official reports to be resurrected after the next series of riots.

Since the recommendations never have been acted upon, it is probably irrelevant to point out that our research (and much of the research of the Kerner Commission staff) found little direct effect of education, housing, and welfare upon riot participation. Blacks did have grievances in these areas and, indeed, discrimination, police mistreatment, and merchant exploitation must be eliminated, and insensitivity and indifference must be reduced in service agencies, among white politicians, and the media. All of these problems are well known. They are thoroughly documented in the official government reports, in many journalists' books and articles, and in our own data on blacks' perceptions. Blacks' grievances reflect genuine reality problems about life in the ghetto and these obviously ought to be attacked directly. At the same time, our data suggest caution in blindly pursuing these standard liberal recommendations.

Lack of Faith in Standard Procedures.   Our society needs to go considerably beyond an attack on these proximate causes of black grievances. For it must be recognized by whites that blacks, even in 1965 and 1966, did not have great faith in the standard American mechanisms for dealing with reality problems. A large minority—especially among the New Urban Blacks—perceived these grievance redress mechanisms as being biased and ineffective in dealing with the particular and possibly unique needs of blacks.

Each of the standard grievance mechanisms we examined is indeed biased to suit the special aptitudes and habits of the white middle class. At this date, the justification for this observation should be nearly self-evident (but, if not, see Silberman, 1964; Jacobs, 1967; Milbrath, 1965; Coleman et al., 1966; Moynihan, 1970). Everything else being equal, a child of the white middle class is bound to find it easier to be a material and status success, to get redress "through channels," and to affect government policy in conventional politics. The very "rules of the game" have been written to favor the advantaged. Invisible and powerless groups in our society are rarely consulted in the drafting of these standard procedures.

Thus the reflexive liberal reaction to the riot was as erroneous as the conservative reaction, though the error was subtler. Conservatives denied that the grievances were legitimate or that they even existed. The liberal's response was to say that these problems existed and that what we had to do was to apply more rigorously our fair, just, honest, efficient, normal mechanisms for handling such problems, so that we would deal with people on their merits, fairly and impartially, reasonably and objectively. This misses the point. The point is that, as long as the "rules of the game" are drawn up and administered by middle-class whites, they are bound to be biased to favor the status quo and particularly middle-class whites. "Impartiality" means making decisions on the basis of dimensions that middle-class whites are good at (for instance, getting good grades, as opposed, for example, to being warm and tender); "efficiency" means keeping costs (and the taxes paid by the white middle class) down, not helping the disadvantaged more; "honesty" means disregarding friendship, kinship, and so forth, and considering only individualistic attributes; "law and justice" means placing one's fate in a system of rules made up by and applied by middle-class whites.

We do not wish to imply, by any means, that the "standard procedures" are invariably unfair to blacks. We do suggest, however, that many blacks' lack of faith in the standard procedures has a sound reality basis, that such procedures are bound to be biased in the long run as long as blacks have little or no power over them. And we suggest that, unless whites understand this, their recommendations will miss the mark.

Education and Disaffection.   Many proposals for dealing with urban disorder have implied or assumed that the disorder resulted from the inadequacies or failures of the schools as agents of social control. Recent polls have shown that Americans put particularly great faith in education as a means of dealing with our racial conflict (Erskine, 1967). Indeed, most white leaders place programs for increasing blacks' educational opportunities near the top of their list of recommendations for easing racial tensions.

Our comparison of better and lesser educated respondents in Chapter 5 may help us to perceive the direction in which increased education for blacks would lead us, in politics, race relations, and urban conflict. Let us quickly review those findings. First, education increased political disaffection. This is the exact opposite of the effect education typically has had upon whites. Moreover, education either increased or did not reduce specific grievances with the local welfare, administrative, and enforcement agencies, and it did not improve evaluations of the local political structure. Second, education increased politicization: political contact, activity, and sophistication. More important, it did so selectively, increasing the attention paid to the world of black politics more than to that of white. White officeholders were regarded in the same way by both educated and uneducated blacks but the educated were much more favorable to black politicians, black national leaders, and black interest groups. The picture of the educated black which these data suggest is of a sophisticated political person—one who participates fully in politics, knows the political actors, and can discriminate his friends from his enemies.

For both the high school and college educated, cynicism and disaffection were quite high. The educated black was working in the political arena and felt some possible power but he did not trust the system. Furthermore, the effects of education were quite similar at all age levels. Young blacks may have become more vocal but the cynical feeling was present among the educated of every generation.

Those who speak rather glibly of education as *the* solution to our urban racial conflict are convicted of naiveté by these data. Without other reforms, which will open the opportunity structure and make the political system more responsive to the legitimate grievances and aspirations of blacks, the principal effect of more education could be increased politicization and increased conflict. Conflict is not an evil in and of itself. It is an integral part of the political process. It is the nature of the conflict that is important for a creative, just, and stable society. When the conflict becomes violent, all suffer a loss of freedom, even those not directly involved.

In our black sample, increased education was accompanied not only by increased political sophistication but also by a sense of cynicism and distrust. These latter were strongly related to the endorsement of violence and participation in the riot. Thus, increased education in conjunction with few other opportunities and a frozen or repressive political structure could produce greater cynicism leading to the politics of violence. Increased education accompanied by an open system could produce greater political efficacy leading to the politics of negotiation and nonviolent conflict. In either case, increased education will not serve to pacify the New Urban Blacks.

Symbolic Changes.   As Edelman (1971) has pointed out, politics is only partially involved with tangible benefits, and the politics of violence was no exception. Symbols and abstract values were more central to the rioting and the post-riot polarization than were more concrete expressions of materialistic self-interest. Our black respondents' most vivid grievances concerned white authorities' and agencies' mistreatment of blacks (or residents of the Curfew Zone) as a group, rather than complaints about their own personal problems. Some respondents said they had been victims of police mistreatment—but much more common was the feeling that it happened often to blacks in the area. Some had suffered racial discrimination—but much more common was the feeling that it happened to blacks generally. The New Urban Blacks were especially sensitive to symbolic politics. Their discontents and attitudes were more focused upon generalized political disaffection (the feeling that there is something wrong with the system) and black pride than upon deficits in their own personal life situations.

Thus, if somehow all the reality-based grievances were to be removed overnight, it is highly unlikely that generalized political disaffection would be reduced substantially or that there would be a change in the relative balance of black pride and anti-white antagonism. This is not to suggest that efforts to reduce the tangible grievances should be dispensed with. Rather, it is a caution that recommendations that focus mechanically on the "nuts and bolts" of personal economic interest probably will not have the impact anticipated by white leaders.

Furthermore, we are not suggesting a cynical manipulation of symbols to produce quiescence. Jobs, housing, education, anti-discrimination laws— all of these are necessary, but insufficient answers to mounting black disaffection. In addition, *symbolic gestures* are called for, to deal with symbolic discontents. That a presidential candidate or a mayor would walk through the streets of Harlem or Watts or that a President would use the phrase "we shall overcome" in a message on civil rights has a profound positive effect. When a President places white southerners of known segregationist sympathies in high executive or judicial places, or when a mayor stands staunchly behind policemen involved in reckless shoot-outs with minority individuals, the effects are equally profound.

With these cautions we conclude our "recommendations." It is obvious that America does not lack for recommendations. What she lacks is equally obvious and very simple: the will to implement them. Since we doubt that white America is on the verge of suddenly acquiring this will, we feel little compulsion to add further to the list of recommendations. True to our role as social scientists, however, we will make a series of predictions that grow out of our research.

Predictions for the Future

Increasing Ghetto Tensions.   Our data point to increasing tensions in the ghetto, stemming from three separate sources: socialization, grievances, and education.

The new socialization of the New Urban Blacks is replacing the trusting but more naive and unsophisticated older generation with more disaffected and sophisticated persons who personally have been exposed to considerably more police mistreatment, who have had more experience with protest demonstrations or riots, and who are a little less likely to have engaged in conventional political activity. Hence, there will be an increase in the number of persons who are willing to use violence and confrontation rather than tedious bureaucratic actions as strategies for social change.

To this must be added the high grievance level of older generations toward specific authorities and agencies. These elders were strongly aggrieved about many aspects of their lives and we see no obvious reason to predict that these grievances will diminish. Furthermore, as the educational level continues to rise, our data give every reason for predicting even greater disaffection.

Thus the "tinderbox condition" of the modern black ghetto is not simply a matter of the generation gap in black society. Rather, the explosive mixture is created by a high level of grievance across all generations and subgroups, combined with a generation gap regarding strategies and approaches to politics. The New Urban Blacks have experienced, and are willing to try, a wider variety of possible political approaches than their elders—including the politics of violence. Since the demographic trends that produced the New Urban Blacks will not be reversed and the grievances will not be redressed as long as whites remain indifferent or preoccupied, tension will increase. Whites probably will interpret their own indifference as indicating a reduction in tensions among blacks but that will be a grave error, one with equally grave consequences.

Strategies for the Future.   In what ways might we expect blacks to attempt to force whites to pay attention to them in the years ahead? What strategies can we expect to see in the future?

The easiest prediction to make is that we shall have more violence. Given the stormy history of American race relations, this is the safest prediction we can make. However, the violence we foresee will not take the form of many large-scale riots. The psychological benefits of the large riots offset their terrible cost to blacks but new riots would have diminishing returns, especially in view of the massive anti-personnel armaments concentrated in the hands of the police and national guard. Instead of large riots, we shall see a series of guerrilla-type attacks upon the police and other white agents in the ghetto. Already we have seen the first stages of this form of violence.

This violence, however, seems likely to be only one of many techniques that will be tried. Already blacks have used countless ingenious and often novel techniques: sit-ins, bus boycotts, protest marches, assassinations, demands for reparations, quotas for blacks' admission to the white opportunity structure, kidnapping of dignitaries, memberships on corporate boards of directors and student-faculty committees in universities, strikes, tutoring, studying, legal action, and formation of caucuses. Some will fail miserably. Others will be successful, as many efforts to open up universities and scholarly societies to blacks and their special concerns have been. The range and ingenuity of the techniques used in the past 15 years has added an entirely new dimension to American political action and we can expect great creativity and enormous flexibility in the years ahead.

Many of these strategies will involve some form of conventional politics. Despite the New Urban Blacks' considerable political disaffection, we foresee no mass withdrawal from electoral politics. Rather, black voters seem more likely to vote selectively and en bloc. Black candidates, in particular, appear to be able to accumulate mass support from all segments of the black electorate. Even the New Urban Blacks are likely to support them regularly, probably showing considerably more enthusiasm for candidates who express a little disaffection than for moderates dedicated to "the system" or for radicals who do not share their basically positive evaluations of black leaders and white liberals. Yet it is most unlikely that the New Urban Blacks will place sole reliance upon electoral politics due to their preferences for strategic flexibility.

This, then, is our major prediction for blacks' actions in the future: there will be violence, yes, but it will take many forms and it will be accompanied by an unimaginably broad range of other techniques for social action, including conventional politics. Nothing would be a greater error than to expect a stereotyped repetition of any single technique attempted in the past.

American Institutions. The manner in which whites conduct their political affairs will have a major effect upon the strategies chosen. In Chapter 4, we pointed out the sharp contrast, in blacks' perceptions, between the indifferent and intransigent proximate local whites and the benevolent and sympathetic, though more remote, federal establishment. The riot contained a two-pronged "message" for whites. The angry retaliatory element in the message was directed at these immediately frustrating local institutions. They were perceived as the direct instigators of the blacks' frustration and the anger was directed at them. On the other hand, the plea for sympathetic attention, we believe, was addressed to the broader American institutions, and indeed the broader American public, which were thought to be basically sympathetic.

The presidency in particular has symbolized the basic benevolence of these national institutions. From Franklin D. Roosevelt through Lyndon Johnson, the American presidency (and the judiciary it has appointed) has been viewed by blacks as a rather paternal, benevolent, and sympathetic institution.

Thus, earlier generations of blacks have had their hopes for the future, their feeling that there was "light at the end of the tunnel," sustained by the belief that the presidency and the federal government as a whole could be trusted to work in their behalf to remove the frustration and discrimination at the local level. The strategies of the many civil rights groups, whose actions also helped to sustain the hopes of the older generations, were clearly predicated upon this local-federal dichotomy. They attacked local conditions in a manner designed to invoke sympathetic action from the President, the Congress, and the federal judiciary.

The future is less hopeful on this score. From the beginning of the New Deal to the death of John F. Kennedy, race was scarcely ever a partisan political issue outside the South. With the Goldwater candidacy and myriad other local and national events since then, it has quite clearly become a central one (Burnham, 1970; Scammon and Wattenberg, 1970; Sears and Kinder, 1971). As racial fears have increased among northern whites, there has been a natural tendency for conservative white political candidates to attract white votes with semi-racist appeals that essentially abandoned the black population. This has happened at all levels of government and in all parts of the nation, running from Nixon's "southern strategy" in 1968 to the "law and order" mayoralty candidates in New York, Philadelphia, Minneapolis, Los Angeles, and numerous other cities in the late 1960s and early 1970s.

Victory by an "anti-black" faction over a "pro-black" faction would be dangerous to any of America's institutions, whether political, educational, business, or whatever. But most dangerous of all would be such a victory at the presidential level. This, we fear, tampers with blacks' attachment to the prevailing political system at a very vulnerable point, for three reasons: (1) the historical role of the federal government in redressing wrongs to blacks; (2) the centrality of affection for the presidency in the early socialization of attachment to the political system, for all Americans; and (3) because of its great power, and its election by a simple popular vote of all Americans, the presidency is even more a symbol of America than are the other referents of the New Urban Blacks' generalized political disaffection.

Here, then, all we can do is raise the question: would (or will) the abandonment of blacks' interests by a presidency dominated by white conservatives dim or remove hope and faith in the future for the mass of black citizens and unite them in bitterness and disaffection with the New Urban Blacks? We are not sure but perhaps the mere raising of the question expresses our concern.

Racial Isolation.   Finally, it is easy for us, along with the Kerner Commission, to predict continuing, even increasing, racial isolation. The races in this country always have been isolated. Hence, the apparent increase in isolation is in part the result of invisible blacks becoming visible to whites, revealing two cultures where whites thought there was only one white culture. But, we feel that the new black pride and the blacks' concern with "getting it together" and the greater fear of whites now that they have glimpsed the New Urban Black (a much more frightening fellow than old

Uncle Tom) will weaken attempts, feeble as they may have been in the past, to bridge the chasm between the races. A consequence of this new isolation for whites will be a lack of opportunity to test their stereotypes, rumors, and fears against reality. Thus, many (or most) white-originated programs for dealing with racial conflict may have an unrealistic quality to them, from programs for "welfare reform" proposed by cost-conscious political conservatives to perhaps the most central and difficult question of all—the integration of suburban housing and schools.

A second consequence of this isolation, this greater sense of racial turf or territoriality, for both whites and blacks, will be a more rapid emergence of attitude and opinion consensus about racial affairs within each hermetically sealed group. Thus, any action that seems hostile on the part of either side, whether it is the "wanton" murder of a policeman or the killing of apparently innocent blacks, will result in further racial polarization. Each side will feed on the other, terrorize the other, and there will be no one to insist on reason and mutual understanding.

If the races are to be reconciled, we feel that the initiative must come from whites. Whites must realize that the New Urban Blacks will not go away. The halcyon, quiet days of yore, when blacks knew their place and did not stir up trouble, are gone forever.

The final resolution of racial conflict in America cannot be anticipated with any confidence. We are not optimistic about the near future. It seems clear that much conflict is ahead of us. Surely, the long-range future of the black minority in America will tax American ingenuity to its utmost. The process of accommodating to a changed black population is certain to be a difficult one, in the short run, for many whites and for many social institutions. But as the need for such accommodation is inevitable, our only hope is that in this period of transition, the opportunities for social creativity will come to dominate the feelings of threat to a comfortable status quo. For, the process of interracial accommodation can enrich us all, and our lives together, if we will let it.

Appendix A
Methodology: Sampling, Schedules, Interviews

Four survey samples interviewed in 1965–1966 have been utilized in this volume: (1) blacks in the Curfew Zone, (2) arrestees, (3) Mexican Americans in the Curfew Zone, and (4) whites outside the Curfew Zone. A detailed methodology for the first three of these may be found in T. M. Tomlinson and Diana L. TenHouten, "Methodology: Negro Reaction Survey," in Cohen (1970). For the white sample, the details may be found in Richard T. Morris and Vincent Jeffries, "The White Reaction Study," also in Cohen (1970). Therefore, we shall give only the most important features here. In addition we have presented some data from a 1969 survey of whites in the San Fernando Valley, details of which are presented elsewhere by Sears and Kinder (1971).

Sampling

The Black Curfew Zone Sample. The main sample for the Curfew Zone was drawn from records supplied by the U. S. Census Bureau from its 1960 census. The Curfew Zone, cordoned off for riot control by order of the Lt. Governor, included 128 census tracts and our sample was drawn from 119 of them. Names and addresses were drawn by a simple random procedure but the sample was stratified to conform to the age/sex proportions of the area in the 1960 census. Using this procedure, 471 interviews were collected.

To compensate for the residential transience of the very poor (under $3,000 per year income) and their underrepresentation in the 1960 census, an additional 125 interviews were garnered, using a cluster sampling technique developed by the National Opinion Research Corporation. Thus, both samples were selected by a random procedure.

In sum, 586 randomly selected black residents of the Curfew Zone were interviewed. The sample was proportionally representative of the 1960 census by age and sex and each respondent was assigned according to random procedure. This sample will henceforth be identified as the Curfew Zone sample.

Arrestee Sample. A true random sample from all persons arrested during the riot could not be drawn because defense attorneys did not wish their clients to discuss the rioting with strangers and prison officials could not find a way to separate the rioters from the many other persons arrested each day during the riot for various types of unrelated offenses. A sample was drawn from the files of the American Civil Liberties Union which was providing free legal aid. Thus, our arrestee sample of 124 persons cannot be assumed to be unbiased.

Mexican American Sample. A sample of 65 Mexican American residents of the Curfew Zone was drawn by a cluster technique. Though we desired a larger sample since the Mexican Americans form the third major ethnic group in Los Angeles, a shortage of funds prevented us from completing the full target sample. Nevertheless, this sample meets all of the criteria of a true random sample and inferences based upon the completed interviews are limited only by the size of the sample.

White Reaction Sample. A sample of 586 whites was drawn by the same clustering procedure used in the Curfew Zone sample. These whites lived outside the curfew area and the sample was stratified according to socioeconomic status and racial composition of the neighborhoods. Integrated and non-integrated high, middle, and low SES levels were represented in six Los Angeles communities and the sample was evenly divided between males and females according to the age proportions found in the 1960 census. This sample is thus not wholly representative of the county, overrepresenting high SES and racially integrated areas.

The Black Interview Schedule

Content. Individual interviewers contacted the respondents and asked questions from a prepared schedule. The schedule had three principal sections: (1) political attitudes, grievances, and personality attributes; (2) riot information, including attitudes, perceptions, and participation; and (3) demographic data.

Format. The schedule included both open- and closed-ended questions. Both types of questions were accompanied by extensive probes. Questions of both types were staggered throughout the schedule but an open-ended question always preceded a closed-ended question on the same topic. In order to refine the questions, the schedule was pretested on UCLA employees, the interviewers themselves, and others known to the interviewers (some of whom were active in the riot).

Interviews and Interviewers

Method and Length.   The interviews averaged about two hours each but community interest was high and very few persons refused to be interviewed. The interviewers attempted to gain as much privacy for the interviewees as possible, after introducing themselves with a standard statement and giving their names and indicating that UCLA was the sponsoring institution. If an interview could not be completed at one sitting, it was resumed at a mutually convenient time. Complete anonymity was assured the respondent (and adhered to by the project staff), even though this meant that we could not conduct verification interviews.

Age, Sex, and Recruitment.   Indigenous interviewers were recruited from a church supported project very close to the center of the rioting in the Curfew Zone. While it might have been possible to obtain reliable interviews through professional interviewers, it was felt that the tensions and suspicions in the Curfew Zone made it highly unlikely that professional, middle-class interviewers (white or black) could achieve the rapport necessary for valid inferences. Therefore, we chose to use nonprofessional blacks residing in the area and to give them the training necessary.

Candidates were screened by a written I.Q. test and a brief interview. From the original pool, 38 persons possessing verbal ability and interpersonal poise were chosen to begin training. Of these, 11 survived to make up the corps of interviewers. The working crew was composed of one man and one woman, both under 30 years of age, two men over 30, and seven women between the ages of 30 and 50. The female interviewers were mostly homemakers, only one having had training in field interviewing previously. Two of the three males were high school graduates and one a college graduate. All were unemployed at the time of interviewer selection.

Training Procedure.   During a three-week period immediately following the riot, in a field station set up within the Curfew Zone, members of the survey project gave instructions on interviewing. Avoiding bias in questioning, making nondirective probes, handling queries and complaints, and becoming familiar with the questionnaire were emphasized. For two days, human relations groups were operated to give the interviewers a chance to become acquainted with one another and to work out some of the grievances they had about each other and the meaning of the survey project. These groups were a valuable experience for the interviewers and apparently continued informally throughout the training period.

Possible Bias.   The extent of bias resulting from interviewer involvement with the issues raised in the wake of the riot was assessed statistically and the results were reported in Tomlinson and TenHouten (1970) and Raine (1970). Very little evidence of interviewer bias was found. The evidence did indicate a possible relationship between interviewer age and respondent selection. However, the age stratification requirement for the entire sample was met by all interviewers taken together. Therefore, sampling bias among certain interviewers apparently exerted negligible effect on the total data pool.

Coding Reliabilities

A staff of undergraduates at UCLA coded the closed-ended questions. A 10 per cent recode of randomly selected questions yielded a reliability of .98. The open-ended items were coded for explicit (manifest) and affective (latent) responses. The undergraduate coding staff, assisted by the interviewers, coded these responses also. For manifest content, the code-recode reliability was .93. For latent content, it was .95.

Appendix B
Scales and Reliabilities

Survey research in a riot-torn black residential area cannot be as "clean" as the purest standards would dictate. Our study is no exception to this. Our interviewers were quite inexperienced and had time for relatively little training before they went into the field. The interviews often were conducted under tense and confusing circumstances. And the interview schedule was unusually long for a survey instrument, due to the complexity of the phenomenon under study and the participation of multiple investigators from various disciplines. For these reasons, and despite the extraordinary patience and conscientiousness of the interviewers, it seemed almost inevitable that measurement error would be a greater problem in our data than in, for example, a much shorter standardized survey carried out by an experienced and established survey firm.

To deal with this error (as well as with the problems of reducing the vast amount of data collected), we made the decision to use scales, rather than individual items, wherever possible. These were scales of the simple Likert type, which involved summing the responses over a series of items in a single category (for instance, all items on perceived police brutality) to form a composite measure of the underlying dimension (for instance, belief in police brutality in general).

We were aware of two main disadvantages of this procedure. The first was that we were thereby taking an individual's response to reflect a latent underlying disposition rather than resting content with its manifest meaning. While this is a common enough procedure in social science, it can lead to disagreements about the interpretations of various patterns of response, since it does not take responses at face value.

The other disadvantage follows from our decision to use a priori scales rather than ones based on factor analysis or some other empirical, a posteriori technique. Hence we could justly be accused of imposing our own preconceptions upon the data. Instead of asking, "how do the items hang together for the respondents?," we simply asked, "do they hang together the way we expected them to, at least up to a minimum criterion?" As will be seen, our data analysis provided some protection for us in this regard, in that scales measuring conceptually related dimensions fit related patterns. Thus our a priori notions received some validation. But it should be clearly understood that our data-analysis procedure throughout the book followed a hypothesis-testing, deductive, theory-testing strategy, rather than a blindly empirical, inductive one.

The exact procedure by which the scales were generated was as follows. Weights were assigned to various item responses and the scale scores were obtained by summing these weights across items chosen a priori for similar content. The final set of items for a given scale was chosen according to the procedure specified in Scott (1968). For each item in a particular scale, the correlation of the item with the sum of the other scale items (excluding the item in question) was obtained. When the overall reliability of the scale under consideration was too low or when an item was too deviant from the scale (correlation too low), then that item was removed and a new set of correlations was computed. For most of the contingency tables in this volume, we split the scales into high and low at the median of the distribution of scores along the scale.

In this appendix we shall report the final items included in the Likert scales and, in parentheses afterwards, the correlation of the item with the sum of the other items in the scale (excluding the item under consideration). Other relevant data may be obtained by most on request from the first author at UCLA: the mean, the standard deviation, the cutting points used to divide it into high and low (or occasionally high, medium, and low), the percentages of respondents at each level, the exact items included, and the weights assigned responses to each item. Data here are from the Curfew Zone sample only ($n = 586$).

Riot Participation

Events Witnessed: A high score refers to those who saw at least four of five major riot events.

"We would like to know a little bit about what you saw during the (RRI).[1] Did you see: Stores being burned?" (.58), "Stores being looted?" (.73), "Shooting?" (.83), "Stones being thrown at people?" (.80), "Crowds of people?" (.79)

---

[1]RRI was a symbol in the interview schedule for "riot, revolt, insurrection," the three most common responses to the question, "What would you call it?" After establishing the respondent's preferred term, the interviewer always used it when referring to the event.

Riot Attitudes

Riot Approval: A high score indicates strong approval of the riot.

"Now that the (RRI) is over, how do you feel about what happened?" (.81), "What kinds of people supported it; what kinds of people were against it?" (.80), "What did you like about what was going on? What did you dislike about what was going on?" (.84)

Perceived Community Involvement: Perceiving larger numbers of people involved in or supporting the riot.

"What per cent of the people in the area participated?" (.71), "What per cent of the people in the area supported it?" (.82), "What per cent of the people in the area were against it?" (.82), "How active were the people in your neighborhood?" (.53)

Protest Interpretation: Interpreting the riot as a meaningful Negro protest.

"Do you think the (RRI) had a purpose or goal?" (.66), "Some people say the (RRI) was a Negro protest. Do you agree with that point of view?" (.71), "Why do you think they happened to get attacked? Was it chance or was there some reason why they in particular were attacked?" (.72), "What caused the (RRI)?" (.65)

Riot Optimism: Believing riot would have beneficial effects.

"Do you think the (RRI) increased or decreased the gap between the races?" (.67), "Since the (RRI), do you think whites are more sympathetic to Negro problems?" (.59), "What do you think the main effects were or will be? What do you think will come out of the whole thing?" (.73), "Do you think the (RRI) helped or hurt the Negro's cause?" (.74)

Local Grievances

Agency Discrimination: Having experienced or believing in discrimination in local agencies.

"Here is a list of some other areas of life in which some people have said there is discrimination against the Negro. Tell me which of these, if any, you have heard about or experienced." Schools (.65), garbage collection (.66), welfare agencies (.71), fire department (.68), park department (.72)

Perceived Police Brutality: A high score indicates belief that at least five of these six events happened to people in the area.

Each item follows the following format: "Some people say policemen . . . Do you think this happens to people in your area?" Show lack of respect or use insulting language (.76); roust, frisk, or search people without good reason (.81); stop or search cars for no good reason (.79); search homes for no good reason (.73); use unnecessary force in making arrests (.81); beat up people when they are in custody (.77)

Biased White Media: Belief that the local media do not cover problems of the Negro community fairly.
     Los Angeles Herald-Examiner (.75), *Los Angeles Times* (.67), radio in general (.83), television in general (.81)

Merchant Exploitation: Experienced difficulty as consumers of goods and services.
     "Here are some complaints often heard about stores and merchants": "Do you have trouble with unfair credit policies?" (.67), "Do you often think you are overcharged for goods?" (.63), "Do you think you are sold inferior goods?" (.62), "In stores, are insulting remarks made to you?" (.53), "Do you have trouble cashing checks?" (.58), "Do you have trouble with quick repossession of goods?" (.61)

Local White Political Structure: Unfavorable attitudes toward local white political leaders and institutions.
     Mayor Yorty (.52), Los Angeles County Board of Supervisors (.72), *Los Angeles Herald-Examiner* (.63), *Los Angeles Times* (.61), Los Angeles City Council (.72)

Inadequate Service Agencies: Unfavorable attitudes toward performance of local service agencies.
     Aid to Dependent Children (.87), Bureau of Public Assistance (.89), State Employment Agency (.82)

Blocked Mechanisms of Grievance Redress

General Political Disaffection: Distrust and disaffection toward political representation in general.
     "Do you think elected officials can generally be trusted?" (.70), "How about Negro elected officials?" (.72), "How do you feel about the way you are represented?" (.74), "Who do you think really represents the Negro?" (.43)

Political Participation: Past conventional political activity.
     "Did you vote in the 1964 presidential election?" (.57), "Did you do anything besides voting in that election?" (.23), "Did you vote on Proposition 14?" (.53)

Political Contacts: Having any political contacts.
1. "Do you know anyone who is politically influential?" (.80)
2. "Do you know anyone else who is politically influential?" (.65)
3. "Anyone else?" (.69)
4. "How well do you know each of these persons?": Person named in question #1 (.61), person in question #2 (.46), person named in question #3 (.42).

The Status Deprivation Index

One of our combined measures cannot be considered a Likert scale. In Chapters 5 and 6, we reported the results from our Occupational Status Deprivation Index. This index was formed by creating nine approximately equal frequency clusters on the NORC Socio-Economic Index for Detailed Occupation. The clusters used were 0–60, 61–70, 71–80, 81–90, 91–100, 101–110, 111–120, 121–140, and 141–184. After assigning a score of 1–9 depending upon the rank of the cluster (high SES = 9), the ranking of the job currently held by a respondent was subtracted from that of the job to which he aspired in order to form the final index.

Though it was possible to produce a nine-step index ranging from zero to eight, by our procedure, we chose to treat the distribution as dichotomous in order to minimize the built-in ceiling for those already at higher occupation levels and in order to minimize any impression we might convey that this index is an interval scale or something even more elegant. Thus, those scoring 0 (30 per cent of the sample) were said to have been satisfied with their current status and those scoring from 1–8 were said to have been deprived.

Political Sophistication

White Politician Familiarity: Knowledge of white politicians and groups.
Governor Brown (.46), Senator Murphy (.62), Mayor Yorty (.51), City Councilman John Gibson (.65), County Supervisor Kenneth Hahn (.66), Republican Party (.39), AFL-CIO (.49)

Poverty Program Familiarity: Knowledge of local poverty program agencies.
Economic and Youth Opportunities Agency (.78), Youth Opportunities Board (.83), Neighborhood Adult Participation Project (.81), Youth Training and Education Program (.81), Operation Head Start (.76), Teen Crash Program (.77)

National Negro Familiarity: Knowledge of nationally prominent Negroes.
Ralph Bunche (.43), Elijah Muhammad (.34), Louis Lomax (.43), Martin Luther King (.29), Thurgood Marshall (.55)

Local Black Politician Familiarity: Knowledge of local black politicians.

City Councilman Thomas Bradley (.65), City Councilman Gilbert Lindsay (.61), Assemblyman Mervin Dymally (.60), Assemblyman F. Douglass Farrell (.52), Congressman Augustus Hawkins (.61), City Councilman Billy Mills (.65)

White Media Exposure: Knowledge of the media's fairness to Negro community.

Uses the same items as "Biased White Media" above but scores only for having an opinion and disregards the nature of the opinion. Reliabilities were .46, .48, .49, and .41, respectively.

Negro Media Exposure: Knowledge of Negro-originated media.

Los Angeles Herald-Dispatch (.39), *Muhammad Speaks* (.37), KGFJ (.28)

Evaluation of Black Leadership

Negro Assimilationist Evaluation: A high score indicates approval of prominent assimilationist leaders and groups.

Ralph Bunche (.71), Martin Luther King (.56), Thurgood Marshall (.68), CORE (.63), NAACP (.63)

Civil Rights Groups Evaluation: A high score indicates approval of the most prominent Negro interest groups *c.* 1965.

CORE (Congress of Racial Equality) (.68), NAACP (.65), SCLC (Southern Christian Leadership Conference) (.61), SNCC (Student Non-Violent Coordinating Committee) (.64), Urban League (.65), UCRC (United Civil Rights Committee) (.72)

Local Black Politician Evaluation: A high score indicates approval of local black politicians.

Same items as "Black Politician Familiarity" scale. Correlations are, respectively, .71, .71, .66, .53, .68, .69.

Black Muslim Evaluation: Approval of the Black Muslims.

Black Muslims (.82), Elijah Muhammed (.85), John Shabbaz (.78), "How fairly does *Muhammad Speaks* cover the problems of the Negro community?" (.60)

National Politics

Evaluation of White Liberals: A high score indicates approval of white liberal leaders and institutions.

President Johnson (.66), Governor Brown (.71), Democratic Party (.67), AFL-CIO (.70)

Republican Party Evaluation: Approval of the Republican Party.
Approval of "Republican Party" (.92), "Does the Republican Party represent you?" (.92)

Poverty Program Evaluation: A high score indicates approval of the poverty program agencies.
Economic and Youth Opportunities Agency (.76), Youth Opportunities Board (.84), Neighborhood Adult Participation Project (.71), Youth Training and Education Program (.84), Operation Head Start (.75), Teen Crash Program (.71)

White Officeholder Evaluation: A high score indicates approval of these local, state, and national officeholders.
President Johnson (.58), Governor Brown (.64), Senator Murphy (.50), Mayor Yorty (.56), City Councilman John Gibson (.49), County Supervisor Kenneth Hahn (.48)

Church Evaluation: A high score indicates a favorable attitude toward the church (see McConahay, 1970a for details).
Approval of "your church" (.78), "Does your church represent you?" (.77), "How often have you attended religious services in the last year?" (.71)

Appendix C
Validity of the Participation Measures

Participation Defined

Since it was impossible to interview people engaged in rioting at the time of the event, the measures of riot participation used in this study were based, with one exception, upon various forms of retrospective self-report. Thus, except for the arrestee sample, we have considered those people as participants who reported themselves to be participants and we have sought to analyze the social, psychological, and political factors related to this claimed participation.

To put it more-formally, we are interested in the social and political properties of a psychological type or group. We defined this group as those persons who claimed some level of participation in the Watts Riot. We think that the properties of those willing to claim participation in the riot are quite interesting in their own right. However, we shall attempt to show in this appendix that the overlap between those *claiming* participation and those *actually* participating was considerable. The reader nevertheless should be aware of this distinction.

Operational Definitions

The questions designed to measure participation were necessarily of a somewhat indirect nature. The overt, aggressive acts that constituted the most active level of riot participation were illegal, and blacks in the community were suspicious of all investigators. Moreover, we had been advised by legal counsel that our interviews were subject to subpoena if the authorities suspected they might contain incriminating evidence.

Thus, we had to distinguish participants from nonparticipants in our Curfew Zone sample on the basis of two rather unspecific measures. The first of these was the response to the question: "We are not interested in the details of what you actually did, but just generally would you say you were very active, somewhat active, or not active at all?" Those saying they were "active" or "very active," we treated as participants. Those saying they were "not active," we called nonparticipants.

Our second measure relied upon responses to the five questions: "We would like to know a little bit about what you saw during the [riot]. Did you see stores being burned?," "Did you see stores being looted?," "Did you see shooting?," "Did you see stones being thrown at people?," "Did you see crowds of people?" These five items formed a Likert type scale which we have called the "Events Witnessed Scale." (The details of this scale are given in Appendix B.) Respondents scoring among the top 30 per cent of this scale, that is, those reporting that they witnessed at least four events, we called active.

Finally, the properties of the persons participating were also assessed by comparing the random (Curfew Zone) sample with the arrestee sample. (See Appendix A for the methods used to obtain these samples.) When this was done, the arrestee Sample was considered the more active group and the Curfew Zone Sample, as a whole, was considered the less active group.

Reliability of the Measures

The reliability of our estimate of the number of persons participating was discussed in Chapter 1 and the reliability of our Events Witnessed Scale was reported in Appendix B. In both cases the reliabilities were quite adequate. Since we have used multiple measures throughout and since we have drawn conclusions only when the pattern of data tended to converge on all three measures, we feel that unreliability was not a threat to our participation measures.

Direct Threats to Validity

Though reliability was high and multiple measures were used, distortions in the interview situation may have affected validity. Here, we consider data which allow us to assess the order of magnitude of these threats, if not the precise amounts.

Distortions by Respondents.   One can imagine several reasons why the respondents deliberately might have overestimated their own activity. For instance, exaggerating one's participation might have been thought to impress the black interviewer. In the days and months following the rioting, possession of goods allegedly stolen during the riot became something of a status symbol. If the desire to impress was an important source of distortion, one would expect the participation rates to be especially high among those last interviewed, on the grounds that over time the danger of prosecution for participation would have receded, while the glory of participation would have become magnified.

However, the proportion claiming "very" or "somewhat" active status was no greater among those interviewed in January, five months after the riot, than among those interviewed in October, two months afterward. In each month 21 per cent said they had been active. This suggests that grandiose retrospective distortions did not greatly inflate estimates of participation.

Censure by Interviewers. There are also obvious reasons why one might underestimate participation. Some respondents may have had stolen goods in their homes. Police interrogation was a constant threat. Or the respondents may have wished to avoid possible disapproval by a representative of a middle-class university. Again, there are some data that help us gauge the possible magnitude of such distortions. The interviewer, at the conclusion of the interview, rated how cooperative the respondent had been. If our interviewers explicitly or implicitly censured riot activity, presumably they would have felt more negative toward participants than toward stay-at-homes and thus would have rated participants as more uncooperative. However, there was no relationship at all between self-reports of activity and the interviewer's rating of cooperation. Fifty-three per cent of the "very" or "somewhat" active gave "very good cooperation," as did 53 per cent of the "not active." Fourteen per cent of the active and 15 per cent of the non-active gave "fair" or "poor" cooperation. This suggests that any such pressures within the interview situation to suppress reports of activity were minor in consequence.

The Arrestees as a Criterion Group

The validity of our indexes of participation may be checked further by comparing the Curfew Zone respondents with the arrestees who were interviewed. Even if some innocents actually were apprehended, the arrestees as a group most likely participated in the rioting more vigorously than did persons in the Curfew Zone sample, who were randomly selected as representative of the general population in the area. (There is some evidence that arrests, too, were made more or less at random during some phases of the riot but surely they were less random than our sampling of Curfew Zone residents.)

The two samples were compared in Table 1.1 on the other indexes of participation. The arrestees were considerably more involved in the rioting, according to each measure. Most noteworthy is that 62 per cent of the arrestees, as opposed to 22 per cent of the Curfew Zone sample respondents, reported themselves "very" or "somewhat" active. The data presented in the last column of Table 1.2 reemphasize the point. "Rioters" made up 52 per cent of the arrestee sample and an additional 26 per cent were close spectators. Therefore, 78 per cent of the arrestees were in the action or were close enough to it to be cheer leaders. This was substantially greater than the 15 per cent and 31 per cent of the Curfew Zone sample making up these categories. The arrestees, of course, had a vital interest in concealing any possible criminal activity. The fact that they said they were more active in rioting than the respondents in the Curfew Zone sample provides further confidence in the validity of the self-reported participation measures as indexes of actual participation.

For discussions of the estimates of participation made systematically and unsystematically by other observers, and of estimates in other riot-torn cities, see Sears and McConahay, 1969; Sears and McConahay, 1970a; and Fogelson and Hill, 1968.

References

Abeles, R. Unpublished research, Harvard University, 1972.

Abelson, R. P., Aronson, E., McGuire, W. J., Newcomb, T. M., Rosenberg, M. J., and Tannenbaum, P. H. (eds.) *Theories of cognitive consistency: a sourcebook.* Chicago: Rand McNally, 1968.

Aberbach, J. D., and Walker, J. L. Political trust and racial ideology. *American Political Science Review*, 1970, *64*, 1199-1219.

Adams, J. S. Inequity in social exchange. In L. Berkowitz (ed.), *Advances in experimental social psychology*, Vol. 2. New York: Academic Press, 1965.

Asch, S. E. *Social psychology.* Englewood Cliffs, N.J.: Prentice-Hall, 1952.

Banfield, E. C. *The unheavenly city.* Little, Brown, 1970.

Barber, J. A., Jr. Social mobility and political behavior, Ph.D. dissertation, Stanford University, 1965.

Beardwood, R. The new Negro mood. *Fortune*, 1968, *78*, 146 passim.

Becker, J. F., and Heaton, E. E., Jr. The election of Senator Edward N. Brooke. *Public Opinion Quarterly*, 1967, *31*, 346-358.

Benham, T. W. Polling for a presidential candidate: some observations on the 1964 campaign. *Public Opinion Quarterly,* 1965, *29,* 185-199.

Berelson, B. R., Lazarsfeld, P. F., and McPhee, W. N. *Voting: a study of opinion formation in a presidential election.* Chicago: University of Chicago Press, 1954.

Bloom, B. S. *Stability and change in human characteristics.* New York: Wiley, 1964.

Brink, W., and Harris, L. *Black and white.* New York: Simon and Schuster, 1966.

Bureau of Labor Statistics. *Social and economic conditions of Negroes in the United States.* BLS Report No. 332. Washington, D.C.: U.S. Government Printing Office, 1967.

Burnham, W. D. *Critical elections and the mainsprings of American politics.* New York: W. W. Norton, 1970.

Campbell, A. *White attitudes toward black people.* Institute for Social Research, University of Michigan, 1971.

Campbell, A., Converse, P. E., Miller, W. E., and Stokes, D. E. *The American voter.* New York: Wiley, 1960.

Campbell, A., Gurin, G., and Miller, W. E. *The voter decides.* Evanston, Ill.: Row, Peterson, 1954.

Campbell, A., and Schuman, H. Racial attitudes in fifteen American cities. In *Supplemental studies for the National Advisory Commission on Civil Disorders.* Washington, D.C.: Government Printing Office, 1968, pp. 1-67.

Campbell, D., and Stanley, J. Experimental and quasi-experimental designs for research on teaching. In N. L. Gage (ed.), *Handbook of research on teaching.* Chicago: Rand McNally, 1963.

Caplan, N. S. The new ghetto man: a review of recent empirical studies. *The Journal of Social Issues,* 1970, *26,* 59-74.

Caplan, N. S., and Paige, J. M. A study of ghetto rioters. *Scientific American,* 1968, *219,* 15-21.

Cash, W. J. *The mind of the south,* New York: Knopf, 1941.

Caughey, J., and Caughey, L. *School segregation on our doorstep: the Los Angeles story.* Los Angeles: Quail Books, 1966.

CBS News. *White and Negro attitudes towards race related issues and activities.* Princeton: Opinion Research Corp., 1968.

Clark, K. B. *Dark ghetto.* New York: Harper and Row, 1965.

Cohen, J. Availability and useability of social services in the South Central area. In N. E. Cohen (ed.), *The Los Angeles riots: a socio-psychological study.* New York: Praeger, 1970.

Cohen, N. E. (ed.), *The Los Angeles riots: a socio-psychological study.* New York: Praeger, 1970.

Coleman, J. S., et al. *Equality of educational opportunity.* Washington, D.C.: United States Government Printing Office, 1966.

Colfax, J. D., and Sternberg, S. F. The perpetuation of racial stereotypes: blacks in mass circulation magazine advertisements. *Public Opinion Quarterly,* 1972, *36,* 8-18.

Conot, R. *Rivers of blood, years of darkness.* New York: Bantam, 1967.

Converse, P. E. The nature of belief systems in mass publics. In D. E. Apter (ed.), *Ideology and discontent.* New York: Free Press of Glencoe, 1964, pp. 206-261.

Converse, P. E. Attitudes and non-attitudes: continuation of a dialogue. In E. R. Tufte (ed.), *The quantitative analysis of social problems.* Reading, Mass.: Addison-Wesley, 1970, pp. 168-189.

Converse, P. E., Clausen, A. R., and Miller, W. E. Electoral myth and reality: the 1964 election. *American Political Science Review,* 1965, *59,* 321-336.

Couch, C. J. Collective behavior: an examination of some stereotypes. *Social Problems,* 1968, *15,* 310-322.

Cox, K. K. Changes in stereotyping of Negroes and whites in magazine advertisements. *Public Opinion Quarterly,* 1969, *33,* 603-606.

Crawford, T., and Naditch, M. Relative deprivation, powerlessness, and militancy: the psychology of social protest. *Psychiatry,* 1970, *33,* 208-223.

Davies, J. C. Toward a theory of revolution. *American Sociological Review,* 1962, *27,* 1-19.

Dawson, R. E., and Prewitt, K. *Political socialization.* Little, Brown, Boston, 1969.

Detroit Urban League. A survey of attitudes of Detroit Negroes after the riot of 1967. Detroit, 1967.

Dollard, J. *Caste and class in a southern town.* New York: Anchor, 1957. (Originally published, 1937.)

Dominick, J. R., and Greenberg, B. S. Three seasons of blacks on television. *Journal of Advertising Research,* 1970, *10,* 21-27.

Downes, B. T. Social and political characteristics of riot cities: a comparative study. *Social Science Quarterly,* 1968, *49,* 504-520.

Downes, B. T. A critical reexamination of the social and political characteristics of riot cities. *Social Science Quarterly,* 1970, *51,* 349-360.

Drake, S. C., and Cayton, H. R. *Black metropolis.* New York: Harper and Row (Torchbook), 1962.

Easton, D., and Dennis, J. *Children in the political system: origins of political legitimacy.* New York: McGraw-Hill, 1969.

Edelman, M. *Politics as symbolic action: mass arousal and quiescence.* Chicago: Markham, 1971.

Engstrom, R. L. Race and compliance: differential political socialization. *Polity,* 1970, *3,* 100-111.

Erskine, H. G. The polls: religious prejudice, Part I. *Public Opinion Quarterly,* 1965, *29,* 486-496.

Erskine, H. G. The polls: demonstrations and race riots. *Public Opinion Quarterly,* 1967, *31,* 655-677.

Erskine, H. G. The polls: recent opinion on racial problems. *Public Opinion Quarterly,* 1968, *32,* 696-703.

Feierabend, I. K., Feierabend, R. L., and Nesvold, B. A. Social change and political violence: cross-national patterns. In H. D. Graham and T. R. Gurr (eds.), *Violence in America.* New York: Signet, 1969, pp. 606-667.

Festinger, L. A theory of social comparison processes. *Human Relations,* 1954, *7,* 117-40.

Festinger, L. *A theory of cognitive dissonance.* Stanford: Stanford University Press, 1957.

Festinger, L., and Carlsmith, J. M. Cognitive consequences of forced compliance. *Journal of Abnormal and Social Psychology,* 1959, *58,* 203-210.

Festinger, L., Pepitone, A., and Newcomb, T. Some consequences of de-individuation in a group. *Journal of Abnormal and Social Psychology,* 1952, *47,* 382-389.

Finifter, A. W. Dimensions of political alienation. *American Political Science Review,* 1970, *64,* 389-410.

Fogelson, R. M. *The fragmented metropolis: Los Angeles, 1850–1930.* Cambridge: Harvard University Press, 1967

Fogelson, R. M. *Violence as protest: a study of riots and ghettos.* Garden City: Anchor, 1971.

Fogelson, R. M., and Hill, R. B. Who riots? A study of participation in the 1967 riots. In *Supplemental Studies for the National Advisory Commission on Civil Disorders,* 1968, pp. 217-248.

Ford, W. F., and Moore, J. H. Additional evidence on the social characteristics of riot cities. *Social Science Quarterly,* 1970, *51,* 339-348.

Frazier, E. F. *The Negro church in America.* New York: Schocken, 1966.

Freedman, J. L., Carlsmith, J. M., and Sears, D. O. *Social psychology.* Englewood Cliffs, N.J.: Prentice-Hall, 1970.

Freud, S. *Group psychology and the analysis of the ego.* London: Hogarth Press, 1922.

Gamson, W. A., and Modigliani, A. Knowledge and foreign policy opinions: some models for consideration. *Public Opinion Quarterly,* 1966, *30,* 187-199.

Ginzberg, R. *One hundred years of lynchings.* New York: Lancer, 1962.

Goldberg, A. S. Discerning a causal pattern among data on voting behavior. *American Political Science Review,* 1966, *60,* 913-922.

Governor's Commission on the Los Angeles Riots [McCone Commission]. *Violence in the city—an end or a beginning?* Los Angeles, 1965.

Greeley, A. M., and Sheatsley, P. B. Attitudes toward racial integration. *Scientific American,* 1971, *222,* 13-19.

Greenberg, E. S. Children and the political community: a comparison across racial lines. *Canadian Journal of Political Science,* 1969, *2,* 471-492.

Greenberg, E. S. Children and government: a comparison across racial lines. *Midwest Journal of Political Science,* 1970a, *14,* 249-275.

Greenberg, E. S. Black children and the political system. *Public Opinion Quarterly,* 1970b, *34,* 333-345.

Greenberg, E. S. *Political socialization.* New York: Atherton, 1970c.

Greenstein, F. *Children and politics.* New Haven: Yale University Press, 1965.

Gurr, T. R. *Why men rebel.* Princeton: Princeton University Press, 1969.

Gurr, T. R., and Ruttenberg, C. *The conditions of civil violence: first tests of a causal model.* Princeton: Center of International Studies, Princeton University, 1967.

Hensler, C. The structure of orientations toward government: involvement, efficacy, and evaluation. Paper presented to the annual meeting of the American Political Science Association, Chicago, 1971.

Hess, R. D., and Easton, D. The child's changing image of the President. *Public Opinion Quarterly,* 1960, *24,* 632-644.

Hess, R. D., and Torney, J. V. *The development of political attitudes in children.* Chicago: Aldine, 1967.

Hofstadter, R. *The paranoid style in American politics, and other essays,* New York: Knopf, 1965.

Hovland, C. I. Reconciling conflicting results derived from experimental and survey studies of attitude change. *American Psychologist,* 1959, *14,* 8-17.

Hyman, H. H. *Political socialization.* Glencoe, Ill.: Free Press, 1959.

Jacobs, P. *Prelude to riot: a view of urban America from the bottom.* New York: Random House, 1967.

Jeffries, V., and Ransford, H. E. Ideology, social structure, and the Yorty-Bradley mayoralty election. *Social Problems,* 1972, *19,* 358-372.

Jennings, M. K., and Niemi, R. G. The transmission of political values from parent to child. *American Political Science Review,* 1968a, *62,* 169-184.

Jennings, M. K., and Niemi, R. G. Patterns of political learning. *Harvard Educational Review,* 1968b, *38,* 443-467.

Jiobu, R. M. City characteristics, differential stratification, and the occurrence of interracial violence. *Social Science Quarterly,* 1971, *52,* 508-520.

Johnson, P. B., Sears, D. O., and McConahay, J. B. Black invisibility, the press, and the Los Angeles riot. *American Journal of Sociology,* 1971, *76,* 698-721.

Kassarjian, H. H. The Negro and American advertising: an historical analysis.

Paper presented to the annual meeting of Western Psychological Association, Los Angeles, 1970.

Kleiner, R. J., and Parker, S. Social-psychological aspects of migration and mental disorder in a Negro population. *American Behavioral Scientist*, 1969, *13*, 104-125.

Kornhauser, W. *The politics of mass society*. Glencoe, Ill.: Free Press, 1959.

Kraut, R. E., and McConahay, J. B. An experimental study of the effects of "Public Opinion Polling" and alienation reduction upon voter turnout in primary elections. Paper read to the annual meeting of the American Political Science Association, Chicago, 1971.

Lambert, W. E., and Klineberg, O. *Children's views of foreign peoples*. New York: Appleton-Century Crofts, 1967.

Lane, R. E. *Political life: why people get involved in politics*. Glencoe, Ill.: Free Press, 1959.

Lane, R. E. *Political ideology: why the American common man believes what he does*. New York: Free Press, 1962.

Lane, R. E., and Sears, D. O. *Public opinion*. Englewood Cliffs, N.J.: Prentice-Hall, 1964.

Lang, G. E., and Lang, K., Some pertinent questions on collective violence and the news media. *Journal of Social Issues*, 1972, *28*, 93-110.

Laurence, J. White socialization: black reality. *Psychiatry*, 1970, *33*, 174-194.

Lazarsfeld, P. F., Berelson, B., and Gaudet, J. *The people's choice*, 2nd ed. New York: Columbia University Press, 1948.

Le Bon, G. *The crowd*. London: Unwin, 1903.

Levy, S. G. The Detroit riot of July, 1967: communication processes and reactions. Paper read to the annual meeting of American Psychological Association, San Francisco, 1968.

Lieberson, S., and Silverman, A. R. Precipitants and underlying conditions of race riots. *American Sociological Review*, 1965, *30*, 887-898.

Lupsha, P. On theories of urban violence. *Urban Affairs Quarterly*, 1969, *2*, 273-296.

Marx, G. T. Civil disorder and the agents of social control. *Journal of Social Issues*, 1970, *26*, 19-57.

Marx, G. T. *Protest and prejudice: a study of belief in the black community*. New York: Harper and Row, 1967.

Matthews, D. R., and Prothro, J. W., *Negroes and the new southern politics*. New York: Harcourt, Brace and World, 1966.

McClosky, H., Hoffman, J., and O'Hara, R. Issue conflict and consensus among party leaders and followers. *American Political Science Review*, 1960, *54*, 406-427.

McConahay, J. B. Religion and discontent, I: attitudes of Negroes toward the church following the Los Angeles riot. *Sociological Analysis*, 1970a, *31*, 12-22.

McConahay, J. B. Religion and discontent, II: Negro attitudes toward the church and participation in the Los Angeles riot. Paper presented to the annual meeting of the Society for the Scientific Study of Religion, New York, 1970b.

McGuire, W. J. Cognitive consistency and attitude change. *Journal of Abnormal and Social Psychology*, 1960, *60*, 345-353.

McPhail, C. Civil disorder participation: a critical examination of recent research. *American Sociological Review*, 1971, *36*, 1058-1073.

Merton, R. K., and Kitt, A. S. Contributions to the theory of reference group behaviour. In R. K. Merton and P. F. Lazarsfeld (eds.), *Continuities in social research: studies in the scope and method of "the American soldier."* Glencoe, Ill.: Free Press, 1950.

Meyer, P. *Miami Negroes: a study in depth.* Miami, 1968.

Milbrath, L. W. *Political participation.* Chicago: Rand McNally, 1965.

Milgram, S. Behavioral study of obedience. *Journal of Abnormal and Social Psychology*, 1963, *67*, 371-378.

Milgram, S., and Toch, H. Collective behavior: crowds and social movements. In G. Lindzey and E. Aronson (eds.), *The handbook of social psychology*, 2nd ed., vol. IV. Reading, Mass.: Addison-Wesley, 1969.

Mischel, W. Continuity and change in personality. *American Psychologist*, 1969, *24*, 1012-1018.

Morris, R., and Jeffries, V. The white reaction study. In N. E. Cohen (ed.), *The Los Angeles riots: a socio-psychological study.* New York: Praeger, 1970, pp. 480-601.

Moynihan, D. P. (ed.) Toward a national urban policy. New York: Basic Books, 1970.

Moynihan Report. See *The Negro family.*

Muller, E. N. A test of a partial theory of potential for political violence. *American Political Science Review*, 1972, *66*, 928-959.

Murphy, R. J., and Watson, J. W. The structure of discontent: the relationship between social structure, grievance, and riot support. In N. E. Cohen (ed.), *The Los Angeles riots: a socio-psychological study.* New York: Praeger, 1970, pp. 140-257.

Myrdal, G. *An American dilemma.* New York: Harper and Row, 1944.

National Advisory Commission on Civil Disorders, *Report of the National Advisory Commission on Civil Disorders* [Kerner Commission report]. New York: Bantam, 1968.

The Negro family: the case for national action [Moynihan report]. Office of Policy Planning and Research. United States Department of Labor, March, 1965.

Newcomb, T. M., Koenig, K. E., Flacks, R., and Warwick, D. P. *Persistence and change: Bennington College and its students after 25 years.* New York: Wiley, 1967.

Niemi, R. G. A methodological study of political socialization in the family. Ph.D. dissertation, University of Michigan, 1967.

Oberschall, A. The Los Angeles riot of August 1965. *Social Problems*, 1968, *15*, 322-341.

Paige, J. M. Political orientation and riot participation. *American Sociological Review*, 1971, *36*, 810-820.

Parker, S., and Kleiner, R. J. *Mental illness in the urban Negro community.* New York: Free Press, 1966.

Pettigrew, T. F. *A profile of the Negro American.* Princeton, N.J.: Nostrand, 1964.

Pettigrew, T. F. Social evaluation theory: convergences and applications. In D.

Levine (ed.), *Nebraska symposium on motivation, 1967*. Lincoln: University of Nebraska Press, 1967.

Proshansky, H. M. The development of intergroup attitudes. In L. W. Hoffman and M. L. Hoffman (eds.), *Review of child development research*, Vol. 2. New York: Russell Sage Foundation, 1966, pp. 311-371.

Rabinowitz, F. F., and Lamare, J. After suburbia, what?: the new communities movement in Los Angeles. In W. Z. Hirsch (ed.), *Los Angeles: viability and prospects for metropolitan leadership*. New York: Praeger, 1971, pp. 133-168.

Raine, W. J. The ghetto merchant survey. In N. E. Cohen (ed.) *The Los Angeles riots: a socio-psychological study*. New York: Praeger, 1970, pp. 602-637.

Rainwater, L., and Yancey, W. L. *The Moynihan report and the politics of controversy*. Cambridge: M.I.T. Press, 1967.

Ransford, H. E. Isolation, powerlessness, and violence: a study of attitudes and participation in the Watts Riot. *American Journal of Sociology*, 1968, *73*, 581-591.

Riley, M. W., and Foner, A. *Aging and society*, Vol. 1: *An inventory of research findings*. New York: Russell Sage, 1968.

Rodgers, H. R., Jr., and Taylor, G. Pre-adult attitudes toward legal compliance: notes toward a theory. *Social Science Quarterly*, 1970, *51*, 539-551.

Rodgers, H. R., Jr., and Taylor, G. The policeman as an agent of regime legitimation. *Midwest Journal of Political Science*, 1971, *15*, 72-86.

Rogin, M. P., and Shover, J. L. *Political change in California—critical elections and social movements, 1890–1966*. Westport, Conn.: Greenwood, 1970.

Rossi, P. H., and Berk, R. A. Local political leadership and popular discontent in the ghetto. *The Annals*, 1970, *391*, 111-127.

Rudé, G. *The crowd in history, 1730–1848*. New York: Wiley, 1967.

Scammon, R. M., and Wattenberg, B. J. *The real majority*. New York: Coward McCann, 1970.

Schwartz, M. A. *Trends in white attitude toward Negroes*. Chicago: National Opinion Research Center, 1967.

Scott, W. A. Attitude measurement. In G. Lindzey and E. Aronson (eds.), *Handbook of social psychology*, 2nd ed., Vol. II. Reading, Mass.: Addison-Wesley, 1968, pp. 204-273.

Sears, D. O. Riot activity and evaluation. Paper presented to annual meeting of American Psychological Association, New York, 1966.

Sears, D. O. Review of "The development of political attitudes in children" by R. D. Hess and J. V. Torney, *Harvard Educational Review*, 1968a, *38*, 571-578.

Sears, D. O. The paradox of de facto selective exposure without preferences for supportive information. In R. P. Abelson, et al., (eds.), *Theories of cognitive consistency: a sourcebook*. Chicago: Rand McNally, 1968b.

Sears, D. O. Political behavior. In G. Lindzey and E. Aronson (eds.), *The handbook of social psychology*, 2nd ed., Vol. V. Reading, Mass.: Addison-Wesley, 1969a, pp. 315-458.

Sears, D. O. Black attitudes toward the political system in the aftermath of the Watts insurrection. *Midwest Journal of Political Science*, 1969b, *13*, 515-544.

Sears, D. O., and Kinder, D. R. Racial tensions and voting in Los Angeles. In W. Z. Hirsch (ed.), *Los Angeles: viability and prospects for metropolitan leadership*. New York: Praeger, 1971, pp. 51-88.

Sears, D. O., and McConahay, J. B. Participation in the Los Angeles Riot. *Social Problems*, 1969, *17*, 3-20.

Sears, D. O., and McConahay, J. B. Riot participation. In N. E. Cohen (ed.), *The Los Angeles riots: a socio-psychological study*. New York: Praeger, 1970a, pp. 258-287.

Sears, D. O., and McConahay, J. B. The politics of discontent: blocked mechanisms of grievance redress and the psychology of the New Urban Black Man. In N. E. Cohen (ed.), *The Los Angeles riots: a socio-psychological study*. New York: Praeger, 1970b, pp. 413-479.

Sears, D. O., and McConahay, J. B. Racial socialization, comparison level, and the Watts Riot. *Journal of Social Issues*, 1970c, *26*, 121-140.

Sears, D. O., and Tomlinson, T. M. Riot ideology in Los Angeles: a study of Negro attitudes. *Social Science Quarterly*, 1968, *49*, 485-503.

Sears, D. O., and Whitney, R. E. Political persuasion. In I. de S. Pool et al. (eds.), *Handbook of communication*. Chicago: Rand McNally, 1973.

Seeman, M., Bishop, J. M., and Grigsby, J. E., III. Community and control in a metropolitan setting. In W. Z. Hirsch (ed.), *Los Angeles: viability and prospects for metropolitan leadership*. New York: Praeger, 1971, pp. 133-168.

Sheatsley, P. B. White attitudes toward the Negro. *Daedalus*, 1966, *95*, 217-238.

Silberman, C. E. *Crisis in black and white*. New York: Random House, 1964.

Singer, B. D. Mass media and communication processes in the Detroit riot of 1967. *Public Opinion Quarterly*, 1970, *34*, 236-245.

Spilerman, S. The causes of racial disturbances: a comparison of alternative explanations. *American Sociological Review*, 1970, *35*, 627-649.

Spilerman, S. The causes of racial disturbances: tests of an explanation. *American Sociological Review*, 1971, *36*, 427-442.

Steinbeck, J. *The grapes of wrath*. Viking, 1939.

Stouffer, S. A. *Communism, conformity, and civil liberties*. New York: Doubleday, 1955.

Stouffer, S. A., et al. *The American soldier*, Vol. 1: *Adjustment during army life*. Princeton: Princeton University Press, 1949.

Taeuber, K. E., and Taeuber, A. F. *Negroes in cities*. Chicago: Aldine, 1965.

Taeuber, K. E., and Taeuber, A. F. The Negro population in the United States. In Davis, J. P. (ed.), *The American Negro reference book*. Englewood Cliffs, N.J.: Prentice-Hall, 1966.

Thibaut, J. W., and Kelley, H. H. *The social psychology of groups*. New York: Wiley, 1959.

Thompson, W. S. *Growth and changes in California's population*. Los Angeles: Haynes Foundation, 1955.

Tomlinson, T. M., and Tenhouten, D. L. Methodology: Negro reaction survey. In N. E. Cohen (ed.) *The Los Angeles riots: a socio-psychological study*. New York: Praeger, 1970, pp. 127-139.

U.S. Bureau of the Census. *Current population reports: the social and economic status of Negroes in the United States, 1970*. Washington, D.C.: U.S. Government Printing Office, 1971.

U.S. Bureau of the Census. *Negro population, 1790-1915*. Washington, D.C.: U.S. Government Printing Office, 1918.

U.S. Bureau of the Census. *U.S. census of population: 1960. Subject reports.*

Mobility for metropolitan areas. Washington, D.C.: U.S. Government Printing Office, 1963.

U.S. Bureau of the Census. *U.S. census of population: 1960. Subject reports. Mobility for states and state economic areas.* Washington, D.C.: U.S. Government Printing Office, 1963.

U.S. Bureau of the Census. *Current population reports*, Series P-20, No. 192, Voting and registration in the election of November, 1968. Washington, D.C.: U.S. Government Printing Office, 1969.

Wanderer, J. J. 1967 riots: a test of the congruity of events. *Social Problems*, 1968, *16*, 193-198.

Wanderer, J. J. An index to riot severity and some correlates. *American Journal of Sociology*, 1969, *74*, 500-505.

Wicker, A. W. Attitudes versus actions: the relationship of verbal and overt behavioral responses to attitude objects. *Journal of Social Issues*, 1969, *25*, 41-78.

Williams, R. *Strangers next door.* Englewood Cliffs, N.J.: Prentice-Hall, 1964.

Wilson, J. Q. A guide to Reagan country: the political culture of southern California. *Commentary*, 1967, *43*, 37-45.

Wolfinger, R. E., and Greenstein, F. I. The repeal of fair housing in California: an analysis of referendum voting. *American Political Science Review*, 1966, *62*, 753-769.

Wolfinger, R. E., and Greenstein, F. I., The political regions of California. *American Political Science Review*, 1969, *63*, 74-85.

Zellman, G., and Sears, D. O., Childhood origins of tolerance for dissent. *Journal of Social Issues*, 1971, *27*, 109-136.

Zimbardo, P. G. The human choice: individuation, reason and order versus de-individuation, impulse and chaos. In D. Levine (ed.), *The Nebraska symposium on motivation, 1969.* Lincoln: University of Nebraska Press, 1969.

Index

Abeles, R., *cited,* 86
Abelson, R. P., *cited,* 111, 116
Aberbach, J. D., and Walker, J. L., *cited,* 64
Adams, J. S., *cited,* 48
Administrative procedures: attitudes of the New Urban Blacks toward, 80–81; attitudes toward, and riot ideology, 179; blacks' lack of faith in, 202–203; as a conventional mechanism of grievance redress, and black attitudes toward in Los Angeles, 61, 62, 68; faith in, as a function of age and socialization, 79 table 5.6; faith in, and riot participation, 99, 100 table 6.5. *See also* Routine procedures
Age: and approval of the riot, 174 table 11.2; and black identity, 70–71, 71 table 5.1; of black migrants to the North, 39; of the black population in America, 36; of blacks in Los Angeles, 40 table 3.3; in the definition of New Urban Blacks, 34; and optimism about the effects of the riot, 175, 175 table 11.3; and participation in the riot, 26–27, 28 table 2.2; and perceived community involvement, 174, 174 table 11.2; and political disaffection, 74, table 5.3; and political experience, 79 table 5.6; and political leadership evaluations, 75 table 5.4; and political sophistication, 77, 78 table 5.5; and riot ideology, 173–177; and protest interpretation of the riot, 174–175, 175 table 11.3; and status deprivation, 87, 86 table 5.8; and strategies for social change, 79 table 5.6, 185 table 11.8. *See also* Generation gap; Youth Agency discrimination, scale of, defined, 216. *See also* Local agencies; Racial discrimination
Agitators as a cause of riots, 18, 110, 150, 167, 160 table 10.2
Anderson, Glenn (Lieutenant Governor of California), 6–7, 149
Animal spirits and riot participation, 107, 110–111, 123–125. *See also* Banfield, Edward C., his theory of riot participation

Approval of the riot: as a function of age and place of origin, 174 table 11.2; of the black public, 163; and events witnessed, 182; and grievances, 178 table 11.5; and merchant exploitation, 182 table 11.7; nationwide, 166; and participation in the riot, 112–113, 114 table 7.1; and police brutality, 182 table 11.7; and protest interpretation of the riot, 181, 182 table 11.7; and racial discrimination, 182 table 11.7; and riot ideology, 171 *ff.,* 172 table 11.1; scale of, defined, 216; and strategies for social change, 180 table 11.6; as a function of time, 117–118, 117 table 7.2; of whites and Mexican Americans, 165
Arrestees: as a criterion group, 15, 223–224; sample of, defined, 211
Asch, S. E., *cited,* 109, 111
Aspirations: of the New Urban Blacks, 84–85, 89; and participation in the riot, 95–97, 97 table 6.3
Attitudes: consistency of, and riot ideology, 171–173, 172 table 11.1; political, of the New Urban Blacks, 46; political, and political socialization, 41–44; toward Watts Riot, of crowds, 14–15; toward Watts Riot, and political socialization of blacks, 47–48

Banfield, Edward C.: his theory of riot participation, 22, 26, 106, 110, 123–125, 201; *cited,* 27, 55, 106, 110, 123, 184, 201
Barber, J. A., Jr., *cited,* 42
Beardwood, R., *cited,* 166, 191, 192
Becker, J. F., and Heaton, E. E., Jr., *cited,* 42
Benham, T. W., *cited,* 113
Black identity: and education, 189; level of, in samples used, 187–188; and political estrangement, 187–195; and political sophistication, 189; positive, as an effect of the riot, 195, 199, 200; positive, and the generation gap, 81 table 5.7; positive, and hostility toward whites, 189–190; positive, of New Urban Blacks, 46, 70–72, 81–82, 88, 197, 200, 71 table 5.1;